the Music Business

Also by Dick Weissman
The Folk Music Sourcebook (with Larry Sandberg)

the Music Business

Career Opportunities and Self-Defense

by Dick Weissman

CROWN PUBLISHERS, INC./NEW YORK

Printed in the United States of America
Published simultaneously in Canada by
General Publishing Company Limited

Library of Congress Cataloging in Publication Data
Weissman, Dick.
    The music business.

    Bibliography: p.
    Includes index.
    SUMMARY: Discusses the music industry and describes
a wide variety of careers. Focuses on popular music.
    1. Music—Vocational guidance.   2. Music trade—
United States. [1. Music—Vocational guidance.
2. Vocational guidance.   3. Music trade]   I. Title.
ML3790.W4   780′.23   78-27397
ISBN 0-517-53433-9
ISBN 0-517-53687-7 pbk.

Contents

Acknowledgments   ix

Introduction or How I Got into the Music Business
and Why I Wrote This Book   1

PART ONE   THE MUSIC BUSINESS:
Records, Agents, Managers, Music Publishing,
Commercials, and Unions

1 Getting Started   12

2 Records   19
Records Are the Vehicle   19
Recording Contracts and How to Get Them   20

3 The Recording Process   24
Selling the Demo   27

4 The Record Industry: A Brief History   30

5 Record Companies   35
Classical Records   39
Specialty Records   40

6 The Record Producer   42
Cost of Records   51

7 Record Company Contracts   52

8   How Records Are Sold and Distributed   60
     Promoting Records   63

9   Agents and Personal Managers   68

10   Music Publishing   75
     Music Publishing Contracts   77
     The New Copyright Law   79

11   Performing Rights Societies   82

12   Commercials   88

13   Music Trade Papers   95

14   The American Federation of Musicians   98
     Other Unions   103

15   Radio   105

PART TWO   CAREERS IN MUSIC

16   Studio Work and Engineering   112
     Engineering   117

17   Careers in Records and Radio   119
     Radio   120

18   Composing, Arranging, and Film Music   122
     Film Music   123

19   Concert Promotion and Careers in Publicity   126
     Careers in Publicity   130

20   Careers in Music Performance   131
     Classical Music Performance   135
     Jazz Performance   138

21   Songwriting as a Career   140

22   College: Getting the Education You Need   145

23   Careers in Music Education and Private Teaching   150
     Private Teaching   152

24   Careers Related to Music in Print:
     The Writing, Publication, and Sale of Written Music   154
     Jobs in Music Publishing   159

25   Music Criticism   161

26   Music Library Careers   165

27   Musical Instrument Manufacturing   167

28 Music Retailing and Wholesaling   170
    Wholesaling   172

29 Music Therapy   173

30 Piano Tuning, Instrument Repair, Music in the
    Armed Forces, Church Music, and Careers in Law   176

    Piano Tuning   176
    Instrument Repair and Building   177
    Music in the Armed Forces   177
    Church Music   178
    Music Law   178

31 Arts Management   180

32 Grants   183

33 Minorities in the Music Business   187
    The Position of Women   187
    Black Participation in the Music Business   192
    Other Minority Groups   194

34 Power in the Arts and Alternative Media   195
    Alternative Media   197

APPENDIX

College Music Business Programs   201
    Colleges Offering Music Industry Programs   201
    Colleges Offering Music Therapy Programs   204
    Colleges Offering Church Music Programs   206
    Colleges Offering Arts Management Programs   206
Lists of Music Business Organizations   208
    Unions   208
    Performing Rights Organizations   208
    Other Organizations   208
List of Publishers of Printed Music   210
Union Scales   211
Schirmer Brochure for Piano   212
Schirmer Brochure for Rock Guitar   213
Sample Lead Sheet   214

GLOSSARY OF MUSIC BUSINESS TERMS   215

ANNOTATED BIBLIOGRAPHY   218

Recording   218
History of Recording   219

Agents and Managers   219
Publishing, Performing Rights, Copyright   220
Commercials   220
Radio   221
Studio Work   222
Audio Engineering   222
Film Music   222
Promotion and Publicity   223
Music Performance   223
  Classical Music   224
  Blues and Soul Music   225
  Country & Western Music   225
  Electronic Music   226
  Folk Music   226
  Jazz   227
  Rock   227
  Popular Music in General   229
Songwriting   229
Careers in Music   230
Music Education   230
Music Criticism   230
Music Library Careers   231
Music Therapy   231
Piano Tuning   232
Church Music   232
Law   233
Arts Management   233
Grants and Scholarships   234
Women in Music   235
Other Minority Groups   236
Power in the Arts   236
Miscellaneous Music Books   236
Periodicals   237
  Music Trade Papers   237
Other Periodicals   238

INDEX   243

Acknowledgments

My thanks go to Rick Abramson, Diane Deschanel, Cathy Hourigan, and Tom MacCluskey for initial encouragement and support. Jim Campbell, Dan Fox, Ed Hinshaw, Ron Lockhart, Andy Robinson, and Harry Tuft contributed specific ideas and comments that influenced my thinking, but they are in no way responsible for my conclusions. My thanks go to The Bookstore in Woodstock, New York, the Woodstock Public Library, Craig Liske, and the library at Colorado Women's College for various favors.

I enjoyed working with Pat Winsor, my editor, who made a number of useful suggestions that helped me organize and complete this book.

Because I teach at a women's college, I am particularly conscious of the usually exclusive use of the pronoun *he*, especially in reference to people in professional jobs. In an attempt to avoid this stereotyping, in this book I have alternated the use of *he* and *she*.

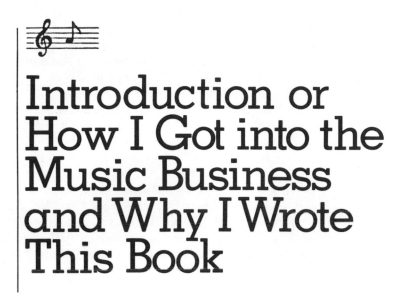

Introduction or How I Got into the Music Business and Why I Wrote This Book

When I was seven years old and my brother was eleven we started out together to take piano lessons. He was a more serious individual than I, and my parents assumed that he would take lessons and I would tag along. It turned out that he was virtually tone deaf, so he quit after a couple of weeks, and I ended up taking piano lessons for about seven years. We lived in northwest Philadelphia in a section called Mount Airy, and every Tuesday I would take the railroad train downtown for my lesson. I played classical music only, and all of the music was written. There was no improvisation. I played the Mozart Sonata no. 3, scales, and exercises, and so on. I never had any idea about what chords I was playing or any other aspect of music structure. I would practice each piece until I had learned it reasonably well, and then go on to the next one. By the last year of my lessons I had reduced them to every other week, and had pretty much given up practicing.

About the same time that I gave up on the piano I heard Pete Seeger play the banjo. This was in 1948, and I was thirteen years old. I had never heard of American folk music, and found it kind of intriguing. At that time the music that was played on Philadelphia radio was a boring collection of insipid love songs, performed by such musical luminaries as Vaughn Monroe, Patti Page, Doris Day, Guy Mitchell, etc. Soon after this, 78 rpm records were phased out, and I discovered an army-navy surplus store that sold 78s by Pete Seeger, Brownie McGhee, Lonnie Johnson, Woody Guthrie, and other folk and blues singers. I bought quite a few of these records at about a quarter a record, and through reading the liner notes of one album I sent for Pete Seeger's book *How to Play the 5-String Banjo*.

At this point I was going to an academically oriented and boring high school in Philly called Central High. I hated it so much that I went to summer school so that I could graduate in three and a half years. I decided not to go to college right away because I felt tired of school. I got a job running a mimeograph machine in a downtown department store. Sometime during that year (1951) I bought Pete Seeger's first LP, *Darling Corey,* a 10-inch LP for Folkways Records. I used to listen to that record every night before going to sleep—in fact to this day it is the only LP that I have ever worn out. Under the spell of the book and the record I decided to go out and buy a banjo. Following Pete's instructions I went to a pawn shop and bought a banjo for $25. I took it home, breathless with excitement, and proceeded to break two of the strings while trying to tune them to the piano. I had never seen anyone tune a stringed instrument before, and didn't know how to match the pitch to the piano. I took the banjo and put it in a closet. It stayed there for about a year and a half.

A year later I entered Goddard College, a small progressive college in north-central Vermont which had no marks, no tests, and almost no students. I met a girl there named Lil Blos, who played the banjo, and she offered to show me how to play. That Thanksgiving I went home to Philadelphia and got the banjo.

For the next two years I played the banjo almost incessantly, much to the discomfort of anyone within earshot. One friend of mine used to refer to it as the tin can with strings. I was quite ruthless about my practicing, sitting in front of the campus community center playing hour after hour, destroying the peace of the Vermont countryside by playing in the woods, and dragging the banjo to parties and picnics. At no time during this period did I decide to become a professional musician. My interests were in the social sciences and literature, and my dream was to write the Great American Novel. I had a friend named Burrill Crohn who played the trumpet, and he and I started jamming, with me playing piano. Burrill played blues and dixieland jazz. I had never played any piano without reading music, but I had learned how to play the banjo without any written music at all. I managed to find a couple of jazz piano

books, including one by Mary Lou Williams that included helpful hints about chord structure.

By the time I was ready for my junior year of college I
realized that I didn't want to stay at Goddard for four years. At
that time it was very difficult to transfer credits because Goddard was not yet accredited by the regional accrediting association. I arranged to divide my junior year between New York and
New Mexico. In the fall I went to the New School for Social
Research in New York, and in the spring I went to the University of New Mexico. As part of my fall plan, I persuaded Goddard to agree to my taking six credits of banjo and guitar
lessons. I remember the registrar writing me a very serious note
saying that these credits might not be applicable to a graduate
school transcript should I go on for an advanced degree. Since I
am now teaching both banjo and guitar for college credit at
Colorado Women's College, and there are guitar programs at
almost every major American college, it seems funny in retrospect. In those days guitar was considered a bit suspect in the
American academic world, and banjo was not recognized as an
instrument worthy of serious study.

I took four months of banjo and guitar lessons from Jerry
Silverman at the Metropolitan Music School in New York City,
and I also had some theory and ear-training classes. In the
spring I went on to Albuquerque and took some sociology and
anthropology classes. I also met a marvelous banjo player
named Stu Jamieson, who lived in the nearby Sandia Mountains. I spent two long evenings at his house listening to him
play, and I did a number of goofy things in Albuquerque, such
as playing on KOB-TV in Albuquerque with Glen Campbell's
uncle, Dick Bills, dressed in full but borrowed cowboy regalia,
and a couple of concerts at the university. When I returned to
Goddard for my senior year I started work on my senior thesis,
which combined sociology and what is now called black studies
(but was then called Negro history) with my interest in folk
music. It concerned the relationship between the life and the
music of Huddie Ledbetter (Leadbelly), the black folksinger-
composer. Mostly I focused on a content analysis of the lyrics of
his songs.

That spring I wrote a suite called *A Day in the Kentucky
Mountains*. It was a five-part piece for the banjo with a song in
the middle, and although I had written a few songs by that time
this was the first original work I had tried to compose for the
banjo. I played the piece at a graduation concert, and settled by
the end of the summer in New York City.

I decided to go to graduate school, and after being rejected at the New York School of Social Work I entered Columbia University in the graduate sociology program. This was a rough period in my life because I didn't think I had the talent to make it as a writer of fiction, I still hadn't conceived of the possibility of becoming a musician, and I really had no idea of how I could earn a living. I didn't especially want to go into the army, which was breathing fairly close down my neck, so I finally decided to pursue some kind of social science research.

I found graduate school to be an elaborate rerun of my high school experiences. I never could understand what my fellow students were talking about, due to my limited background in formal sociology. In fact, I found them harder to understand than my teachers. I didn't know too many people in New York, and I didn't like my academic compatriots much. I started to support myself by teaching banjo and guitar. During the year and a half I was taking courses at Columbia some friends and music-store owners told some other musicians and arrangers that I could play the five string banjo, and I got a few good jobs doing commercials and playing on some records. Before long I was taking my banjo with me to classes, leaving classes early to play jobs, or not going to classes at all. Finally it came time to write my thesis. I wanted to write about a number of blind black street singers, some still alive and some dead. I had a theory that blind street singers who were basically nonliterate people reflected and upheld the traditions that were alive when they were children, rather than changing their beliefs and attitudes as the society itself changed. I tried to explain what I wanted to do to my adviser. He looked at me with some confusion, probably at least partly the fault of my explanation, and acknowledged that he didn't know much about what I was talking about. He informed me that his wife was an artist. In other words he was used to dealing with eccentrics. The sociology department at Columbia mostly welcomed very structured statistically oriented studies of voting behavior, consumer product choices, etc. This kind of study was statistically sound, used specific data, and didn't involve abstractions or much in the way of loose theorizing. In other words they were safe. Sometime during this conversation with my adviser I decided to become a full-time musician. I realized I would never write a thesis at Columbia. I didn't officially quit school, but I started teaching guitar and banjo six days a week, four in New York and two in my hometown of Philadelphia. I got some jobs teaching classes at Ys, neighborhood art centers, and so on.

Gradually more calls came in for studio work, and I studied some jazz guitar, worked on reading music for guitar, and met some good professional musicians, particularly my guitar teacher, Dan Fox. In 1960 I met John Phillips, and he and I and Scott Mackenzie formed a group called The Journeymen. We recorded three albums for Capitol, did college concerts and played nightclubs all over the United States and Canada, and did some commercials and television. Without any real foresight or planning I had become a professional musician.

How and Why I Wrote This Book

Anyone writing a book seeks a certain amount of recognition or some degree of financial success. I also have some other specific motivations in mind which should be of greater value to the reader. I hope that everyone reading this book will be able to learn from a few of the unfortunate experiences I have had in the music industry over the last twenty years, and I hope that some of the more positive experiences will be of interest and value.

In 1959–60 I was a member of what probably was the world's first folk-rock group. It was a collection of singers and musicians called The Citizens, put together by two Broadway songwriters named Sid Jacobson and Lou Stallman. By Broadway songwriters I mean a corps of professional writers of that time who literally wrote two or three songs a day most days of the week year after year. Sid and Lou had written a few hits, and were the owners of a huge bunch of demonstration records and lead sheets of their songs. They had put together a concept album consisting of a group of songs describing life in New York City. They auditioned a number of singers and musicians and I was accepted into the group as the principal guitarist, banjo picker, and occasional singer. Lou and Sid had a deal with Laurie Records, the company that recorded Dion and the Belmonts, the Chiffons, and others. Lou and Sid gave us contracts, which signed us to them as our personal managers. I no longer remember whether we were under contract to Lou and Sid as independent record producers or whether we had a direct contract with Laurie Records. In the record deal it was stated that we could not record for any other record label. Since I was starting to make a good part of my living doing free-lance recording for various record companies, I insisted that this provision be changed so that I could continue to record for other labels. Lou and Sid agreed to revise this part of the contract.

Considering my lack of experience at the time, in retrospect I am amazed I even read the contract that carefully. Anyway the contract was not revised, so I never did sign it. We finished the record, but Laurie held on to it for a long time before issuing it. Perhaps they didn't think it would sell, wasn't any good, or whatever. While this was dragging on I had met John Phillips, and he and I and Scott Mackenzie ended up signing a recording contract with Capitol. One day the phone rang, and Sid called to remind me that I was still under a contract with them as managers, and that they would expect to get 20 percent of my earnings. I reminded Sid that I had never signed the contract because they had failed to rewrite it. I mention this because if I had signed the contract I would indeed have had to pay Sid and Lou commissions. The moral of this story is to be very careful about the contracts that you sign because some months or years later you may find yourself in a situation which you never anticipated. In this instance I was very lucky.

When The Journeymen got together we went through the Schwann LP catalog and decided on eight record companies which we thought were likely prospects. John, who was the smoothest talker in our group, called them on the phone and asked to speak to the artist and repertoire department. None of them were willing to have us do a live audition except MGM Records. Since we had very little money, and we all had some recording experience, we didn't want to go to the time, trouble, or expense to do a demonstration tape. We sang and played for MGM and they liked us and offered to sign us. Meanwhile John and Scott were under contract to Decca Records because they had been in a group called The Smoothies who recorded for Decca. None of us wanted to record for Decca, which we felt was a dated and musically unsympathetic company, so we adopted the following strategy. The Smoothies' producer was a man named Milt Gabler, a noted jazz buff who hated banjos. We positioned ourselves with me slightly in front of the other members of the group and with my banjo pointed directly at Milt's head. John then had me play as loud as I could so that I virtually drowned out anything else. John and Scott got their release from Decca after we sang two or three songs.

In the midst of our negotiations with MGM we picked up a manager named Rene Cardenas, who was in a sort of limited partnership with Frank Werber, who then managed the Kingston Trio. The Trio was then the most successful pop-folk group around. The Kingston Trio recorded for Capitol, and Werber and Cardenas felt they would have no trouble getting us a deal with Capitol if that proved necessary. We went back to MGM with Rene Cardenas. He asked for a guarantee of two albums a year, and a $5,000 guarantee for promotion of the first album. Besides the three of us and Rene, two people represented MGM at this meeting. One of them was Danny Davis, who later became a producer for RCA and then left to form the Nashville Brass, and Jim Vienneau, who now produces records in Nashville. Danny was very friendly but not optimistic about the deal that Rene had outlined. Vienneau played the bad guy (which he did quite well) and looked us straight in the eye and said, "You'll never get a deal like that in the record business." Ten minutes later we walked into the New York office of Capitol Records, and sang a few songs for Andy Wiswell, their eastern production chief. He called Capitol's head office in Hollywood in our presence, and within a half hour of Vienneau's speech we got exactly the deal that he had described as impossible. At that moment and forever more I learned not to believe people in the music industry when they describe a deal as impossible, or a contract as nonnegotiable.

The sequel to this story has a less happy conclusion. After some months of management by Werber and Cardenas, we became convinced that our careers were not progressing as quickly as we had hoped. The Kingston Trio was breaking up, and we felt that most of our manager's energies were directed toward finding a replacement for Dave Guard, who was leaving the Trio. Since the Trio was an exceptionally valuable show business property this was somewhat understandable. We spent several months starving in San Francisco, and Scott and I moved into a $9-a-week Chinese hotel in North Beach, while John worried a lot because he had relocated his wife and two children to Mill Valley, California, from their home in Virginia. We got about six weeks of work on our own at a club in San Jose, and finally Werber and Cardenas got us a couple of jobs in Spokane and Phoenix. Most of the money was eaten up in travel expenses, but we were happy to be working at all. In Phoenix we were fired from the steak house in which we were playing, because the owner thought we were arrogant and was annoyed that we weren't drawing any customers.

Just about this time our first Capitol single came out. It began to get heavy radio play in New York City. Our original booking agency, International Talent Associates (ITA), had been in New York, but Werber and Cardenas had pulled us out of that agency and started trying to book us themselves, and in the case of the abortive Phoenix job through another outfit called ABC (Associated Booking Corp.). We got in touch with the people from ITA, who had been hearing our record on the way to work every day, and possibly thought it would be a hit. They offered to book us again, and we fired our managers and went back to New York. Unfortunately, we had a binding contract with Werber and Cardenas, which we had to buy out of with cash. It cost us $6,000 and some monies they had advanced us, and a lot of anxiety and bitterness. The money was paid in deferred payments, since we were penniless. Ever since this experience I have been very careful about signing contracts. Contracts can be broken, but it is a long and expensive process, which consumes time and energy as well as money.

The Journeymen stayed together for three and a half years, did three albums for Capitol, and several hundred concerts and a bunch of nightclub gigs all over North America. By 1964 it became apparent that the folk boom was ending, and I had done about enough living out of a suitcase. I had met my future wife, and decided to leave, get married, and move back to New York. I did all of that, and resumed my career as a free-lance studio musician, also doing some songwriting and record producing. John tried to keep The Journeymen alive for a year, calling them The New Journeymen. They never got a record deal, and broke up, eventually evolving into The Mamas and the Papas. Scott Mackenzie made a number of 45s that were unsuccessful, and then scored with the big hit " If You Go to San Francisco," written and co-produced by John Phillips.

In 1972 I moved to Denver, Colorado. I had gotten tired of the New York studio scene, and decided to get a music degree and study a bit about composing and arranging. In 1975 I met Tom MacCluskey, head of the music department at Colorado Women's College. He offered me a job organizing and teaching courses in the music industry program at the school. This is one of a number of such programs at schools throughout the United States that teaches music students about jobs available in the music industry. As I started to organize the courses, I looked around for a good textbook. I found the available books either vague, technical, or purely autobiographical. In my opinion they were not valuable or clear to someone who is trying to enter the music business but lacks knowledge or experience about it. This book is my attempt to convey what goes on in the music industry to a young, aspiring musician, or to the curious lay person. It tries to explain what the various people in the business do, how record companies function, what agents and personal managers do, the role of songwriters and publishers, unions, etc. Basically I am trying to explain how a young person can make intelligent career choices, how to get started, and how to progress.

I will also explore alternatives to going after the big money for those interested in a more personal, less popular sort of music. Other topics to be discussed are contracts, lawyers, commercials, studio work, music therapy, and arts management. I hope that this book will answer some of the questions you may have and point out some directions that will be of use to you in making a career in music.

The Music Business: Records, Agents, Managers, Music Publishing, Commercials, and Unions

1 | Getting Started

Before I discuss the structure of the music industry, I'd like to take you through the complete process that a beginner or a near beginner in the industry might need to experience in his efforts to start a music business career. This is only a single example of someone getting started, and the situation may not apply to you or your own problems in starting a career. This is intended as a road map, not a complete guide to the territory.

I am basing this part of the book on questions that people have asked me or that I have heard them ask others in the last few years. Denver, the city where I have been living for the last six years, is a fairly typical American city in the sense that there are some reasonably good recording studios, a few very small record companies, a number of clubs to perform in, and a reasonably good symphony orchestra. Denver is not a center for national recording, so that some of the frustrations or career roadblocks felt by the person in this example may not be true if you live in Nashville, New York, Los Angeles, or Toronto. On the other hand, you may be living in one of these cities, be aware that the industry is there, and have no way of getting yourself in touch with the existing industry apparatus.

Let's say that you are a singer-songwriter, you live in a medium-sized town, say Dubuque, Iowa. You have had a little bit of performing experience, but nothing of an extended nature. In other words you haven't been on the road or played outside the immediate area in which you live, but you do have twenty or twenty-five songs that you have written, and you're really not sure what to do with them. Let's further assume that you have not copyrighted the songs, you don't have an agent or a manager, don't really know anyone making a living in the music business, and are not a member of the union. I am assuming that you have made a commitment in your own mind to try to pursue a successful career in music.

The first thing that you need to do is to get as much performing experience as possible, on whatever level it is available. Offer your services, probably without charge at this point, to hospitals, old age homes, schools for the retarded, public and private schools, parties, or for any other group that might enjoy watching a musical performance. As you begin to get more comfortable with performing, try to notice what is working well in your performances and what doesn't work at all. Try a few of your own songs in your shows, but don't restrict yourself to your own material. What songs do people like? Solicit comments on what you are doing, and listen to unsolicited comments. Have your friends attend some of these performances and ask them to listen to what people are saying about you. Think of this period in your career as a growth or experimental period, where you are putting together a show that will hopefully make you some money in the future. Experiment with your material and your musical arrangements. Make some songs longer than you originally wrote them, take some instrumental solos if you can, use different tempos and try different keys, do some sections of a song louder or softer than others, and so on. If possible, tape some of your performances and some of your rehearsals, and try to be objective about the results. Tape a song before and after you have changed the arrangement and compare the results. Some things will work, other things may not.

After this period of trial and error you should have put together some kind of a coherent show, including some of your own songs. Do guest sets in clubs, and begin to start asking for money for your performances. Find some other musicians to jam with through music stores, music school bulletin boards, friends, and so forth. At this point you may want to decide whether you want to play in a band or pursue a solo career. What kind of music are you playing? If you play hard rock you will need to have a band to get the effect you want. Do you have enough original songs of your own? Are you a great harmony singer who doesn't have a wonderful solo voice? Do you have some friends who have good sound equipment who are looking for an additional performer who plays rhythm guitar, or piano, or whatever you play?

With or without a band, you will need to make a demo tape for the club owner or school staff person who wants to hear a sample of your work. It doesn't have to be a professional tape recorded in an expensive studio. It should represent what you do well enough to give an accurate impression of your sound. Take some time in doing the tape to achieve that result. Sometimes people working in high-fidelity stores or at college radio stations have reasonably good sound equipment and enjoy recording tapes of this kind. See if you can find someone like that to do your tape. Often they will be happy to do your tape for the cost of the tape itself, or for a very small fee. A 16- or 24-track studio will cost you between $80 and $200 an hour, plus $100 or more for each reel of tape. Don't go into the studio thinking you will make a cheap tape.

You should limit the number of tunes on your tape to three or four. In the early stages of your career it is unlikely that anyone will listen closely to much more than that. Don't put very long or esoteric songs on a tape for a club owner—show the range of what you can do, perhaps a ballad, an up-tempo song, and a unique arrangement or song of your own. It is always possible to do a live audition and sing other tunes for a club owner who expresses real interest in what you are doing. You will also need some photos of yourself—you might again try your friends or someone studying photography at an art school. This will minimize your costs.

Let's say that you are now beginning to get work in some local clubs, as a solo act or as a member of a group. Should you copyright your songs? The copyright fee for each song is now $10, so that for twenty songs you are looking at $200. It is possible to copyright a group of songs under one name, such as The Jane Smith Songbook. This will cost you $10, and will protect your songs. As each song gets recorded or published in the future you will have to copyright it separately, but this will save you some money for now. To copyright a song you must include a lead sheet with the melody line, lyrics, and chords of your song (see the Appendix of this book for a lead sheet and the address of the copyright office). In my opinion at this stage no one is apt to steal your songs. It is possible, but unlikely, that someone will run off with your song and copyright it themselves. If someone else has to write your lead sheet for you because you don't read or write music they will probably charge you from $5 to $20, depending on their experience. Music school students are a good source for relatively cheap lead sheets, if you need them. With your demo tape you should include any favorable reviews that you have received in local newspapers or magazines.

Take your demo to various club owners or managers together with your photos and any good reviews of your work. Offer to do a live audition if they want you to do so. As you start to get local club jobs and build a reputation, you will probably be approached by local booking agents, who will flatter you and make promises of work if you sign exclusive agreements with them. Avoid signing any exclusive or long-term contracts at this time, if you possibly can. If you are headed for New York or Los Angeles, why tie yourself up with an agent in Dubuque who will continue to collect commissions on your jobs in New York, but who doesn't have the contacts to get you work outside the immediate area? Don't sign with a personal manager in a small town unless you are convinced that she is as ambitious as you or more so. Will she go anywhere it is necessary to go to promote your long-range career? Do take local jobs from booking agents, and pay them the required commissions on the work they get for you. If necessary sign a relatively short-term contract, say for six months or a year, to book you exclusively. Don't do this either until you have some definite offers of work. They should be for reasonable amounts of money in clubs that you are familiar with, and should specify the number of shows, wages, etc. Take the advice of your booking agent about the union—you may have to join the local in your city of the American Federation of Musicians (AFM) as you start to work in better clubs or in concerts. Before you join the union go down and talk to the officials about the dues, the initiation fee, any possible work dues, and what will be required of you as a union member.

Let's say you are now ready to leave Iowa and try for the big-time in a major recording and talent center. Before you go you may want to take a few precautions. First of all, save up a certain amount of money—enough to sustain you for at least three or four months as you attempt to become established in your new city. You can't reasonably expect to start working right away, and you will need a cushion to sustain you while you get to know the new city, make contacts, and so on. Upgrade your sound equipment. In a larger city you can't get away with inadequate equipment—the competition is too rough. Plan on getting new instruments or amplifiers if you need them—

maybe even a whole new sound system. Make another demo tape. This time pay more attention to the sound quality, and be sure to include some original songs. The purpose of this demo will be to interest a major agent or manager in a big city in your talents. Have some new photos taken, put together your best reviews, and possibly buy some new stage clothes. Where will you live in the big city? Do you have any contacts in the business there? Perhaps a local agent in your hometown knows an agent, a manager, promoter, or record company employee who can put you in touch with the business in your new town. Do you have any other marketable skills? In other words do you have another way to support yourself while you are knocking on music business doors? Have you ever been a waitress, waiter, or temporary office worker? It may take you some time before you become self-supporting with your music in a new environment.

You have now arrived in the big city. Look for clubs that have open stage nights, hootenanny nights, and showcases. Some of these clubs may be famous places, like The Troubadour in Los Angeles, and some may be unknown small bars. Try to meet other composers and musicians through music stores, music schools, clubs, and ads in papers like the *Village Voice* in New York. As a member of the Iowa union you will be allowed to accept one-night jobs in union clubs in New York or Los Angeles, but you will be prohibited from accepting steady work in a club unless you transfer your card (which usually takes six months) or unless you get a card in your new local. The larger locals of the musicians' union generally charge higher initiation fees and dues than the unions in smaller towns. There is also usually a residency requirement of some minimum amount of time. Sometimes the union will waive this residency require-ment, formally or informally, if you can pay the full initiation fee in cash or have someone already in that local of the union vouch that their groups must include you in order to continue working. If you have not joined the union before, you almost certainly will need to do so now.

As you start to get some jobs in clubs you will meet agents again. Most of them will dress better (or flashier), talk faster, and be harder to figure out than the agents in your hometown. Beware of signing long-term agreements based on verbal prom-ises without actual contracts that offer specific jobs. Find out what acts the agent is currently booking, and if possible talk to the acts about the agent. If possible go through a trial period until you are convinced of what the agent can do for you. It is also a good idea at this point to make sure that the agent has a union franchise. If you are in the union you may not work for agents unless they have a union franchise, nor can you work with nonunion musicians.

At this point you need a personal manager. While an agent solicits work for clients, a manager is a person with a career plan for their acts. A manager should have relatively few clients, while a good agency may have a number of agents and a huge number of clients. Which people does the manager currently handle? What do they think of him? What percentage of your earnings does the manager want? Does the manager know many people at record companies? Beware of managers who mention top acts they "used to" manage. Perhaps these people left them, and then went on to fame with no help whatsoever from this manager. Agency contracts are usually fairly cut-and-dried, but no one should sign a personal management contract without having an experienced music business attorney check through the contract. This lawyer should have other clients in the business, and be used to dealing with managers and record companies. A hometown lawyer who is an old friend of the family won't do; after all, you wouldn't go to a heart surgeon to treat an ear infection. Don't use the same lawyer your manager uses to go over your management contract; with all the goodwill in the world he can't reasonably represent both of you. In a year or two you and your manager may end up in court. This could create a conflict of interest for your lawyer, and might leave you without proper legal help.

Be sure that your manager and agency can get along. One of the most important jobs of a manager is to make sure that the artist is getting good agency representation. This includes such matters as replays at higher prices, limitations on the number of shows per night, limitations on traveling between jobs, and more. Your manager and agent should not be the same person, generally speaking, although in the early stages of your career your manager may also help you to find work.

Armed with an agent and a manager and a lawyer you are now ready to go after a recording contract. You should consider making a final demo tape. Perhaps your agent or manager can get a reduced rate at a studio, or even own an interest in one. Your manager should be the key person working on a record deal, but some lawyers and agents are quite knowledgeable and experienced in dealing with record companies. Such an individual may help or spearhead the process. After a record deal is made, attention can be devoted to such matters as where the record will be produced, who the producer should be, what kind of promotional guarantees you can get out of the record company, will the record company advance you some money to buy new instruments or sound equipment, provide some tour support to help transport you to high-exposure but low-money jobs, and so on. Now you are on your way.

There are some things that I have left out of this beginning portrait of the business. I haven't discussed percentages that go to agents and managers because that material can be found in later sections of the book that deal with these specific roles. Similarly I have omitted any description of music publishing or the nature of the record deal. In general, it doesn't help to make unsolicited tapes and send them to a record company where you don't know a soul. Once in a while this rule is successfully violated. The Doobie Brothers were signed on the basis of an unsolicited demo tape sent to Warner Brothers Records, but most unsolicited tapes are thrown away or listened to very quickly by people who are office boys or secretaries. These people cannot sign an act to a record company, but they can reject a tape. If they like a tape, it is simply passed on to someone further up the corporate ladder. At each level your tape can experience a rejection, but you cannot get signed until you have crossed over several levels. It is the job of the personal manager to get your tape to someone at the company with deal-making power, and then to negotiate a deal together with your lawyer, the record company lawyer, and a record company executive.

In this description I don't mean to imply that you are doomed to a life sentence in a music industry center. You may well end up recording in such a town, but if you become successful ultimately you can live wherever you wish. You will always have to maintain some kind of contact with the lifelines of the industry, which run most strongly in New York, Nashville, Los Angeles, and Toronto.

2 Records

Records Are the Vehicle

There are numerous ways for an artist to establish popularity with the general public, including concerts, nightclub performances, and television, but at the present time records are the lifeblood of the music industry. Without making records, an artist's popularity is generally limited to a specific city or region of the country. This is true for every kind of music, from soul to Country & Western to hard rock, jazz, or classical music. Records are the catalyst for music business careers, and without them these careers will not get off the ground. As electronic technology develops it is possible that in the future records as a medium will be replaced in popularity by video cassettes, where the consumer can see as well as hear the performer. It is true that tapes are cornering a larger percentage of the market from year to year, but tapes are essentially the same medium as records. It would also be a mistake to disregard that rare performer, such as Lena Horne, Sammy Davis, Jr., Ben Vereen, or Jim Bailey, who has achieved comparatively little success on records but does very well in nightclub appearances. Nevertheless, at the present time an artist must generally make successful recordings in order to pursue a fruitful career in the music business.

Recording Contracts and How to Get Them

There are a number of ways to get a recording contract, but these methods usually follow the same general pattern. First of all it is necessary to make some sort of contact with a record-company representative and get her excited about your music. There are producers (in the old days referred to as A & R or artist and repertoire people) who look for talent in clubs or concerts. Naturally these visits will occur most frequently in the cities where record company headquarters are located, but some companies will have producers seeking talent in different parts of the country. Sometimes these people are not record producers themselves but are in a department of the company called talent acquisition. Once in a great while one of these people will chance upon a group or an individual performer by accident, but the chances are heavily in favor of their visiting an act that they have heard about through a manager, agent, promoter, lawyer, or another person who works for the record company itself. In New York and Los Angeles there are certain clubs, such as The Troubadour in Los Angeles or The Bottom Line in New York, where industry people often hang out. If you should capture a booking at a club like this, it is very likely you will be seen by some record company people.

The most common way to make contact with a record company is by making a tape which contains a sampling of your music. This is usually called a *demo,* short for demonstration tape. Let's examine the way such a tape is made before we get into such details as how to get it to a record company.

A demo tape should be a succinct summary of the things that you or your group can do, highlighting your special skills or talents, presented in such a way that a busy record executive will sit up and take notice. In my opinion there should be no more than four tunes on such a tape, and none of the tunes should be much longer than three minutes. The reason for this is very simple: the way that a typical record company person will listen to a demo is that she will put it on and listen to the beginning of the first tune. If nothing catches her interest in the first ten or fifteen seconds, she will wind the tape forward to the second cut. By the time she gets to the third tune, if the auditioner doesn't like its beginning, she will probably wind the tape and take it off, regardless of how many selections are on the tape. I have also not yet mentioned that you may not have the listener's complete attention: she may be talking on the phone, reading a music industry trade paper, or doing paperwork. This is not necessarily a function of the executive's uninterest in your tape, but a problem of how many such tapes she must listen to and how many distractions there may be in a busy office.

The reason that a demo is best presented on tape is that tapes can be listened to over and over again without any resulting scratches, while a demo record will wear out very quickly. Althought the sound quality of cassette tapes is poor unless the machine is plugged into a stereo system, many people in the business prefer cassette tapes because they are so convenient. They also can be played in cars that are equipped with cassette recorders.

I said that if a record company person listening to a tape doesn't like the introduction they will often go on to the next cut. Although albums are the key to a long career in the music business, most listeners look for the hit single that will establish a new act in the public eye—the song that can serve as a promotional tool to help identify the group to the average person. If you pay any attention to hit records you will have noted several things about their structure. First of all, most hits have some sort of an introduction that serves to whet your appetite for what is coming next. It may be an unusual musical figure, an instrument recorded in an unaccustomed way—anything that will serve to involve you with the song. Sometimes this figure will recur in various parts of the song, sometimes played in an identical way, sometimes arranged in a different manner as the song continues. This device is called a *musical hook*. It is one technique used in writing and arranging popular songs.

Another rule of thumb is that the opening cut of a demo should be up-tempo and enthusiastic. Make sure that your first song is a song that the listener will want to come back to and hear again. Don't do three consecutive songs in the same key with similar tempos and arrangements. This will expose your group's inability to do more than one thing. On the other hand, the sound of each song should be recognizably that of your group, with whatever strengths you have going represented on each cut. Too much variety may cause a company to feel that your product is not commercial.

What songs should be on your tape? In the competitive record business of the late seventies most record companies prefer talent that writes its own material. If you or the members of your group don't write songs, your best bet is to seek out someone that you know who does write. It may be a fellow musician in another band, an ex-band member who doesn't want to leave home, a sister or brother, or anyone else that happens along. Why do record companies like to see original songs on these demos? There are a number of reasons. If you or your group are going to sustain a career over a long period of time, it will be necessary for you to keep coming up with songs. If no one in the group writes, it means that the band, your manager, and your record producer will spend many hours looking for new songs that are suitable for your style. If you write songs the material is already there, and probably in a style that is compatible with your group. Not being able to write songs doesn't necessarily destroy your career. Linda Ronstadt, Andy Williams, and Glen Campbell are not songwriters to any great extent, but they have been very successful as performers. Sometimes a performer who writes only words or music will establish a long-term collaboration with someone who can supply the missing part of the song. Examples are Carole King's collaborations with Gerry Goffin or Neil Sedaka's work with Howard Greenfield or Phil Cody.

Another reason that record companies like the artist to be a songwriter is so they can publish the songs. This represents a considerable source of money if the artist is successful. (See Chapters 21 and 24.)

You have now come to a critical point in doing your demo tape. You have decided on three or four tunes, you have a fairly good idea of how they will be arranged—who the lead singer will be, what instruments will be played, etc. How good should the tape be? Should you record on a friend's 4-track Teac tape recorder, on your cassette player, or should you go to a 16- or 24-track studio? At this point sit down and use every bit of common sense you and your fellow musicians have. What kind of sound does your group have? Is it a hard-rock band, or are you a singer-songwriter who has a friend add occasional second guitar parts? Does someone in the group have a really incredible voice, one that sounds great in person but doesn't pick up on your $35 cassette recorder? Remember, you are going to be judged on the basis of your demo. Record people get dozens of tapes that include letters excusing the quality of the tape, explaining how broke the group is, that the arrangement is sketchy, the lead singer had a cold, and so forth. Imagine yourself listening to these tapes. What would you do with them?

Do you know anyone who has good tape equipment? You may know an engineer who works for a radio station, a college student who has access to the college's brand-new recording studio (some colleges have good 16-track studios), or there may be a high-fidelity store that would love to engineer a demo by a group that goes on to become famous. These are all ways of doing your tape for little or no money beyond the cost of the tape itself. Keep in mind that someone is doing you a favor. They may not be professional engineers, and your tape may take a bit longer to do and may not come out sounding like a hit record. Remember your goals. You want the tape to reflect the strongest part of your sound. Be sure to feature your strong points—instrumental solos, lead singer, or backup harmonies. What stands out about the sound of your group that would excite a record company? Be sure these qualities get on the tape. If they're not there, go back and do it again.

Assuming that your group hasn't been together for fourteen years, there are also some weaknesses that you recognize. If possible try to keep these weaknesses from being obvious on your tape. Maybe in performance your drummer sings backup harmonies, but he can't sing and play well at the same time. On the actual recording let someone else sing, or put his vocal parts in later.

3 | The Recording Process

I am going to assume that you have gained access to either a 4 or an 8-track recorder through friends, relatives, or whatever. Recording is quite a different procedure from live performance. If you have ever heard a tape of yourself or your group you know what I mean. Some things that work beautifully in performance, such as drum solos or spontaneous shouts, can sound dull and artificial on a tape or record. Weaknesses that are barely noticeable in live performances, such as rhythm sections that are not quite together or vocal harmonies that are slightly out of tune, can be much more serious defects on tape. In a live performance the audience itself is often making quite a bit of noise, and the performance may have an excitement to it that covers up minor flaws.

Modern tape recorders have a number of available tracks on each piece of the tape. Semiprofessional or professional studios have machines that have anything from four to thirty-two tracks. This means that information can be recorded on a different section of the same piece of tape. If the machine has four tracks, four separate bits of information (we can call them programs) can be recorded on a different section of the same piece of tape. If your group has piano, bass, and drums, a lead singer, and some background vocals, you might record the bass and drums on one track, the piano on a second, the lead vocal on track 3, and the background vocals on track 4. This can be done simultaneously or later. The studio can be set up in such a way that the piano track does not "leak" onto the bass and drum track. This is done through careful microphone placement or by setting up wooden *baffles*—soundproof barriers that keep the sound of one instrument from leaking into the microphones of other instruments. When these baffles are used, it is often necessary for the musicians to wear headphones so that they can hear one another. This is a strange experience if you are not used to it. Some people wear one headphone on and one off, which enables them to hear the natural sound of their own instrument while the other instruments are coming through the headphones.

If you don't like the sound that is coming out on the tape, it is possible to experiment with changing microphones, moving the microphones to different positions, or adjusting your own instruments or amplifiers to modify the sound. In the case of guitars or electric basses, it is possible to use or discard various types of picks. Drum heads may be tightened or loosened; pedals on a keyboard instrument can be used more or less.

The lead vocal may be recorded at the time the rhythm section plays, but the final lead vocal is usually done again afterward. Having the vocal there keeps the rhythm section more aware of the song with its lyrics and musical dynamics, but rerecording the vocal enables the performer to concentrate on getting a richer performance without distractions.

Some other recurrent studio problems: make sure that guitar and bass strings are new enough to sound bright, but not so new that a lot of time is wasted in constant tuning; make certain that your drummer has tuned the drum set, that any keyboard instruments are in tune; and if you are using an acoustic piano, have it tuned in the recording studio, just before the session if possible.

You have now finished recording your 4- or 8-track demo, and the next step is to mix it down to a stereo tape, just as you would do for a record. Don't listen to your demo for long periods of time at high volume levels or you may wear out your ears and your patience. Make sure that whatever unique qualities your group has are prominent on your final tape. At this stage of the game don't get too involved with subtleties. If the lead vocals are good, the band is coherent, and the lyrics are understandable, that should be good enough to demonstrate what your group can do. If you are having trouble making decisions, rely on the judgment of the person who did the engineering. Don't bring in friends, lovers, relatives, or other nonprofessional experts or you may get involved in time-consuming and meaning-less arguments.

You will note that I have assumed that you worked out some way of doing the demo without renting a studio. My feeling is that if this is the first time you've worked in a studio with any seriousness it is best not to spend your money there. A 4-track studio might rent for $25–$50 an hour, and an 8-track studio might cost $35–$75 an hour. In addition you will be paying studio tape charges, which can mount up considerably, and you will be charged professional prices for copies of your demo. Very few young bands can afford to go into a studio and burn up thirty or forty hours of studio time at these prices. This is a time for experimentation and learning, not for professional-ism and quickness. If you live in a small town and have no way of getting your tape done, perhaps you will be forced to rent a studio. Talk to the engineer ahead of time, explain what you are trying to do, and find out exactly what it is going to cost. In some instances it is possible to make some sort of trade-off for studio time, such as doing free studio work for the owner of the studio. Perhaps you can sing or play on someone else's sessions in exchange for the studio time. Some engineers who are also musicians arrange to do free engineering in exchange for free studio time for their own projects. Don't make promises to come back and use the studio for your album, and don't give away publishing rights or a percentage of your group's record rights to the studio. Commitments of that kind could prove impossible for you to fulfill at a later date and could involve you in a law-suit.

How good should you make your demo? Try to be realistic. A typical album today costs $50,000 to record. You are not in a position to compete with that sort of studio production. What you are trying to do is to convince a record company to invest that kind of money in your career. Don't be intimidated by insignificant mistakes. Be sure that the main strengths of your group get on the tape and can be heard.

It is possible to make a demo that is a finished product intended for commercial release. This is called a master. Think of the amount of time and money this may take. Also think of your comparitive inexperience. A record company can find you a producer who has experience in putting records together. String parts, horn parts, additional vocals, or other touches may then get added to your record. Unless you have some experience in the studio and unrestricted use of free time, it is best not to think about the possibility of doing a finished product at this time.

This brings up another question. How good are the ears of the person who will ultimately judge your tape? Will they be horrified at the wrong bass note on the second verse of your song? The people who work at record companies vary wildly in their musical tastes and backgrounds. Some of them are ex-musicians or arrangers with tremendous ears—the kind of people who can write out the third saxophone part of a big band record after hearing it once. Others are lawyers or ex-salespeople. Some of them have a good feel for music, but wouldn't know a C from an F#. If there is a glaring deficiency in your band, such as a bad drummer, you may want to use a friend or a fellow musician to play on your tape. You may want to add an instrumental part on one song, such as a flute solo, but not have anyone in the group who plays flute. It is always possible to hire someone to play the part for you. Unless you really think the sound is vital for your demo, it is better to leave it off the tape. When you get a record deal your producer will have access to many fine flute players, and you can hear your idea in finished form.

Selling the Demo

Now that you have completed your demo tape, what are you going to do with it? Let's assume that you are for the most part pleased with the fruit of your labors, and you have your 7½ ips tape copies (that is the best speed for demos) or you have some cassette copies in hand ready to go. At this point you need to get your product to the record company in order to make a deal.

First off, let's deal with the subject of unsolicited tapes. Most large companies employ people who listen to unsolicited tapes that come in through the mail. Your chances of getting a record deal this way are probably something worse than a million-to-one odds working against you. There are always exceptions, of course.

There are some very good reasons why sending an unsolicited tape usually is unsuccessful. The people who listen to these tapes are generally very young people with very little experience. They listen to hundreds of such tapes a week. These "screeners" cannot sign an act to the company. If they do like your tape they will pass it on to the next person up the chain of command. That person hopefully is a record producer and with the approval of the A & R administrator they might sign you. The point is that the person who first heard your tape can pass your tape up to the next rung of the ladder or they may reject your tape. In no case can they make a deal. It is much better to deal with someone higher up in the record company hierarchy in the first place—someone who has decision-making power. Who this person is will vary from company to company. An executive like Clive Davis, president of Arista Records, likes to involve himself with creative decisions. He will go out and sign talent personally. Some other record company presidents don't involve themselves in creative decisions, but might take your tape and give it to a company staff producer to get an opinion.

At this point you probably have already guessed the next part of this dissertation. That is that you need to have someone to sell the tape for you. Ideally this person is your personal manager. It can also be an agent, or a lawyer who specializes in show business law, or a concert promoter who has good connections with a record company. The person attempting to sell the tape must know and believe in the product. They also should have some financial stake in your success as an additional incentive. They have to be able to spend time knocking on doors in New York, or one of the other major music industry towns, and they need to know which doors to knock on.

It is better to have almost anyone try to sell the tape than a member of the group itself. Record companies do not like to talk business with artists. Most artists don't understand the way record companies work, and later they will often feel that the company has taken advantage of them (which it may well have done). Unhappy artists don't make good records, and over a period of years record companies have learned that it's better for the manager and the record company executives to handle business negotiations, which can get quite complex.

Selling a demo requires as much skill, labor, and determination as recording it takes. The person doing the selling needs to be enthusiastic, mature, patient, and good at selling. A personal manager is someone with a career plan for an act, and with the contacts and expertise to make it all happen. If you don't know someone with this sort of capability, you may want to put off the selling, and use the demo itself to find the right person to handle your career. Don't wait too long because records become dated very quickly. Today's new sound is tomorrow's cliché. Above all, don't rely on a personal friend (it usually turns out to be someone your own age) to sell a demo. Not only are the chances minute that someone like this will sell your demo, it may also destroy your friendship when they can't sell it.

It is sometimes possible to get in touch with record companies through people who work at a local branch of a record company or at an independent distributor. Major companies have such sales and promotion branches in most major cities. The problem in having such a person help you is that they may be great at selling or promoting records, but the home office may not have any particular respect for their opinions of talent. If the local person really has a good relationship with a record producer that works for the company, that might work in your favor. Sometimes people in the record business have a tendency to exaggerate, and your idea of friendship might not be the casual relationship that they in fact have with the producer. Everyone in the music business seems to be on a first-name basis with everyone else, but this does not necessarily mean that they are really close to one another.

Be sure to include some photos and any favorable reviews with your demo, much as you did in selling the group long ago to local club owners. If you can write out music, include lead sheets with the melody line, words, and chords written out. Since so few pop musicians are musically literate, this itself may impress the person examining the tape. If you can't write out the music, at least include typed copies of the lyrics. Be sure that these lyric sheets or lead sheets are neat and readable. Include some leader (blank tape) between the songs, so that whoever is listening to the tape can go back and find each song without wasting any time. Write the names and author or authors of each tune on the tape box, so that the listener knows which songs are originals. You might also type out a brief history of the group.

Remember to be patient. Record people often put off appointments or inquiries from people they don't know, or even people they do know, when things get busy. When I worked as a record producer at ABC I once listened to a tape of a group from West Virginia. The seventeen-year-old boy who came to see me was one of the members of the group. A producer at RCA had made him wait eight hours before he would listen to the tape, even though the poor fellow had received an appointment after writing to this particular producer.

The person selling your demo is representing you and your group. He should make a good first impression and be able to answer any questions that the company may have about the group—where it has worked, the age of the people, career plans, education, or anything else the record company wants to know. Often when a good manager doesn't know the answer to questions like these, he will make up a convincing story.

4 The Record Industry: A Brief History

The first phonographs date back to the nineteenth century. Thomas Edison in the United States and Charles Cros in France both came up with similar ideas independent of one another in 1877. In 1893 a phonograph cost $193, a considerable sum at that time. In the early days, records had music on only one side of the record; the other side was blank. In 1904 a German company called Odeon produced the first double-sided records. The first big record star was Enrico Caruso, the opera singer. According to Gelatt,* Caruso made over $2 million in royalties, and his estate collected about as much after his death. Some Caruso recordings are still available today. The first jazz recordings were by the Original Dixieland Jazz Band, a white group that recorded in 1917. Freddie Keppard, a black New Orleans trumpeter, had been offered the chance to record, but he refused, feeling that other musicians would steal his ideas.

The early recordings did not use microphones. Edison had a solid brass horn, which was 135 feet long and tapered to 1 inch wide where the sound was actually being recorded. The records were wax cylinders, and the horn was attached to them. If a mistake was made, the process would start over again. Victor

---

* Much of the material in this chapter was extracted from an excellent book, *The Fabulous Phonograph: 1877 to 1977,* by Roland Gelatt.

introduced electrical recording with microphones in 1925. By 1931 Victor had come up with the idea of long-playing records, but none were produced until after World War II.

Sales of records moved right along, and got as high as 987,000 records in 1927. Shortly thereafter the Depression struck, and sales plummeted to 40,000 in 1932. Gradually the country recovered, and record sales started to go up again. In 1948 Columbia Records introduced the 33⅓ rpm long-playing record. Victor tried to compete with the 45 rpm disc, resulting in several years of costly competition until a compromise was reached, and singles issued on 45 with albums on 33⅓.

Three other innovations changed the character of the record business. The 10-inch LP was eliminated in favor of the 12-inch record, and stereo or 2-channel sound was introduced. Many small companies were badly hurt because they were left with overstocks of 10-inch and monaural records. By 1958 stereo had taken over 69 percent of the business. In the late sixties Columbia tried to introduce quadraphonic sound but met with consumer resistance. Many people do not have a room suitable for 4-channel sound, or don't wish to buy four speakers and an additional amplifier. Whenever I think of quad, I think of my friend Ron Lockhart, who used to be a producer for the Columbia Record Club. I remember him sitting in his cubiclelike windowless office with the walls covered by four speakers in a room smaller than the average kitchen. Possibly if the CBS people had seen Ron's office they wouldn't have pursued quad sound.

The most fundamental change of all in the business was the switch to tape recorders, which were brought back from Germany after World War II. The first tape recorders used only one track, but in the early days of rock 'n' roll someone discovered a process called overdubbing. In overdubbing, after you finish recording, you run two tape recorders at one time, and besides recording the information on the first recorder onto the second machine, you can also add whatever additional sounds you wish at the same time. This was revolutionary for its time, but as you went from one tape recorder to the next, you went to what is called another generation of sound, with a resulting loss of fidelity. This didn't necessarily bother some rock producers, notably Phil Spector, because they were seeking new sound techniques to play with, and an overall thickness of texture in the sound was their goal, not clarity as such.

The next step was the introduction of 2-track tape recorders, quickly followed by 3- and then 4-track machines by the early sixties. With these multitrack machines by recording in the sync mode, which is marked on the machine, the new information could be put onto other tracks of the same tape without any loss of fidelity in adding generations, as was necessary in overdubbing. This is the way modern recording is done at present. Although the process is called sel synchronization, many people still refer to it as overdubbing.

Tracks soon jumped from 4 to 8, briefly to 12, and then came the major leap to 16 tracks in the middle sixties. With 16 tracks the technology that we know today was born. Not only could most instruments have their own tracks, but some instruments, such as the piano, were recorded on two tracks initially, with the high notes of the piano on one track, and the low notes on another track. The drum set was separated on as many as five or six tracks; each track was devoted to a different part of the drum set. All of this also required a necessary refining of microphone techniques so that leakage could be avoided from one track to another. In the middle and late sixties noise-reduction systems came into use to remove tape hiss. The first system that became popular was the Dolby system. Then came DBX, and today Telefunken and others are also in use. These systems work in somewhat different ways, and different engineers and producers prefer one or another. Many studios have only one of the systems because each one of them represents a considerable expense, since the noise reduction must be added to each track separately. When you use one of the systems on a record, if you mix the record in another city you must use a studio that has the same noise reduction equipment.

Today 24-track studios are common, and 32-track tape recorders are also being manufactured. At times two 24-track machines are linked together. The linkage uses up 2 tracks, thereby keeping 46 available tracks. I suppose the technology will continue until someone records a symphony with 105 tracks, one for each instrument.

It is a wonderful thing to have so many tracks to experiment with, but it has a tendency to make a producer put off decisions about the final product until the very end of the process. In the final mix the producer, together with an engineer, and sometimes the artist, must mix down the 24 tracks to a stereo tape. Generally speaking, the original tape is recorded flat—that is, no echo or special effects are added on the original tape—but at this point in the process it is possible to add echo, and to add or subtract the high, medium, and low frequencies on the top. This is called equalization, or EQ. Many producers spend hours and hours equalizing the various tracks, especially if there is some sound that they don't like on the original tracks.

Other special effects are available through the use of a graphic equalizer, limiters, tape-delay devices, and a recent mixing toy called the Aphex aural exciter. Many of the smaller studios cannot afford all of these devices, which is one reason not to make records in places like Dubuque, Iowa. It isn't so much that you can't make good records without these devices as it is that not having the technology puts you at a competitive disadvantage. You should have access to these devices, whether or not you elect to use them.

Once the tape is completed, and approved by the record company, it is taken or sent to a mastering studio. At this point in the process it is still possible to influence the sound of the tape, but the decisions are on a different level. Again, you can add or subtract from the high, middle, and low ends of the sound spectrum. However, at this point your information is on 2 tracks only. If you don't like the sound of the bass and you boost the bass frequencies, everything else on that channel (left or right) will also have its bass frequencies boosted. It is therefore fairly radical surgery to make this kind of decision at this time. It is advisable to have someone at the mastering session who worked on the record, preferably a producer or engineer. The mastering engineer usually does nothing but master records for eight or more hours a day and will not be familiar with your record. If you have one cut on your record that is too loud, for example, rather than cutting the volume on that song alone, the engineer may simply set all the volume levels low. Consequently your record will sound dull and lifeless, especially on the radio.

What actually goes on in the mastering is that the engineer is cutting your tape onto a record. This lacquer then gets covered with silver nitrate. From this "mother" record is made a stamper, and the stamper is mounted onto a hydraulic press which turns hot plastic into records. Dozens of these presses work at one time, and each stamper is good for about 500 records, after which another stamper must be made from the mother.

The newer tape recorders run at 30 ips. Some artists are starting to record at 30, and do not use the noise-reduction systems. Some people feel that the Dolby system takes quite a bit of brightness out of the sound of a record, and in the case of the DBX you can actually hear the sound of the noise-reduction device pumping along with the music if you have a particularly acute ear.

In the last several years a few high-fidelity-oriented companies have returned to the pretape days and have been recording direct to disc without tape recorders. Such recordings are harder to do because any serious mistake causes a scrapping of that master disc. You must rely on musicians who make few or no mistakes. The resulting sound is unquestionably cleaner and brighter than the sound of records made from tapes. The records are also about twice as expensive at the moment, so that it appears they will remain a specialty item for sound enthusiasts. Since rock 'n' roll usually entails so much experimentation in the studio, it is hard to imagine rock 'n' roll recorded in this way.

5 Record Companies

There is a wide variety of record companies in North America. Some of them are small specialty labels that may press as few as 500 copies of a record at a time. Others are full-service companies recording all styles of music and with worldwide distribution. RCA, Columbia, MCA, and the Warner Brothers Elektra-Atlantic-Asylum complex (WEA) are examples of full-service record companies. Even in such companies there may be specific areas of weakness or concentration; for example, WEA consigns its classical music to the small Nonesuch label, which itself is a subsidiary of Elektra.

Below these supersize record companies is the large independent company, of which there are really only two today. These companies are Arista* and Motown. The independent companies do not own and operate branch offices in various cities as do the full-service companies. Instead they rely on independent record distributors in various cities, which do the distribution and selling. The large independent record companies do have their own promotion people, but many of the smaller record labels also farm out their promotion to these independent distributors.

---

* Arista is owned by Columbia Pictures, but uses independent record distributors.

Another difference between the independent and the giants is that the medium-size record companies are essentially in the record business—they do not make movies or manufacture refrigerators, own television networks, parking lots, guitar companies, funeral parlors, or other businesses.* All of these activities and others are pursued by some of the major companies mentioned above.

Below the medium-size record company is the specialty company that makes records in a specific field, such as gospel music, blues, Country & Western, modern jazz, or other kinds of music. Some of these labels, such as Philadelphia International Records, may be quite powerful in their own field—in this case pop-soul—but they generally avoid recording other styles of music. When the smaller companies try to market diversified products they often find that they lack not only the expertise but also the image to sell products in other areas of music.

The largest record companies have a fairly complex operating structure. Companies like Columbia or WEA have someone at the top of the structure who sits on the board of directors of the parent company (CBS or Warner Communications), for example, and who is responsible for overall supervision of the record division of these corporations. Just below this person is the president of the company. The president of a major company may have a creative background, coming from work as an artist, musician, songwriter, arranger, composer, or performer; or he may have a business-administrative background, coming out of sales, promotion, law, or accounting. The way in which presidents of large record companies operate will vary as widely as do their backgrounds. Clive Davis, president of Arista Records, likes to become involved with the artists and their records. He advises the artists on directions, tries to match them with appropriate producers, often signs artists after actually seeing them perform or auditioning them, and likes to participate in decisions about which songs are produced. The heads of RCA Records have always tended to be somewhat anonymous—they seem to frequently come out of sales and marketing backgrounds and generally stay out of the creative areas.

It is important to know what kind of company you are

---

* A & M is an independently owned record company, but its records are now distributed by RCA. Since A & M was one of the most successful independently distributed record companies, its decision to go with RCA in early 1979 has caused shock waves in the entire record distribution system.

recording for because it may have a strong influence on your career. It is a cliché in the business that RCA has in the past been run by committees, and that it often took an endless amount of time to get a decision from them on a specific artist. On the other hand, RCA has also demonstrated more patience with the development of an artist's career than many of the other companies have. John Denver, for example, didn't really start to become popular until his fourth or fifth solo LP for RCA. Many companies would have given up on him after his first, or perhaps second, record.

Below the president of a record company are positioned the various departments of the company. Many of the department heads have titles as vice-president of something or other, such as A & R, marketing, etc. The titles in themselves don't necessarily have any significance, but may or may not reflect the importance of a particular job. Below is a chart that will convey some idea of how a major record company might be organized.

In addition to the people shown on the chart, there may be others working at subsidiary labels, such as Epic, in the case of Columbia. Some of the same people, such as lawyers, might do work for both companies but the subsidiary may have its own creative and marketing staff, at least to some extent. Columbia and RCA have their own record clubs with their own staff. Production work at a record club is largely a matter of thinking up intelligent reissue projects, and deals must be made with various companies to lease their material. Some record companies have their own recording studios, with a staff of engineers, maintenance engineers, and setup people. The studio manager may also rent the studio out to other record companies or individuals to do recording sessions. Some companies, such as CBS, have their own mastering facilities and even press their own records. They will have manufacturing and warehousing facilities in various parts of the country, and business people and factory workers in these plants. Premium divisions deal with special projects, such as the Christmas records which are sold at tire stores. When a major label has its own pressing plant, it also may be used by other record companies to manufacture their records.

The major record companies all have publishing divisions. Most of these operations are there simply to pick up the publishing of some of the artists who record for the company, but a few of them, such as United Artists Music and Warner Brothers Music, are large operations in their own right. Both of these companies also have print divisions, where they publish sheet

RECORD DIVISION SUPERVISOR ON BOARD OF DIRECTORS OF PARENT COMPANY

PRESIDENT OF RECORD COMPANY

A&R (Artist and Repertoire)	Marketing Division	Creative Services	Business Staff	Publishing
Chief	Sales and Promotion	May be national director	Legal, accounting dept., cost analysts, personnel specializing in foreign rights	Head of company
Staff	Each may have a national director			Staff
	Staff	Staff of various sizes in advertising, publicity, graphics-album covers, or free-lance people may be hired for specific projects	Secretarial help	Professional managers, staff writers
Independent producers hired for specific projects	May be broken down into specific kinds of music (national director of promotion for soul-disco music, etc.)			If there is a print division, it includes extensive personnel, such as staff arrangers
Secretaries includes executive secretaries and people who have specific functions, such as dealing with unions, studios, publishing licenses, etc.	May be a national director for singles promotion			
	Product managers and artist-relations staff			
	Secretarial staff			

Miscellaneous

May include people working on special projects, premium records, or whatever. Record clubs would be a separate division.

Subsidiary labels would have their own creative staffs and smaller business and marketing staffs.

music and folios of their own and other artists. They also print music for high school and college bands and choral groups, and instruction methods for specific instruments.

Occasionally a record company will have a talent management wing to handle its own artists. None of the giant companies do this, but some of the smaller companies do.

Some companies have people in the A & R department who do not produce records but who are involved in the process of talent acquisition. In other companies the producers themselves would be expected to pursue this function. The staff of the various departments will vary in size according to the size and policy of the company. For example, at the present time there is a tendency for companies to develop their own A & R departments. Five or ten years ago many staff producers were fired, and the companies were using more independent producers to produce records.

At the bottom of this hierarchy, working in a cubbyhole in the A & R department sits the office person who listens to unsolicited tapes that are received in the mail. Looking at the chart you can see why you are better off never having to deal with this person.

Classical Records

The merchandising of classical music is a very different matter from the selling of a pop record. The market tends to be concentrated in an older age group, and the audience is quite particular about the sound quality of records. Liner notes often contain detailed information about the music and a particular performance. In classical music there are certain staples of the repertoire, such as Beethoven's Fifth Symphony, that are recorded over and over again, so the quality of a particular performance is important to the buyer. Compared to popular music or jazz, a very small amount of new repertoire is recorded.

Favorable reviews by important critics are an important means of influencing a record company to contract a new artist. As with pop music the record company will be impressed by a well-qualified manager and by the artist's willingness to tour. Record people working in classical music often have considerable knowledge of the music. Many of them are composers, musicians, or ex-musicians.

Certain orchestras, performers, and conductors, such as the Philadelphia Orchestra, Arthur Rubinstein, and Leonard Bernstein, to give an example of each, have the same magical appeal to the classical music buff as do pop stars in their field. In recent years some companies have begun to market classical music in a style similar to the way they sell pop music. Columbia has taken this approach with its composers' greatest hits albums and by featuring eye-catching album covers.

Large-scale orchestral works and operas are often recorded in Europe because the union scales for musicians are one-third to two-thirds less than in the United States, depending on the country where the record is produced. Because classical music constitutes a very small share of the record market in the United States,* many companies don't bother with it at all, or they simply distribute records produced abroad. On the other hand, some small record companies, such as CRI, produce recordings of serious contemporary works for a small, select audience.

Specialty Records

Specialty record companies exist in every conceivable style of music, ranging from polka bands to free jazz. These companies must have a very accurate concept of their audience because when a record is pressed in small quantities there is virtually no promotion budget available. Often the company may have one or two employees, including the owner, so that it is possible to go right to the top level of management for decisions.

Some specialty companies sell records by mail, advertising in appropriate magazines. The artists may also sell the records whenever they perform. Some companies operate regionally, attempting to concentrate their sales in a specific area. This is particularly true of foreign language music. The interest in Cajun music, for example, is clearly centered in Louisiana.

Many specialty companies offer little or no advance money to the artist and they may operate outside the rules of the AFM or AFTRA. Production costs of these records are usually kept very low, especially if the company owns its own studio or uses portable recording equipment.

The audience for specialty music is very particular, and innovative sounds may result in controversy. This may reduce

---

* The share is 3.4 percent of the record market, according to NARM, the National Association of Record Merchandisers.

or increase record sales, depending on the ultimate judge, the consumer. The introduction of contemporary songs and electric instruments into bluegrass music, creating a style called "new-grass," has created this kind of furore.

The owners of these small companies often have a true love for the music and do not really expect to make much money from their records. There are always exceptions, of course. Some of these record people are ambitious and greedy, and some make money without seeking to do so.

6 | The Record Producer

In the forties and early fifties record producers were called A & R men (they were virtually all males) and they were the kingpins of the industry. They found the artists, usually through the efforts of personal managers and agents, and they also found the songs for the artists to record. In those days artists did not generally write their own songs. The songs were brought in by music publishers, who constantly solicited record producers with future "hits." The songs were brought in on records which became known as *demos*. These demos are a peculiar part of the business because up until recent years the unions did not consider demos legal, yet hundreds of them were recorded by union musicians in New York. There were and are certain studios that specialize in this sort of recording and will even hire the musicians for their clients. Generally, in the making of a demo, a small orchestra was used, most often a rhythm section with the piano or guitar playing lead lines or fills. Occasionally, a publisher might add strings or background voices to help convince the producer and his artist that this particular song was especially suitable for the artist. Usually the singer on the demo was told to imitate the style of the artist for whom the demo was intended, without doing too precise a copy. Many singers who record commercials are capable of doing an exact imitation of a current artist, should the client desire, and some of these people developed these skills in the making of demos.

Similarly, quite a few good studio musicians broke into the recording field by playing on demos. It was a good way to break in because, although the sessions were usually completed in an hour, there was relatively little pressure, and the session involved a combination of reading and improvisation. Both of these abilities are important in studio work, as you will see.

The publisher would make a lead sheet of the song, with the melody line, lyrics, and chords written out. This would then be submitted, usually in person, to the A & R man. Often part of the ceremony might include a free lunch at a good restaurant, which is a perfectly legal business device that is practiced in most businesses when a salesperson entertains a prospective customer.

A key part of the producer's job, in that era, was the ability to recognize a hit song. A producer might listen to hundreds of songs to find that hit single and to fill up the resulting album. Then the producer would hire an arranger, or on occasion write the musical arrangement himself. Before the actual arrangement was written the arranger would find the correct key for the artist. The arrangement itself would usually attempt to include some sort of musical catchphrase or gimmick that would be repeated several times in the song. This is called a *hook*. These arrangers were often well-trained musicians with music careers and even careers as soloists or bandleaders behind them. Some arrangers, especially the more jazz-oriented ones, were essentially self-taught but were equally capable.

The producer would then take the artist and the arrangement into the studio. Since recording was done on one or two tracks at that time, it was done live, with the singer and the band recording at the same time. The producer or the arranger generally used a contractor to hire the musicians. When I talk about studio work you will see how that works. The arrangement was usually fairly preset, and most of the music was written out with an occasionally improvised solo. If background singers were used, still another contractor hired them.

Since there was no multitrack recording at the time, special electronic effects were usually minimal, and done at the time of recording rather than in the mix. All that remained by the end of the session was a bit of editing and the record was ready to go.

The ultimate A & R man at that time was probably Mitch Miller. He was an excellent oboe player before he started his career as a producer. As a producer at Columbia in the early fifties he recorded such artists as Doris Day, Frankie Laine,

Johnny Ray, and Jo Stafford. The popular songs of the day were generally saccharine love songs directed at the teenager. Love was presented in dull and romanticized terms and had little to do with life. The titles alone, "Cry," "Be My Love," "Secret Love," and others of that ilk convey the subject matter. Most of these songs were written by professional songwriters, who sat in their little offices in the Brill Building at 1619 Broadway and turned out dozens of slushy love songs, together with an occasional novelty tune. In the period 1950–56 Miller-produced records sold over 80 million copies, according to sociologist R. Serge Denisoff, writing in his survey of the industry entitled *Solid Gold: The Popular Record Industry.*

At the peak of Mitch Miller's career a new, comparatively crude, and energetic music called rock 'n' roll appeared. The early rock 'n' roll records were mostly "cover" records. These were recordings by white artists of black music of the day, prettified and simplified for the white teenager. The first big hit was Bill Haley's "Shake, Rattle and Roll," a sort of countrified rock version of the original rhythm and blues hit by Joe Turner.* In the next few years a number of white artists, such as Pat Boone and Georgia Gibbs had hit after hit in this fashion, by covering songs that were popular in the rhythm and blues field.

There were several reasons why it was the cover records that became national hits rather than the original versions of the songs. Generally the average white teenager had some trouble understanding the lyrics in the original records, as did the average white disc jockey. Many of the large radio stations did not want to play records by black artists, and in some cases the small record labels that recorded the original records lacked good national distribution and promotion. When the cover records were put out by the major labels, the small companies were shut out of the major markets.

Bill Haley and the Comets was an important group for another reason as well. It was a self-contained band that could make its own recordings and didn't require the services of a musical arranger to add strings or horns. It didn't need the production services of a sophisticated musician like Mitch Miller. As a self-contained group the Comets foreshadowed the

---

* In the twenties and thirties black music was called race music; later it was referred to as rhythm and blues; today it is called soul.

revolution that came full force to the industry with the rise of the Beatles.

Most of the Mitch Miller-era producers or arrangers were older, trained musicians. These people did not like or understand rock 'n' roll, but considered it an unpleasant form of musical primitivism. It is amusing to look back on comments that people like Miller, who was producing some of the corniest drivel ever recorded, made about rock 'n' roll. The traditional producers were also beginning to experience the generation gap. They were too old for the kids who were now buying the records. They didn't understand the dances, the black influences on the music, the rebellious nature of the whole experience, or much else about it.

The independent record producers who came to the fore in the middle and late fifties were a different breed of cat from the staff producers for the big companies. Foremost among them were Jerry Leiber and Mike Stoller, who worked as a team, and Phil Spector. These men were songwriters themselves, and they spent a great deal of time rehearsing groups that did not read music before taking the groups into the studio. Spector worked on many of the musical arrangements in the studio itself instead of relying on written music. Besides being younger than the staff producers for the big companies, these independents had a great deal of sympathy for black music, particularly blues and gospel music. If the earlier producers had any interest in black music at all, that interest was usually limited to jazz.

As independent producers developed, a new mode of business operation appeared with them. Sometimes the independents were hired by record companies to produce acts that were in their artist roster but which none of the staff producers felt capable of producing. Soon the independents started to sign acts to contracts, produce the records, and then sell the records to the record companies. In many instances the producers were also songwriters, and they kept control of the music publishing rights when they signed their deals with the record companies. In some cases the producers managed or shared in the personal management of the acts as well. The independent producer replaced the staff A & R person as the glamour boy of the business, and Phil Spector even started his own record company. Spector was a flamboyant example of a style of production that is still practiced today. His productions showcased his production abilities as much or more than the talent of the artists.

Leiber and Stoller worked in a different way with the studio. They wrote and rehearsed their songs with groups like the Drifters or the Coasters, and then they relied on written arrangements by such arrangers as Gary Sherman for the instrumental tracks. It is also important to mention the work of Ahmet Ertegun, one of the founders of Atlantic Records. Although he was not a musician, he was a great fan of black music. Ahmet wrote songs based on black colloquialisms and went into the studio and cut hit records. Most of the Atlantic Records of the fifties and early sixties were too black-oriented to be hits in the white market, but later Jerry Wexler, another brilliant nonmusician producer, was able to come up with all-market hits by black artists, especially Aretha Franklin.

The rise of the independent producer highlighted a basic change in the music business, which is still having its effects at the present time. The producer now fulfills a great variety of functions, whether working on staff or independently. The producer may find the artist through a network of personal contacts that includes personal managers, booking agents, lawyers, friends, concert promoters, musicians, or accidental contacts. When I worked as a staff producer for ABC-Command-Probe Records I found acts through a music store owner in Denver, a local booking agent in Washington, D.C., and one walked in off the street by chance. Other artists were assigned by the president of the company. In looking for talent I made several trips to such towns as Albany, Boston, Washington, D.C., and Philadelphia, and normally saw some acts perform in clubs in New York, which was the company's headquarters.

Once the producer finds an act, she goes to the head of the A & R department, who is often not a record producer but is primarily an administrator, and discusses the situation. What sort of deal is necessary, is the act working, do they have a manager, should the deal include an album or just be for a single release, where can the group promote the record effectively? All of these are questions that the administrator might ask, and if the producer and her boss agree, the legal department (if it is a large company) will prepare a contract. The contractual details will be discussed later, but assuming the contract is signed, rehearsal begins and the producer may prepare a budget, which she and her boss will discuss. If the group is a local group, rehearsal is no problem; the producer will attend some rehearsals, help pick tunes, make suggestions about the musical arrangements, and develop rapport with the group. If the group is from a distant city the producer will probably want to hear tapes of the songs they expect to record. If possible the producer will want to meet with the group. This can be arranged by the producer's going to visit the group or by the group arriving for the sessions several days early and meeting with the producer. It is advantageous for everyone to get to know one another before the sessions start, and to work on some of the musical arrangements together.

The producer will usually choose what studio the group will be working in and also the particular engineer that will do the recording. Some record companies like to use their own studios for obvious economic reasons and also for reasons of convenience. It is most important that the producer and engineer complement each other's abilities because they will be working very closely on this project. Some engineers hate specific kinds of music, and this can create unpleasantness in the studio. If a producer is in a strong bargaining position at a particular record company, she will insist on working with an engineer with whom she is compatible.

Some producers, such as Billy Sherrill, who works for Columbia in Nashville, are also excellent songwriters, and they may actually write a song specifically for the group to record. They also may make suggestions to an artist about recording songs by other songwriters to broaden the appeal of an album. Sometimes these suggestions are motivated by a producer owning part or all of the publishing rights to a song, but a good producer should be motivated primarily by making the best possible album for your group.

There is no one style of producing records, and producers usually come from one of three different kinds of backgrounds. Some are trained or untrained musicians or arrangers who may be particularly skilled at putting together musical sounds. Such a producer is especially valuable when working with a young musical group that really hasn't quite settled on its musical directions yet. Richard Perry and Bob James are contemporary producers who possess this sort of background. Generally this kind of producer will concentrate on the music and let the engineer take care of the equipment. This will vary according to how much background the musician-producer has in engineering, and how comfortable she is with the engineer. Other producers are basically engineers, with little or no formal musical background. Bones Howe and Bill Szymsyck are examples of this kind of producer. An engineer-producer is perfect for a group like The Eagles, which Bill in fact produces. An experienced group has a musical groove that is well worked out, and they don't need much advice about musical arrangements. In such a case the engineer-producer concentrates on getting exactly the right sound out of the equipment. Sometimes such a producer will actually engineer the record as she is producing it. Or she may simply tell an engineer exactly what to do. The third kind of producer is not formally trained in either music or engineering but has a great feel for what constitutes a good record, together with a good natural ear. Lou Adler and Jerry Wexler are examples of this style of producer. A few producers may have both a music and an engineering background, as does Phil Ramone. This is probably the ideal situation, in terms of being able to translate musical conceptions into actual engineering practice.

The skills required to successfully produce jazz and classical music recordings are somewhat different from those of the producer of popular music. A classical music producer needs to be able to follow a musical score in order to guide the engineer in making difficult tape splices and to be able to make decisions as to which parts are important in complex orchestral writing. Similarly, a good jazz engineer will have to be able to balance a horn or saxophone section. Often sections of instruments are recorded on a single track. Does the second saxophone have the melody in a specific section, is one violin playing a countermelody while the others all play the same part? In recording jazz and classical music there is usually relatively little overdubbing, and the emphasis has to be on getting the correct instrumental balances and then going after a quality performance rather than putting the parts in later.

In the recording session itself the producer must demonstrate an ability to work with people. The producer needs to know exactly what will help someone do a better performance in the same way that a sports coach must function with athletes. Some people require attention and encouragement, some are better left alone, some may respond to anger. Different producers may be more or less comfortable with using psychological devices in working with artists, and each must find a style that suits the situation and her own personality.

Producers are also responsible for such details as making sure sessions are reported to the various unions, contracts are delivered to the record company for the recording sessions, and payments are made within the period of time required by the various unions. Other details to take care of include studio rentals, calling in the instrumental setup to the studio ahead of time, renting the instruments, and the hiring of an arranger or additional musicians if necessary.

A producer must be capable of making decisions. Can the group do a song better than they have done it for the last two hours, will one more performance produce the right sound, or was the take recorded an hour ago the best the group can do? Should a take be stopped because of a bad note, or can it be overdubbed later? When should a break be called, and when should the tape be played back for the musicians and some changes made in the arrangement or the microphones be readjusted? All of these seemingly casual decisions can simplify or destroy a recording session, depending upon the timing of when they are made.

After the recording session is over, the producer usually goes home and waits several days, or even weeks, before mixing down the tape to the 2-track stereo master. This waiting period enables her to take a fresh and more objective view of the project. In the mix, as we have already mentioned, each track is equalized, echo or special effects may be added, and decisions may be made to rerecord certain parts of the song. If the mix is for an album, the producer must decide where to place each track in the stereo spectrum. A track may be heard in the left or right speaker alone, it may be in the center, which makes it audible on both speakers equally, or it may be positioned slightly to the left or right. The way the tracks are placed will influence the total sound, and the producer will listen carefully to the effects of each decision, trying to decide when and how the desired result is achieved. To mix a 16- or 24-track tape down to two tracks (for an album) or one track (for a single) can take many, many hours. It will take anywhere from two to six hours for each tune, depending on how complicated the original recording was and what the producer is trying to do in the mix. Often after a whole day of mixing, she will be unhappy with the results, and will come back another day and start over again. In well-equipped modern studios computerized mixing boards are available. They can quickly recreate a previous mix, which the producer may then wish to modify in some minor respect. Before these boards were available (and in studios that cannot afford them), it was necessary for the producer or engineer to write down the settings of each dial or take a Polaroid picture of the dials in order to recreate a mix.

Mixing can be very frustrating because people hear differently on different days, so that coming back to a studio and using the same settings still may not appear to recapture a specific mix. The equipment itself can be affected by variations in temperature, wearing out of tape heads, replacement or exchange of tape recorders, or other seemingly intangible phenomena.

After the mix is completed, the record must be mastered from tape to disc. It is wise for the producer to attend the mastering, if it is at all possible. Once the mastering is completed, she waits for test pressings from the factory. When the test pressings arrive, she must sit down and listen to them for possible defects of skipping, sticking in the grooves, too much surface noise, hisses or pops, or any other disturbances. This is a tedious but essential part of production.

Some producers involve themselves in such matters as the album cover, liner notes, credits, and back-cover graphics. The producer must perform or supervise all of the paperwork that is a standard part of record company procedures. It is necessary to apply for mechanical licenses from the various music publishers that own the songs on the record, the release of the record must be scheduled within the company, and the producer must play the record for sales and promotion people in the company in order to build excitement in the company even before the record is released to the public. Those producers who have contacts in the promotion area, especially at radio stations, will often try to assist in the promotion of the record as well.

The work of the record producer is at the heart of the creative part of the record business. It is because this work is so important that they can earn fabulous wages, particularly independent producers. Their royalties can be from 3 to 5 percent of the retail selling price of the records, and they can often negotiate large advances, as much as $25,000 or more for an album. This is an advance against royalties, and negotiations are similar to artist negotiations in terms of packaging deductions and the like. Producers who work on staff at a record company are paid salaries, have expense accounts, and may or may not earn percentages or points, as they are called, on their productions. In some cases the company may pay a bonus to the whole production staff, which is split among the various producers. A successful producer would much rather be paid according to the success of each production. Other sources of income include songwriting, publishing, or even personal management of the producer's artists.

One of the reasons why producers are so well paid is that the creative life span of a successful producer is usually short. Record producers often have specific styles of working in the studio. As pop music changes these styles may go out of fashion. Most pop artists are young people in their twenties or even younger. These artists may feel uncomfortable working with a middle-aged producer. Older producers may gain a reputation as being old-fashioned, whether musically or in terms of their life-style. Producing a record requires endless patience and dedication, and a producer may become creatively burned out. She may be tired of the endless repetition of the same few songs on an album or the constant musical decisions that are part of the process. A number of producers have said that when they finish producing a record they never want to have to listen to that record again. Lou Adler, Bob Crewe, Dave Appell, Snuff Garrett, and Bones Howe are examples of producers who have been able to sustain their careers over long periods of time, but they have had many ups and downs too. Few producers have a successful production life of more than five years. They may then go on to jobs as record company executives, music publishers, radio station executives, go into the business of making commercials, work for industry trade organizations, or they may leave the business entirely.

Cost of Records

Chris Strachwitz, writing in *Lightning Express,* #3, 1976, estimates the cost of producing small quantities of records as follows:

1,000 copies	cost between $1.86 and $4.13 per record
5,000	cost between $1.41 and $1.86
10,000	cost between $1.35 and $1.58

Price variations reflect use of single or double-fold albums, color or black-and-white covers, and varying amounts of studio time and advances to the artist, plus payments to other musicians. It is obvious that producing as few as 1,000 albums makes the break-even figure difficult to reach.

7 | Record Company Contracts

Record company contracts with artists are long and fairly complex documents. If you want to see what one looks like consult page 544 of *This Business of Music* by Sidney Shemel and M. William Krasilovsky.*

The initial contract that a record company offers is not necessarily the contract that you should sign. Dealing with record companies is a chess-style negotiation process, and you should work with a competent lawyer on any aspects of the contract that you consider undesirable. Some of these areas of contention might involve money, whether in terms of royalty percentages or advances. Others may involve artistic control of the product—who will choose the producer, the album cover, or a number of other possible controversies.

In general you should never sign a deal with a record company without consulting a competent music business attorney. Avoid lawyers who are friends, or friends of friends, or who handle divorces or real estate closings in their practice. It is difficult to find an experienced show business lawyer outside the music industry centers. You may have to use a local lawyer and have him consult with a music industry lawyer in New York,

---

* Be sure to get the 1977 edition, which states on the cover that it is the New Copyright Act Edition.

Los Angeles, or Nashville. I cannot emphasize enough that a lawyer in general practice will not be adequate for your needs. Music industry lawyers charge fees of $50–$200 an hour. Sometimes they are hired for a monthly retainer or even for a percentage of the artist's earnings.

The royalty percentage offered to you should start at 5 percent of the retail selling price of the record. Some record companies express royalty percentages in terms of the wholesale selling price. If this is the case in your contract make sure that the royalty on this price is at least double the retail royalty, or even slightly higher. Make sure that the royalties are expressed as percentages and not flat sums of money. I signed several contracts a number of years ago that expressed the royalties in terms of a precise amount of money. Twenty-five cents is a good royalty on a retail selling price of $3.98, but it isn't too good in terms of the current retail prices of $6.98 and $7.98.

The royalty figure I have given is a good royalty for a starting artist. Superstars may get royalties of as much as 12 percent of retail. Agreements can also be negotiated where royalty percentages increase over certain sales plateaus. There really is no one standard record deal today, but generally record companies will design the contract in terms of a one-year time span, with four additional options of one year each held by the record company. In order to exercise or "pick up" these options the record company must notify the artists or their personal manager thirty days before the end of the first year. This notification must be in writing, and is usually sent by registered mail. You may be able to get a provision written into the contract that if the record company picks up the option your royalty rate will go up.

Advances beyond the minimum union-scale payments are part of negotiating a record deal. The extent of such advances depends on who is doing the negotiating and how badly the record company wants to sign the act. Your lawyer and your personal manager should work as a team to get the maximum amount of money for your group. Advances of $10,000–$20,000 are not unusual for a major record company to pay. If several record companies are bidding for your services it is possible you will be able to get an even better deal. In most cases this money is considered an advance against your royalties. This doesn't mean that you personally must pay the money back if your records don't sell, but it does mean that you will not receive any royalties until all of these costs are paid back in terms of your record sales. When a record company is very eager to sign a particular act, it may be possible for all or some of the advance to be regarded as a nonreturnable cash bonus which will not be charged against future earnings. This is an unlikely event at the start of a recording career, but is the type of negotiation that artists like the Rolling Stones or John Denver can insist upon in renegotiating their contracts after the initial contract expires.

Some understanding must be reached with the company as to where your recording will occur. Who will pay your living expenses while you are making the record, who will pay transportation from your hometown? These questions are of considerable importance early in your career; hopefully at a later date your group will be in better financial condition. Often these details can be worked out in the form of a verbal agreement between your manager and the record company. The record company may be willing to help with your financial difficulties on your first record, but they will probably be unwilling to continue advancing these monies later in your career. Of course, if you are receiving a sizeable advance in the contract, some of that money can be used to pay these expenses. Sometimes the advance is not payable until completion of the first album. Similarly, your union payments for playing or singing on the sessions are not payable for two or three weeks after each recording session. This varies, depending on which union is covering you. Since your first recording sessions are extremely vital, and you will probably be fairly keyed up, worrying about having enough money to stay in a decent hotel is the last kind of problem you will need at this point.

For a young group the initial advance can be a very important item. With that money you may be able to pay off instruments that were bought on the installment plan, purchase a van or truck, or get new costumes or a sound system. In the United States (European contracts work differently) all the costs of recording your records will be charged against your royalties. These charges can include renting the recording studio, hiring a musical arranger, your own union fees, monies paid to other musicians who play on your records, instrument rentals, promotional expenses, and advertising. Most record companies compute their royalties on 90 percent of records sold. This quaint custom reflects the days of 78 rpm records and consequent breaking and shipping losses. If possible your lawyer should renegotiate this figure to 100 percent. Royalties for tape sales are often offered at 50 percent of record royalties. This can be renegotiated to two-thirds or even 100 percent by your lawyer. Record club royalties are also usually 50 percent of ordinary record sales. Often no royalties will be paid on free records given away by the record club. If your lawyer can do so, it is advantageous to place some sort of limitation upon the number of records that can be given away. Records given to radio stations or record stores will not be computed in your royalties, and this is a necessary concession. If your records don't get played they probably won't get sold either. There is a packaging allowance, which can be as high as 15 percent, but which is more typically 10 to 12.5 percent, and which is deducted from your royalties. This means that you are really paying for your album cover and all of the graphics on your record. Your lawyer should endeavor to keep this percentage as low as possible.

The number of sides or albums that the record company must record will be stated in your contract. Sometimes a record company is unwilling to commit themselves to recording more than a single record during the first year of the contract. You should try to get a deal that commits the company to recording at least an album a year. You may want to do at least two albums a year. However, this can be a double-edged sword. Keep in mind that if you are touring extensively you may have trouble getting enough songs together to do that much recording. Some artists, such as Bob Dylan or Paul Simon, may go as long as two or three years before doing a new album. In such a case the normal situation may be reversed, and it is the record company that is applying pressure to get the artist to fulfill the contracted minimum of sides or albums. Sometimes an advance may be written into the contract upon completion of each album, and it may be a sizeable advance if the artist is a successful one. Foreign royalties are usually computed at 50 percent of your domestic monies. Some companies own their own foreign affiliates, and in such instances you might be able to raise this percentage to 75 percent. Many records made here will not be issued abroad, because the foreign affiliate may not think they will sell in their territory. If the American company agrees it sometimes will try to lease the product to another foreign company. That is why some Beatles products appeared in the United States on Swan and Vee Jay Records in the early part of their career. In that case the Beatles recorded for EMI, which owns Capitol Records, and Capitol was not initially excited about the Beatles.

Record company contracts may spell out a company's commitment to record an artist, but may not include any commitment on the part of the company to actually release the recordings. Some artists try to insert a guaranteed-release clause in the contract, which specifies that the record must be released as well as recorded. This is a useful device, but not quite as useful as it appears. The release of a record without any promotion or advertising is not worth much to the artist. To guard against such a situation a powerful artist may insert into the contract some provisions guaranteeing a specific amount of money to be spent on promoting the album.

The record company often wants to publish its artists' songs. The nature of publishing revenues will be discussed in the section on publishing, but it is advantageous for you to control your own publishing rights or to own half of them. This is another provision for negotiation.

Usually the number of recording sessions for which the artist will receive union payments will be determined by a verbal agreement between the manager and the record company. If you spend thirty-eight hours in the studio doing vocal and instrumental overdubs to your songs, it is unlikely that the record company is going to pay you union scale for this time. Instrumental scale is set by the American Federation of Musicians and is $127.05 per three-hour recording session. Singers are paid through AFTRA, and their scale is a bit more complicated, but scale for royalty artists is $81.50 per person per hour or per side, whichever is greater. AFTRA actually limits the amount of scale payments for a record, and this limit is a maximum of three times the scale no matter what the length of the recording sessions may be. Generally singers must join AFTRA and instrumentalists AFM; but in some instances, when a musician sings and plays, he may end up having to join both unions in order to do television performances or sing in commercials.

Union payments for recording sessions can get to be a sticky matter when it is the performer's own record. It is impossible for the union to monitor all recording sessions, and so much overdubbing takes place in popular recording today that union payments should be a matter of good faith and mutual understanding on both sides. Make sure that you know just how many recording sessions you are going to be paid for before you start to work to avoid disputes later.

In return for advances and union payments the record company makes certain demands on the artist. Generally the individual or group will not be allowed to record for any other record company without permission. Often the company will grant such permission in return for a credit on the back of the album, such as, "Jane Bridger appears courtesy of Austerity Records." The record company will demand free access to your photograph or any promotional materials for use in advertising. Some record companies try to reserve additional promotional rights, such as the use of your name or group logo on T-shirts, candy bars, and so on. Naturally it is best to retain such commercial rights for your own use. Record companies will usually put a group and all individuals in it under contract both individually and severally, which means that if you should leave the group, or if the group breaks up, all members are still under contract to the company. The company can then determine whether they wish to continue recording you. Sometimes complex trade-offs occur when a group consisting of superstars forms. The group may be under contract to one company, and each of the individual group members may have separate recording contracts for individual records with different companies. This may reflect some past obligations, such as an artist recording as a group member for Company A. The group breaks up and this artist continues to do solo albums for Company A, but joins a new group which has a deal with Company B. Company A may approve that deal if the artist continues to record as a soloist for them, and if Company B gives Company A some financial compensation, or does the same thing with some other artist that has just joined a group that records for Company B. When Buffalo Springfield broke up, this sort of musical chairs game was played. David Crosby got a release from CBS (he had been a member of the Byrds); Richie Furay went to CBS from the Springfield's home label, Atlantic, to join Pogo; Neil Young ended up as a solo artist on Reprise; and Graham Nash went from CBS to Atlantic, which was the new home label for Crosby, Stills, and Nash. Such negotiations with high-priced superstars can be complex.

Sometimes an artist is contracted to an independent record producer, who in turn makes her own deal with the record company. If you have such a deal with an independent producer, make sure there is some sort of time limitation on selling the completed product. The producer should have to sell the product in a reasonable amount of time—say, six months after completion. Remember it does take time to negotiate with a record company and reach a final agreement. A sample independent production deal appears on page 551 of *This Business of Music*.

Whether you are under contract to a record company or an independent producer you will want to have some provision for auditing upon receipt of your royalty statements. There is usually a specified time period during which the artist must notify the company or producer as to his intention of auditing the books. It is sometimes specified in the contract that if a certain dollar amount of royalties is uncovered that has been unjustifiably withheld from the artist, the company must pay the costs of the audit. Certain accountants specialize in such audits, and are able to smoke out false costs that a record company or producer may be charging to the artist. Most record royalties are paid every six months, so a reasonable notice of audit might be within thirty days of receiving the statement. In record company audits that cover long periods of time as much as several million dollars have been recovered by accountants. This is not necessarily money that has been stolen from the artist but may involve disagreements in defining such matters as packaging allowances, free goods, or other terms of the contract.

Sometimes a music publishing company finances recording sessions, in return for which the artist relinquishes his publishing rights to the publishing company. Hall and Oates had a deal of this sort with Chappell Music, and it worked out well for them. There should be a time limitation on such a deal as well, or you may find that your publishing rights are tied up but you still don't have a record deal. Some record companies may not sign you if they can't get your publishing; on the other hand, you may not want to deal with a record company that takes such an absolute view. Another factor in such a deal is whether the publishing company has good contacts with record people, and whether they are active in contemporary music and will assist in promoting the record.

Another way to get a recording contract is by using a record company's studio facilities on a first refusal basis. The record company gives you free studio time in return for which they have the right to sign your group if they like you. If not you can walk away with a free professional tape. Once again you would want to limit the time during which the company must make up its mind. Do you really want to record for this particular company if they do like the tape, or was it simply a matter of getting the free studio time? If you don't want to record for the company to start with, it is best to avoid this sort of deal.

To sum up, in negotiating with a record company your chief assets are a good lawyer, a good manager, and a lot of patience. At times it seems impossible to get a decision out of a large company. Many artists, such as the Lovin' Spoonful, Don McLean, and Bachman-Turner Overdrive, have been turned down by dozens of record companies and were on the verge of despair when finally making a deal. If you are fortunate more than one company will be bidding for your services. If this is the case for you, you may come out with an excellent contract, with a high royalty rate, a lot of artistic control, and few options on the part of the record company. If you are a beginning artist, do the best you can, but don't sign a contract if you don't feel you can live with it.

If a record company really likes an artist, and the artist has no personal manager or lawyer, the record company may recommend someone with whom they have a good working relationship. However, don't accept a lawyer or a manager simply because a record company has recommended him. Find out what clients he represents, and make sure that he will be representing your interests in any possible conflict with the record company.

8 | How Records Are Sold and Distributed

When you buy a record at a retail record store it is the last step in a rather complicated distribution process that starts with the record company and ends with the consumer. The giant record companies have their own sales and promotion offices in all major cities. These offices service retail stores and radio stations with sales and promotion personnel. Promotion is a key part of the marketing of records. As Top 40 radio has become Top 15 or 20 in some markets it becomes harder actually to get records played on the radio. Top 40 is a radio format where forty records a week are played in a rotation system. Many stations play the top four or five records every hour. Even the so-called progressive rock stations often have play lists for their albums. Disc jockeys today have only a limited amount of control over their own programming. The extent of that control depends upon the station format and the way the program director enforces the use of that format.

Sales personnel from the record company now give away promotion copies of records to retail stores, many of which play records in the store. In some of the giant record stores considerable sales can be generated through the playing of records in the store itself. Retail stores have sixty to ninety days in which to pay the bills to the record company branches. If they don't pay the bills they are placed on what is called credit hold. At that point new merchandise is withheld from the store, or the branch may insist that the store pay cash for all new records on delivery.

Some retail stores, especially small ones, don't like dealing with a number of different companies to get records. Starting in the sixties there arose a middleman called a *one-stop*. A one-stop is a place that stocks records from all record companies, especially the major labels. For a very slight markup the retailer can get all of their records from one place, simplifying book-keeping, traveling, and the time it takes to respond to a customer's order. Jukebox operators also buy their records from one-stops.

When retailers are in financial trouble, they will often juggle buying records from one source against another. While they are on credit hold in one place they will get records from the other source. As they clear up their credit situation in the first place, they then do the same thing to the other. Since operating a small record store is a hand-to-mouth existence, especially with the competition of large discount stores and chains, this situation is not unusual. Sometimes branches of different companies stay in touch with one another to cooperate in pressuring retailers to pay their bills, but few companies can resist a large order. It is worth mentioning that when the record company gets paid late artists and music publishers will also experience delays in getting their royalties.

There is another kind of record distributor called an *independent distributor*. This type of wholesaler may carry records from a large number of minor labels, together with the product of the larger independents, such as Arista or Motown. The independent distributor also may do record promotion for the smaller labels, although companies like Arista and Motown have their own promotion people in each market. Such a record distributor might carry minor labels and some larger ones that deal in specialized products, such as soul, country, bluegrass, progressive jazz, or whatever. When an independent distributor does promotion, the promotion is usually fairly simple—for example, getting new Greek records to the one radio station in town that has a Greek program.

In 1952 another form of record distribution began. This distributor is known as the *rack jobber*. Rack jobbers service supermarkets, variety stores, drugstores, and department stores. The rack jobber actually chooses the records that are sold in these locations, and from the beginning they offered 100 percent return privileges. In this way the owners of these stores simply sell records—they don't have to worry about ordering them, new releases, and so forth. Rack jobbers generally operate from the top albums on the music trade paper charts. Occasionally they will bow to local tastes by including an occasional polka record, or a German record in stores in a German neighborhood. Sometimes the rack jobber leases space in a department or discount store and owns as well as operates the record department. According to Chapple and Garafalo's book, *Rock 'n' Roll Is Here to Pay,** by 1970 rack jobbers and the owners of leased record departments accounted for more than 70 percent of all retail sales in the United States.

Another way that records get to the consumer is by direct-mail sales. Record clubs, such as CBS's Columbia House, the RCA Record Club, or the Musical Heritage Society advertise in newspapers and magazines, or occasionally on radio or television. There are also TV packages, records that are assembled from older recordings, and reissued as Greatest Hit packages, memorial albums, and the like. They are usually leased from the record companies and are sold through television advertising.

The increased dominance of the rack jobber has placed records in supermarkets and rural drug and general stores, but it has also limited the selection of records to what are usually current hits. Artistically this is a somewhat frightening phenomenon, akin to the gradual absorption of book publishers by various conglomerates.

Small specialty record companies often sell their records by mail, direct to the consumer. A few of them have even gone into the record distribution business itself. Some artists for these small companies also sell their records at their performances. This can work very well if the performer doesn't mind doing it. In certain kinds of music, such as bluegrass or gospel music, the audience expects the artist to sell their records, so the artist can proceed to do this at intermissions or before and after the show. Since a good performance is probably the single most effective way to create an immediate demand for a record, this can be a highly successful way to sell records. It also may antagonize local record store owners who may feel that the artist should concentrate on doing performances and let the store owner sell the records.

The sales department of a record company can provide a

---

* Steve Chapple and Reebee Garafalo, *Rock 'n' Roll Is Here to Pay.* This book is an interesting radical political analysis of the record business.

number of promotional aids to the record store that are attractive to the store owner and help promote the company's artist. Some of these tools include giant window displays, posters, special sales displays, browser bins with the record company name printed on them, mobiles, and other store decorations and giveaways.

Promoting Records

Promotion has always been a significant part of the business, and it is crucial to the introduction of new artists. The larger record companies deliver thousands of free records to radio stations. These records are usually marked PROMOTION RECORDS, NOT FOR SALE, or they may have extra holes punched in them or a small part of the cover torn off. Nonetheless it seems as though every major city in the country has at least one record store that sells promotion copies at huge discounts. These promotion records may be extra radio station copies, or records that the stations never played, or they may come from record reviewers for newspapers or magazines.

How does a record get played on the radio? It is important for a promotion person to have a good relationship with the radio stations that she services. Most stations have certain days or hours when promotion people can contact the station manager or program director (sometimes the same person) and deliver the company's new releases. Large companies may release as many as fifteen or twenty albums in a month, especially in September and October. Those months are generally regarded as the best time to release records because of the return of students to schools.

Your manager needs to have convinced the record company that your group is going to make it, and he should have gotten your booking agency to arrange a tour of major cities coordinated with the release of your record.

If the local promotion person knows that you will appear in their market, and that the record company is spending money on various promotional devices, then she will walk into the station with your record on top. This requires good communication between the company and its local branches. The program director or music director is unlikely to program all of a label's new releases. Some will get priority because they are already well known artists. If your group is high on the record company list of new products that he feels can sell (not an actual list but a feeling passed down to local promotion people in the form of suggestions or even commands), it may well be your record that gets played at the station. Without record company support, based on an enthusiasm for your product together with the work of your manager and booking agency, your record may well end up in some obscure spot in the station's record library, at a local used record store, or will be given away to some station employee's family.

Albums may be advertised on the radio, in print ads, or even on television. It is harder to promote singles, but there are a few things that can be done to stimulate sales. T-shirts, bumper stickers, and radio station giveaways have been done many times, but if they are handled in an imaginative way can still work. The record company may also sponsor a contest within the company itself. The promotion person who gets the record on the first Top 40 chart wins money, or a free trip to Bermuda, or whatever the company thinks will stimulate interest. In certain cases the record company may give away extra records to the distributors, or may establish a special discount structure. When the Kingston Trio re-formed with John Stewart replacing Dave Guard, Capitol gave away free records when copies of the new single "Where Have All the Flowers Gone" were bought by stores. This helped stimulate the success of the record, and started a whole new cycle of success for the group, a big seller for Capitol at the time.

A record promotion person today must be fairly flexible. Major cities have so many radio stations with so many formats, and there are also the college radio stations. A few record companies even hire college-age promotion people to concentrate on college radio promotion and on helping promote the artists who are appearing in concert at the colleges.

When a promotion person cannot get a major market station to play a new record she will try what is called a secondary market, a station in a comparatively small city that beams into the major market. Milwaukee radio, for example, can be heard in Chicago, and if a record hits in Milwaukee the promotion person will try to spread its success to Chicago. The trouble is that many of the secondary markets and even the small-town markets may have their own tight play lists. Breaking a record by a new artist takes a lot of work and a great deal of communication with the home office to find out where the record is being played.

It is most important for record companies to have strong staff liaison with the music industry trade papers, which include

Billboard, Cashbox, Radio and Records, and *Record World.*
These liaison people will report any radio or sales action on
records to the trade papers in hopes of getting the record on the
trade paper charts. There are also a number of radio station tip
sheets, such as the *Bill Gavin Report,* which have detailed
weekly reports on what stations are playing what records.

No matter what a record company may do, promotion and
advertising are not guarantees of success. Moby Grape was promoted to the tune of over $100,000 by Columbia Records, and
five singles were released simultaneously. It didn't work; in fact
the built-in hip audience for the group in San Francisco was
alienated by this approach. About ten years ago MGM Records
discovered the "Boston sound," and supposedly dropped several
million dollars because the general public didn't buy it.

When a record company believes strongly in a group they
may finance a series of promotional parties or performances in
key cities. The act will usually do a brief performance and then
will meet the local disc jockeys, music critics, and record store
owners or buyers. These can be useful in introducing a new act,
provided that the record company is able to get them to come to
the party.

At one time the group I played in, The Journeymen, did
such a tour. It worked very well in New York, where we met
quite a few important people in the business, and it was a fiasco
in several other towns, where people didn't come or, in the case
of Cleveland, were more interested in drinking than in listening
to the group.

There is another tool used in promoting records. It is called
payola and is illegal under federal law. It can also operate in a
variety of ways which are legal. The free lunch or dinner is
standard practice in many businesses. This may be abused by
bringing along lots of friends or going to the most expensive
place in town, but it is still legal. Christmas gifts are another
way of keeping goodwill flowing in the industry. Less legal are
such goodies as free drugs, payments of money, cars, other merchandise gifts, trips, illicit sex, or other such favors. It is difficult
to tell just how widespread these practices are, but it may be
worth noting that they are certainly not limited to the music
business. You may recall the Boeing Aircraft bribes of several
national leaders, the South Korean congressional bribes, local
police scandals, or similar episodes. In the total perspective of
American business operations it may be that too much has been
made of payola in the record business.

A problem that has plagued record companies for some

time is that caused by returned merchandise—unsold records
that are returned to the company. If a salesperson for the record
company is too zealous in pushing a new record on the retail
store the company may end up with the product again in a few
months. This usually happens after the demand for the artist
has died down in other markets, so that the merchandise cannot
be resold elsewhere. The rack jobbers have forced the companies' hands on returns with their own 100 percent return
policies. When records are returned it further complicates the
royalty situations of artists and publishers. Many companies
withhold a certain percentage of royalties for what they call
"reasonable returns." Under the new copyright law the register
of copyrights is directed to come up with a time period after
which a record is regarded as being permanently distributed and
after which royalties must be paid. Perhaps this will become the
standard that record companies will set to stores as limitation
on their return privileges.

After records are returned, they may be scrapped for the
vinyl to be reused, or sometimes the records are sold again at
reduced prices. They are removed from the catalog and are
called *cutouts*. When cutouts are sold, not only does the price
get reduced but there will be smaller royalty payments, or no
royalty payments at all to the artist. In effect, the record is
being redistributed.

Another part of record company operations is the creative
services department. Most record companies have some sort of
publicity apparatus that sends out biographies of the artists to
radio stations, newspapers, and magazines. It may also write
record company advertisements. Some record companies even
publish their own magazine, such as Warner Brothers' *Circular*.
Another part of this department is involved in artist relations.
The artist-relations people help to coordinate tours with visits
to radio stations, key record stores, and radio spots. When this is
coordinated properly it is invaluable to the artist.

Another group of people, called *product managers,* sees
each specific product through the whole company apparatus,
scheduling album releases, making sure that the record is completed, arranging for the graphics (which can be done in-house
or by free-lance firms), checking on the progress of liner notes,
label copy, and anything else relating to the record. Without the
product manager there would be a great deal of confusion as to
whether or not a record is being completed on schedule.

We will discuss record company publishing companies in
our section on music publishing. There is often an international

vice-president, who arranges for foreign releases by affiliates or other companies and does the same for their releases in this country. Details such as foreign royalties, subpublishing agreements, and other matters have to be worked out. This executive is often an administrator and not a creative staff person.

The legal staff, which in the larger record companies is an in-house operation, handles contracts with artists, any business problems relating to contracts on mergers or acquisitions, and lawsuits. The legal staff must make sure that artist options are picked up before expiration, and they handle negotiation or renegotiation of contracts. Usually the president of the company will set the general policies that the lawyers who do the actual legal work must follow. When an artist is negotiating with a record company the process may be quite lengthy, going in an endless chain from artist to artist's lawyer, together with a personal manager, to record company lawyer, to record company administrative head of A & R, to record producer, and back again.

There is a business division of the large companies that includes an accounting and payroll department. It is their responsibility to make sure that all bills and royalty statements are paid on time, delinquent accounts are placed on credit hold, and the like. Company policies on such matters may be set by administrators, but the business department will follow through on these decisions.

A few record companies, such as Columbia, operate their own pressing plants, and they can totally control the entire process from initial recording to the finished product. In such operations the company has employees working in its pressing plants, in packing and shipping functions, and in company warehouses around the country.

9 Agents and Personal Managers

Many artists don't understand the differences between an agent and a personal manager. An agent is someone who finds work for performers. Think of an agent in the sense of an employment agency. A personal manager is someone who performs an entirely different function. A personal manager represents the artist as the negotiator in any kind of business deal that involves the artist. The deal may be with a booking agency, a record company, an advertising agency that wants to sign the artist to do commercials, a clothes manufacturer that wants to name a line of clothing after an artist—in short, any activities that will result in revenue and publicity for the artist. In the larger cities a booking agency can be a large office employing quite a few agents. Agencies such as the William Morris Agency have offices in Paris, London, and Rome, in addition to offices in the major cities of North America.

Most agents will seek to sign the artist exclusively. This means that they will represent the artist in all phases of activity in the entertainment world. Sometimes an artist will seek to limit the authority of an agent. This could happen in the case of a good rock artist who has movie ambitions, and has one agency for booking rock shows and another for movie representation. The agent will always seek exclusivity but may be willing to settle for representation in a specific area. Below is a chart that illustrates some of the differences between the agent and the personal manager.

Agent	Manager
Finds employment.	Doesn't find work for an act, except occasionally during initial stages of career.
Large agencies always operate under union contracts.	There is a union agreement for personal managers, but most managers don't use it.
Many agents in an office, may have many offices and a large organization.	Relatively small staff, usually 1 or 2 principals and a handful of assistants. Usually one office, occasionally one on each coast.
Pays own overhead.	Part of overhead, such as trips on the artist's behalf are payable by the artist.
Standard fees, 10–20% of the gross wages, depending on which union covers the contract. Occasionally fees are lower, if a strong manager and a superstar artist are involved.	Considerable variation in commissions. Usually 15–25%. Percentage may be based on artist's income. In unusual cases as low as 10% or as high as 50%.
Possible conflicting obligations to artist, club owner, or promoter.	Primary commitment always to the artist.
Comparatively little personal involvement with the artist.	Considerable personal contact with the artist, may assume counseling role.
Not deeply involved with image or long-range career plan.	Helps formulate image, deeply concerned with long-term career plan.
Rarely has power of attorney.	Often has power of attorney.

Agent (continued)	**Manager** (continued)
Three-year contract or less, under union rules.	Like a record company contract, 1–2-year contract, with options often extending to total of 5 years.
Often books artists that are competitive to one another.	Usually does not manage artists that compete with one another.
Worldwide.	Usually based in New York, Los Angeles, or Nashville.
Not much dealing with record company.	Frequent dealings with record company.
May have limited functions (limited to television, movies, etc.).	Unlimited functions, except for occasional foreign rights. For example, a British act may have separate British and American managers.
Little involvement with promotion of a specific artist.	One-person hype operation. Plants stories in newspapers, constant word-of-mouth publicity to others in the music business.

Let's review some of the material in this chart in a bit more detail. The agent is responsible for finding employment for the artist. This is generally done by telephone, although in the case of local employment it may involve visits to clubs and concert promoters or colleges. She generally tries to ascertain what the budget of a particular location is, then proceeds to sell the employer an act from a large list of acts that the agent books. She usually has photos and records, which she gives to the buyer. An agent is a salesperson and naturally will build up the act verbally so that the buyer thinks he is getting something unusual. This is always easier to do if the act has already had some success. It is difficult for an agent to do much until an artist has a recording on the market. However, it may be possible to find a young artist work as an opening act at a local nightclub, or as an opening act for an established concert performer. The manager needs to stay on top of this action. He is continually working to convince an agency that the record company is behind the act and that the act is going to make it. Meanwhile, he is doing the same thing at the record company—

keeping them informed about any important bookings, telling them about a great new song that the act is working on, and so on. He must spend a great deal of time with the record company people, getting to know the people in the various departments of the company. The album cover needs to reflect the correct image of the group, the release date of the record should coincide with a tour, the promotion people at the company need to know about the tour, and the salespeople should be preparing some special displays to introduce the group to the public. A good manager can deal with record people in an effective and confident way without alienating them by being an obnoxious pest.

An agent works repeatedly with some club owners and promoters, and may be caught in the middle of an argument, not wishing to alienate the employer or the employee. A manager should always look after the interests of his meal ticket, the artist.

One of the main functions of a good manager is to make sure that the agency is representing the artist properly. Agents are paid commissions on a percentage of the gross, so they really are not overly concerned about the amount of traveling that a group must do between jobs. Traveling can be mentally and physically exhausting, and it can also eat up all of the profits of the job itself.

The manager often has power of attorney, which means that he is allowed to sign contracts. This is important because the artist may be traveling at the time an important job offer comes through. Often the agent will require an immediate answer, and the manager should be qualified to give one. A good manager makes sure that the bookings are in reasonable geographic proximity and that if the job is a return engagement (replay) the price of the artist goes up with each booking. Setting a price for a group is a complicated procedure, and it requires cooperation between the manager and the agent. The price for the artist should not be so high as to discourage job offers, but not so low that the group doesn't make a decent living.

Building an image involves such matters as stage costumes, lighting, performance techniques, choreography, programming of the music, and media interviews. Agents usually don't have the time to devote to an individual act in order to deal with such matters. The manager needs to attend some rehearsals and performances in order to gauge how successful the group is in getting the effects for which they are striving. Sometimes specialists may be hired to write special comedy material, stage an act, design costumes, help with choreography and lighting, or do whatever else is necessary. The manager should be an objective judge of whether a group's performance is coming off successfully. Some managers fancy themselves as musicians and may try to intervene in the actual musical arrangements. It should be a matter of judgment by the artist as to whether he feels the manager is qualified to deal in such questions.

It is not unusual for a new act to go on tour with a well-established act, thereby playing to an audience which they themselves are not yet capable of drawing. The manager and agency need to work together to create such a situation. The manager may have such an act in his own roster, or the agent may come up with one. Great care must be exercised so that the acts can share the stage successfully. A soft folk duo might be a very poor choice as the opening act for a hard-rock group. The audience for the rock group will not want to listen to an unknown group playing such a different style of music.

It is necessary for agents to have acts that are competitive to one another because the agency gets hundreds of calls from different parts of the country, and one act couldn't possibly take all of these jobs. It is best for a manager not to work with competing groups because one group will inevitably feel that it is receiving less time and attention than the other group gets.

Any large agency works under standard union contracts. The American Federation of Musicians allows agents to charge 15 percent commission on jobs of two days or longer, and 20 percent on one-night engagements. This commission is charged on the gross wages, with no expenses being deductible. The agency often asks for an advance deposit of 50 percent from the promoter or club owner, which protects the artist and the agency against nonpayment of the agreed wages. Usually an agency is knowledgeable about a particular promoter or club owner. They will warn the artist to demand the rest of the payment immediately after the engagement, or even before going on stage, if there is some doubt about payment. It is often specified in the contract when the additional monies are to be paid, and in what form—cash, certified check, or whatever. In three years of working with the same booking agency the group in which I performed only had three incidents of nonpayment. One was settled by lawyers, one concert promoter in Miami disappeared into the great American night with the remaining 50 percent of our money, and one club in Phoenix eventually went backrupt. Without the services of an agent the artist must turn into a bill collector, and often in a strange town with people that the artist does not know.

Under the rules of the musicians' union, if the agency does not get any work for the artist for four consecutive weeks, or doesn't provide twenty weeks' work in the first year of the agreement and forty weeks' work in the second year of the agreement, then the contract is invalidated. A week is defined as four or more days of work in a seven-day period. AFTRA allows the agents only a 10 percent commission on bookings.

Some of the larger booking agencies today are the William Morris Agency, International Creative Management (ICM), the Agency for the Performing Arts (APA), and in rock Premier Talent Associates and Queen Booking Corp.

In classical music the agent and personal manager are often the same person. This agent-manager takes a 20 percent commission. Classical recitalists operate under the rules of the American Guild of Musical Artists (AGMA). Some of the large classical booking agents are Columbia Artists Management Inc., Shaw Concerts, ICM, and Hurok Concerts, Inc.

There is considerable variation in the commissions paid to personal managers. In some cases a sliding scale is used, and the manager gets more money as the income of the artist goes up. Such a deal might provide for 15 percent commissions on weekly earnings of $1,500, 20 percent up to $2,500, and 25 percent over $2,500. In the case of sliding scales royalty payments, such as record royalties, are usually paid at a flat commission and are not included in the weekly earning schedule. Record royalties are usually paid every six months.

Managers often wish to publish the songs written by an artist. Few managers would own a really active music publishing company. Often a manager may co-own a publishing company with the artist. In such instances his share of the income should be restricted to publishing, and he should not collect additional commissions on the artist's songwriting (songwriter-publisher income is usually split fifty–fifty). Some managers do try to collect this double income.

It is difficult for a young artist to know exactly what constitutes a good personal manager. Most managers are glib and have great plans for the artist, at least verbally. The artist should try to institute a trial period during which he will have an opportunity to see if the manager can justify his words. A good trial period might be six months, or even a year, with a mutual option. Sometimes an earnings limitation may be placed in the contract. The group must earn a certain amount during the first year of the contract or they can get out of the agreement. The second year of the contract might include a higher figure. In the early part of an artist's career, a manager may waive or defer payment of commissions, knowing that the artist is really pressed for money.

When a manager undertakes trips to represent an artist in a business negotiation, this money is payable by the artist. In some cases the manager may be able to represent some of his other clients in other business negotations during the same trip. If this happens then costs should be divided. There is a great deal of mutual trust involved in an artist–manager relationship, and that trust can easily be abused by either side. It is more important that the manager understand the artist as a person, and that there be a mutually agreeable career plan, than that the manager be all that knowledgeable about the artist's music or pursue a life-style similar to that of the artist. Many managers are years older than the clients that they represent.

Occasionally an artist will act as his own manager, as Bobby Vinton does, or actually hire people to run an office for a flat fee, as did The Limelighters. Whether this kind of business activity will interfere with the artist's creative impetus is a decision for the artist to make. Certainly most performers are ill-equipped to pursue the business end of things because they have neither the time nor the expertise.

There is a sort of manager's guild called the Conference of Personal Managers, with an eastern branch in New York and a western office in Los Angeles. You might check out a prospective manager with them. A good manager is likely to be a member of the organization, although not necessarily.

Some artists also have business managers who handle their investments and tax matters. These persons usually work for commissions of 2 to 6 percent of the artist's earnings. The business manager is generally not the same person as a personal manager, although some personal managers may also pursue business management for their acts.

A personal manager may also help an act hire various personnel to work with them. These might include a road manager and an equipment crew, as a group does more traveling and earns more money. A manager will also work with the record company press and advertising people, and at some point may suggest that the artist hire independent press agents. He should oversee any promotional material or photos of the artist.

If possible try to have a trial relationship with your prospective personal manager. As with other situations, contractual obligations are negotiable. It is a matter of how badly an artist wants a manager, and how badly the manager wants to represent that artist.

10 Music Publishing

Music publishing has three primary aspects—mechanical use fees for recordings, performing rights for radio and television, and the actual printing of music. When most people use the word *publishing* they are referring to music in print, whether it is the sheet music of a song, artist collections such as *The John Denver Songbook,* an instrumental method such as *How To Play the Bassoon,* or music for school bands or choral groups. In the early days of the record business sheet music was a bigger seller than records. Piano players demonstrated songs in five-and-dime stores and music store windows and people flocked in and bought the music.

Today the biggest part of the publishing business is in mechanicals and performing rights fees. Mechanicals are the royalties that are paid by record companies to the music publishers. Performing rights are the rights paid by the radio and television stations, and some other users of music, for permission to use that music.

There are little more than a dozen publishers that are active in the actual printing and selling of written music. These publishers license the songs from the original publishers, paying a royalty fee for print rights. There are thousands of music publishing companies in the United States that dream of publishing a song that will become a hit. They vary in size from the publisher with an office in his living room to large companies like Jobete Music, a publishing division of the highly successful Motown Record Company.

Most of the monies that such publishers as Jobete (the nonprint publishers) get come from record sales, as we will see in our discussion of the new copyright law.

The publisher has the right to control the first recording of the song. Thereafter anyone may record it, provided their record company applies for a mechanical license and pays royalties to the publisher. This right to control the first recording may assume some importance because it enables the artist-song-writer to make sure that his version of the song is the first one that is commercially released. In the forties and fifties there were often many versions of a song called *cover records*.* Today the cover record is mostly a thing of the past. When it does occur, the new recording is often done some months after the original record and in a totally different style. Such a modern cover record was Aretha Franklin's version of "Bridge Over Troubled Water," recognizably the Paul Simon song, but not sounding a bit like the Simon and Garfunkel version. In the old days a cover record might even be a close copy of the original. Kay Starr's cover record of "The Wheel of Fortune" used an identical arrangement to the original by Sunny Gale and had a similar vocal treatment. Musical arrangements, by the way, cannot be copyrighted.

Most publishers utilize the services of the Harry Fox office to collect their mechanical royalties. The Fox office charges the publisher from 3¼ to 5 percent of the collections, based on the gross of the publisher. The cheaper rate is in effect if the publisher grosses over $25,000 a year from the Fox office. There are other offices that perform similar services, but the Fox office represents over 3,500 music publishers, and is the undisputed leader in the field.

Another form of publishing rights is called synchronization rights. They are granted to television and movie producers for the rights to use music with a film. These rights are negotiated by the music publisher, except that the Fox office may negotiate the rights for previously published music that is reused in a new film.

---

* A cover record is a recording of a song that has already been recorded. The word *cover* indicates an attempt to compete with the original record.

Music Publishing Contracts

In order to make contact with a music publisher, you pursue the same basic strategy that was described for getting a record deal. The difference is that there are many more companies, and they are more accessible to a new artist. The bulk of the large publishers are headquartered in New York, Nashville, and Los Angeles. ASCAP, BMI, and SESAC can provide you with a list of their affiliates. For their addresses, see the Appendix of this book. You might also try a publisher who publishes material in the vein that you feel is similar to your work. You may want to write an initial letter before sending your tape, asking if the publisher will listen to unsolicited material, and asking whether she prefers the material to be on cassette or reel-to-reel tape. Lead sheets should be included, if you can write them. If not, at least include typed lyric sheets.

When you make a demo for a publisher, the primary idea is to expose the song. It is not necessary that the performance or arrangement be great, only that they be in the correct general context in which you want to place the song. The lyrics should be enunciated clearly, with or without a typed lyric sheet. If you have a number of songs on the tape, remember to place leader between the songs.

If possible, try to convince the publisher to let you be there when she listens to your songs. If you are there, the chances are that she will listen more carefully, and there will be fewer interruptions. Even more important is the possibility that she may have some constructive criticisms to make of your songs, and the two of you will get some feeling as to whether the chemistry exists between you to establish a good working relationship. This kind of contact cannot be established by mail.

If a publisher is interested in your work you will get a contract. The contract may be for one song only, for a group of songs, or it may provide that the publisher will own and publish all of your material. It would be foolish to tie up all of your songs with one publisher unless she is willing to offer you a cash advance or a salary. If you receive a contract from the publisher, there are a number of provisions you will want to place in the contract. If the publisher is unable to get a recording of the song within a specified time (six months to a year is fair), she should either return ownership of the song to you or should pay you some sort of fee to show good faith in keeping the song. As a writer you should receive 50 percent of all monies that the publisher gets, including foreign or any other rights. For sheet music sales you should get a royalty of 3 to 5 cents a copy, and a proportional share of 10 percent of the retail selling price of any songbooks which include your song. Some publishers try to charge the writer up to 50 percent of the cost of any demonstration records or dubs which the publisher makes. Sometimes these dubs might be made directly from your tapes, sometimes the songs may be rerecorded with professional singers and musicians. It is better, of course, to have the publisher pay all such costs. You should have the right to audit the books of your publisher within a specified time after receiving royalty statements. No assignments of publishing rights to other companies should be made without your permission, nor should the publisher be allowed to make any changes in your words and/or music without your permission.

Do not pay any publisher money to make tapes or records of your songs. No legitimate publisher will ever ask this of you. Publishers that operate in this way are known as "song sharks." They advertise in popular magazines hoping to dupe inexperienced writers who have a dream of getting their songs recorded. These sharks may even offer to sell you 500 or 1,000 copies of the recording of your song. I have met people who have been bilked out of as much as $1,000. They end up with some bad records of their songs, a few lead sheets, and an empty wallet. Similarly, you should never have to pay anyone to collaborate on words or music with you. Their payment should be in a share of the song's royalties, when the song is recorded.

If you are worried about your inability to recognize a good writer's agreement, check out an organization called AGAC (American Guild of Authors and Composers). They will provide you with fair songwriting contracts and will collect your writing royalties for a fee of 5 percent of your earnings on the first $20,000 annually, then 5 percent up to a maximum of $1,400 a year. They will audit questionable publishers and expand your knowledge of the music business through seminars, classes, and newsletters. Their address is in the Appendix.

A proven songwriter is sometimes able to attain a position as a staff songwriter for a major publishing company. Such a company may pay the writer anywhere from $50 to $200 a week. This is an advance against the writer's royalties.

Look out for cross-collateralization in contracts. This is a technique where the publisher will charge the royalties made by one song against the expenses of another song. Of course, if you are a staff writer this is inevitable. If you are recording for a record company which also is publishing your music, make sure that the two contracts are separate and that your recording costs as a recording artist will not be charged against your songwriting royalties.

The New Copyright Law

If you are worried that publishers or other artists may steal your songs, you may want to copyright your songs. You must remit $10 to the Copyright Office in Washington (see Annotated Bibliography for further information). If you have written a number of songs this can mount up to a good deal of money. You can copyright all of your current songs as a body, calling it The Collected Songs of Jane Doe. As each song is recorded or printed, you will have to recopyright it individually and pay the proper fee, but it is one way to protect your songs without having to pay so much money. There are also services that will register your songs with the Bureau of Copyrights, but the cheapest way to do it is to register all of the songs under one title. Lyrics without music or music without lyrics can be protected in the same way.

There are two ways to register a copyright. One way is to send lead sheets of your song or songs with the proper fee. A lead sheet contains the title, words and/or music, the name of the publisher, and a correct copyright notice. (See sample lead sheet appearing in Appendix.) The other method of copyrighting a song is to send a tape recording or phonograph record with the copyright form. The actual performance will be protected and so will all of your original words and music. Since many musicians have trouble writing music in manuscript form this protection can be important. The actual copyrighting of a tape or phonograph record is one of the features of the new copyright law.

The new copyright law, which was passed by Congress in 1976 and went into effect January 1, 1978, represents a considerable advance for songwriters and publishers over the old law. Besides the increase in mechanicals from 2 to 2¾ cents per song and additional monies for longer songs (½ cent a minute or 2¾ cents, whichever is greater), jukeboxes will be paying an $8 fee and cable television companies will pay a fee based on their gross income. These are all new sources of income, as is public television, which will pay a fee to be set by the copyright tribunal. This tribunal will be appointed by the President of the

United States and approved by the Senate. The members will serve staggered seven-year terms, and will be reviewing royalty rates and other provisions of the law during their sessions.

Under the old copyright law, if a mistake was made in the copyright notice, the song lost its copyright protection and went into the public domain. Under the new law reasonable time is given to correct any mistakes in the notice of use. The new longevity of copyrights will be the death of the last living collaborator plus fifty years. In cases where anonymous works or works for hire are created the term will be seventy-five years from the first publication or 100 years from the creation of the work, whichever is shorter.

Under the new copyright law, the writer can reclaim a copyright from the publisher after thirty-five years. Under the old law the publisher could copyright work for twenty-eight years and then renew it for an additional twenty-eight years. This represents a considerable advantage to the writer or her estate.

The compulsory license works like this. Within thirty days of recording the record company must apply for a license from the music publisher. Because compulsory licenses require compulsory payment of royalties every thirty days, the procedure usually followed is that the Harry Fox office grants a negotiated license to the record company. This is necessary because most record companies only pay royalties every six months. In fact sometimes the record company tries to get a lower rate on the song than 2¾ cents. This would often be granted if the song is a new work by an unknown writer or if the record contains a number of songs by the same writer. Record clubs usually pay only 75 percent of the ordinary licensing rate, and they negotiate directly with the publishing company instead of with the Fox office. Sometimes this lower rate is granted because the record club agrees to pay on a large minimum order of records. This can be done with a record that the club is confident will sell well. Smaller fees are also negotiated for budget records and premium records.

The structure of music publishing companies is relatively simple. The company may be owned independently, by a record company, or by a number of partners. Below the chief officer of the company or president is a general professional manager. The manager is responsible for signing writers and for placing songs with recording artists and record producers. In the larger company the professional manager may also have a number of assistants who spend much of their time contacting artists and producers. Larger companies have offices in the various music cities, and may even have foreign branch offices.

When a music publishing company also has a print division, as United Artists Music and Warner Brothers Music do, the print division is run separately from the rest of the publishing company. It is considered a different business.

11 Performing Rights Societies

Performing rights are the rights granted for performances of songs in public. This includes radio, television, concerts, night-clubs, and other performance places. The money that a writer makes from these sources is not paid by music publishing companies. Both writers and publishers receive performance money from one of three performing rights societies. They are ASCAP (American Society of Composers, Authors, and Publishers), BMI (Broadcast Music Inc.), and SESAC. To join one of these societies a writer needs to have had at least one song published or recorded.

ASCAP is the oldest of the performing rights groups. It was founded in 1914 and is owned by the membership, who pay annual dues of $10. BMI was founded by the broadcasters in 1940 when they objected to an increase in rates which ASCAP was attempting to negotiate. Historically ASCAP was uninterested in country music and blues, and BMI started with an aggressive open-door policy, welcoming writers of any kind of music. ASCAP now pursues a similar policy, although some of the Nashville publishers still refuse to join ASCAP because of its attitude toward country music in the old days. BMI claims to log more smaller stations in the country and soul fields than does ASCAP, and if you write many songs in these fields you might wish to check comparable hit songs in these areas with BMI and ASCAP and with your lawyer to see which organization will earn more money for you. Although the broadcasters still are the stockholders of BMI, the stock has never paid a dividend, nor was it expected to do so. SESAC is a private company founded in 1931, and it is the only profit-making organization of the three societies.

On the next page is a chart reflecting some of the differences in the three performing rights organizations.

In order to determine the amount of air play, ASCAP tape-records radio station programs for six-hour periods and brings the tapes back to New York for analysis. While this procedure ensures a lack of favoritism since no one at the station knows that the taping is going on, it also relies on the ability of the listener to identify the song if the disc jockey does not identify it clearly. If the song is a current hit, there is little question that the listener will spot it. ASCAP has song files containing all sorts of melodies, and the listeners are musicians, but one may still wonder how much time can possibly be spent on identifying any one song. BMI logs radio stations every twelve to fourteen months. The radio station sends BMI a list of all songs played during a one-week period, with the names of the writer and publisher written on the log. Both ASCAP and BMI have complex formulas for converting air play from a single station into a mathematical factor and multiplying it to produce an index of national play during the time surveyed. Neither system is foolproof, if you have a local hit in a particular place that is being logged, you will get more national credits than you deserve; on the other hand, if it is not logged at all you are being cheated. With ASCAP you must rely on the ability of their listeners, and with BMI you need to hope that the disc jockeys have not played records by friends or associates during the logging week. If this is too obvious the computer will throw out the results, but there is no question that some favoritism can be shown when the station knows it is being logged.

SESAC does only spot checking on air play and devises its writer payments mostly from trade paper activity. Credit is also given for growth of the publisher's catalog within SESAC, seniority, diversity of the catalog, and so forth. SESAC pays the writer and publisher $200 each on release of a pop single, and $80 each for any song recorded on a pop album. The SESAC system is probably the quickest way for a popular music writer to receive payment.

Television payments differ according to the hour of the day; they are the highest during the evening prime-time periods. The networks are easy to monitor; for local programs the so-

ASCAP	BMI	SESAC
$17.50 dues for writers	No dues for writers	No dues for writers
To be a member must have one song recorded or published	Same	Same
17,800 writers * 4,800 publishers	29,000 writers 15,000 publishers	260 publishers
Collected $85,000,000 **	Collected $52,500,000	Collected $2,500,000
Airplay is determined through taping radio stations	Radio stations are logged every 12–14 months	The basis of the SESAC payments is from chart activity in music trade papers. Further explanation in text
Bonuses for songs with 20,000 feature performances, classical music, religious music	Special credits for local FM air play of classical music, songs with 1,000,000 performance credits	Bonuses for longevity on trade paper charts, and crossover from one chart to another—for example, soul to pop
54% 1975 income from television licenses, 31% radio, rest miscellaneous.	Similar to ASCAP	Television 21%, radio 75%
Educational functions include classes for songwriters, speakers furnished for educational purposes	Musical theatre writing workshops, Songwriters' Showcase in Los Angeles, sponsors seminars with speakers on the music business	Provides speakers for educational workshops
Pays reduced credits to composers of commercials	No credit for commercials	Recently began paying composers of commercials
Performing rights only	Performing rights only	Also issues mechanical licenses for records and synchronization rights for movies and television

* Figures from Shemel and Krasilovsky, *This Business of Music.*
** 1975 figures.

cieties rely on local TV magazines and occasional sampling procedures.

All three organizations license radio and television stations for performing rights. The rate for ASCAP and BMI is just under 2 percent of the station's gross receipts. Shemel and Krasilovsky say that BMI charges the stations about a third less than ASCAP does, although in the case of one radio station in the Midwest for which I was able to get data the fee for BMI was exactly half that of ASCAP in summer 1977. SESAC has a national rate card with rates ranging from $180 to $6,000 a year. The average fee for a 10,000-watt radio station is $1,200 a year. Most stations have licenses from all three societies.

BMI used to be more generous than ASCAP in giving advances to writers. At the present time neither one is too free with advances. Advances are usually given only if the society knows that the writer has an album coming out shortly that will be sure to repay the advance. Occasionally they are given in cases of grave need, such as sickness or injury. Ned N. Shankman and Larry A. Thompson, in their book *How To Make a Record Deal and Have Your Song Recorded,* point out that BMI publishers earn 25 percent more than do BMI writers. This is because of the BMI bonus system, where a publisher gets bonus credits based on his entire catalog and the performances of all songs in the catalogs. Bonus credits for writers are computed on a song-by-song basis.

ASCAP has two systems of payment. One is based on performances, the other is a deferred-payment plan called the Four Funds System. Most young writers want payment as quickly as possible, but the Four Funds System may be useful for deferring taxes, or if the writer plans to take a year or two off, say, to write a Broadway show. Despite having no immediate song activity, through the deferred payments the writer may achieve some income.

No matter which society you join, it is most important that you report any recordings or performances of your songs to the society. Some writers rely on publishers to do this for them, but you should fill out a clearance form yourself to insure that you will get the credit. If you do not report the songs the societies are not obligated to pay you.

In my opinion ASCAP at this time offers a better deal to the prospective writer than does BMI. SESAC can be good if you are concerned about getting cash quickly and have good reasons to expect recordings of your songs. ASCAP pays better than BMI because it charges more money to the broadcasters.

In addition, if you are in the commercials business you will get no credit for your works from BMI. If you are your own publisher and you have reason to believe that you might qualify for the performance bonuses, you might want to consider BMI. Performing rights contracts are somewhat negotiable, especially for publishers, and a lawyer might help you improve your deal. I would like to see all the societies place less emphasis on performance bonuses, and give more help to younger writers. They are really the ones that need the money. It is true that both ASCAP and BMI make some special grants to young composers of classical music.

When the new copyright law was being written, there was some heavy lobbying by performers who felt that they should receive money when their performances were played on the radio. The basis of their argument was that the success of radio stations was largely dependent upon playing records by successful performers. Therefore the radio stations should pay the artists for the rights to play their performances. The radio stations took the opposite view, saying that without the radio stations the artist would not become popular. Either point of view makes some sense, but I'm not sure that they don't cancel each other out.

In an article in the AFTRA magazine, summer 1978 issue,* it is pointed out that the unions in the recording field and the record companies have agreed that a performer's royalty is justified. They would give half of the royalty to the record company and the other half would be split in equal shares for all of the background singers and players and the artist. I can see some validity in giving the background performers some share in money contributed by radio stations, after all they get no publicity and relatively little money from the record. I'm not at all sure there is any real justification for giving the record company or the performing artist this additional source of revenue. The artist does get royalties from the sale of the record, and in fact many of the artists are also songwriters and get performance rights money from the stations as songwriters. I can't see the argument that the record companies deserve more money either—logically one has to accept that radio and record companies are interdependent. Without air play records would not sell as well as they do; without records radio stations could not present music in the way they do at present. I would like to see

---

* No author is credited for the article.

some revenue from air play go to the background singers and musicians. They are the people with the most compelling argument for a larger share of the pie. There is a bill currently before Congress that would create a performance royalty, but I suspect that it will take some years before Congress passes it, just as it took quite a while for the copyright law to be revised.

Naturally radio station owners are totally opposed to the creation of a performance royalty of any kind, because it would cut into their profits. Since ABC, CBS, and NBC all own radio stations and record companies, the creation of such performance fees would cost their radio stations money while benefiting their record operations, assuming a bill is adopted as outlined in the AFTRA article as opposed to the way I have suggested.

12 Commercials

Commercials are an amazing phenomenon in American society. Radio and television commercials include technically superb and highly artistic levels of work in such areas as songwriting, filming, music writing, acting, singing, and editing. It would be virtually impossible to put as much care into a complete film or play as is lavished on a thirty-second TV spot for a major product. In fall 1977 it cost from $50,000 to $55,000 to buy a thirty-second spot in prime-time (evening) television. For a top-rated show, such as "Laverne and Shirley," the cost was $100,000.* The cost of filming such a jingle** might come to $20,000 to $50,000. These costs pale to insignificance when one considers that to show such a spot twenty times in prime time would set the sponsor back a million dollars.

The number of people that actually are employed in the commercials industry is small. Terry Galanoy, writing in 1972 in his book *Down the Tube,* estimated that some 500 people write, direct, and produce the majority of national television commercials. The majority of the actual filming is done in Los Angeles because of the easy availability of color labs, experienced crews, and lighting and film technicians. When a major commercial is shot in Boston or Atlanta the chances are that most of the film

---

* *New York Times,* January 8, 1978.
** I use the terms commercial and jingle interchangeably in this book.

crew has flown in from Los Angeles. The music is cut into the picture after the film has been edited. Since most of the advertising agencies have their headquarters in New York the agencies usually record the music there. Some filming is done in New York, and Los Angeles and Chicago are the next largest music centers for commercials. There is a smaller but thriving jingle business in Dallas, particularly for what are called *drop-ins*. Drop-ins are commercials that use the same instrumental tracks but different copy. A radio commercial for Frontier Chevrolet that I have heard in Denver has the identical music track to one for another product that is aired in Cheyenne, Wyoming. The singers are also clearly the same, but in each case they sing the name of the client in the specific market. A drop-in can be used in several dozen different markets.

A good commercial is one that the viewer or listener remembers, and one that helps sell the product. The manufacturer takes great pains to make packages attractive and recognizable, and similarly the advertiser wants you to have their jingle in your head when you see the package. Many manufacturers spend more money on the packaging than they do on the actual contents of the package.

Commercials start with the client, which is the company that makes the product. The client representative goes to an advertising agency. The agency formulates a campaign, with or without extensive consultation with the client. At this point an independent film house is generally assigned to do the actual filming. The commercial is then cast by the agency, with some possible input from the film house. An account executive from the advertising agency who is assigned to the particular product will attend the actual filming. The film is then edited and the agency hires another independent creative group to work on the music. This "music house" will then write the music for the spot. They may also write the lyrics, or the agency people may supply the music house with the lyrics. Some agencies have their own music departments, and the actual jingle may be written by agency people, or these people may act as supervisors over the work of the music house. There is considerable discussion between the agency and the music house about the type of campaign that the client wishes. It may be an aggressive hard-rock jingle for a youth-oriented client, or a friendly down-home country fried chicken commercial, or the music may be written in some other style. The music house will do the musical arrangement or hire a free-lance arranger to do so.

The agency, and even the client, often hears a rough skeleton of the actual jingle. This demo may actually be sung live, or it may be taped with a modest accompaniment, such as a piano, a guitar, or a rhythm section. For the music house this is the most troublesome time in the entire process. Most clients and many agency people are not particularly musical, and making a sketchy demo may not be enough to convince them that the finished commercial will sound good. It is difficult to do a big band arrangement, for example, without a big band. If the demo is approved, then a final recording session will take place. The best singers and musicians are hired to do these sessions. They are readily available because the pay scale for commercials is higher than for any other type of recording. The singers can make fabulous sums of money based on exactly what use is made of the commercial. Many commercials don't actually get on the air, and some are test marketed in one area and then abandoned, but if a campaign is used nationally the singers will make thousands of dollars from a single product. The best jingle singers in New York earn six-figure incomes, but there are scarcely more than a dozen of them who do the bulk of the work. Payments for singers are graded for different-size population markets and for national network use, and reuse payments must be made for commercials that are used on both radio and television. Commercials are generally bought for thirteen weeks at a time, and if they are used for another time cycle the singers get additional payments, called residuals. Residuals are the heart of the singers' income; by comparison session fees are insignificant. Session fees vary according to the size of the singing group; for a soloist the pay would be $90 an hour.

Musicians who play on commercials get $50–$54 an hour, depending on the size of the band. There is an extra 30 percent added for playing more than one instrument. This is called doubling. Musicians also get residuals based on thirteen-week cycles, but they are not paid nearly as well as the singers. Both musicians and singers receive additional payments for their pension and welfare funds.

In recording television commercials a device called a *click track* is often used. This is a click that sounds like the beat of a metronome, and it is heard in the musicians' headphones. This click establishes exactly the right tempo, and that tempo can be varied as different frames of the picture show different things. On some sessions all of the musicians have the click track in their headphones, on others only the drummer hears it, and the other musicians must follow the drummer. Commercials must be timed exactly or the client will be charged additional money by the networks. A thirty-second commercial usually runs twenty-nine seconds, and a sixty-second jingle might be fifty-eight or fifty-nine seconds long.

Sometimes more than one music house competes for the same commercial. Each of them may make a demo, from which the agency and client will choose the winner. In the past many of these demos were made at the expense of the music house rather than the advertising agency. Through an organization called SANPAC the music houses have banded together and tried to formulate some ground rules for working with the advertising agencies. They now generally get a small creative fee and budget for such demos, usually in the area of $200–$500. If musicians are hired on the demos they must be paid union scale as if they were doing a finished commercial. Technically the same rule holds for the singers, but because the rewards of singing on a national commercial are so great singers will sometimes waive the session fees.

Commercials are written in different sections. There is usually some kind of musical introduction, a basic tune, a sort of musical bridge, sometimes with spoken copy,* and a tag at the end. This tag is the product signature and may be used in a number of different campaigns by the same product. It is really the equivalent of what we have called the hook in songwriting. Sometimes a product will run a number of different jingles during the same overall campaign, using the same tag at the end of each one. Usually the product name is mentioned early in the commercial, almost always by the end of fifteen seconds. When an announcer is used the agency generally selects the announcer. Some disc jockeys make quite a bit of extra income doing these announcements, called voice-overs. When a commercial is sung with a videotape the singers are paid through AFTRA, when the commercial is sung with a film the singers are paid through SAG. The AFM sets different scales when a musician is shown on camera playing an instrument.**

I have mentioned that some agencies test-market commercials in one or two markets before airing the commercial nationally. They may also test commercials on theatre audiences, or they may use the Gallup Organization to make phone calls checking on whether people like or remember commercials

---

* The tune used with spoken copy is called a doughnut.
** SAG is the Screen Actors Guild; AFTRA is the American Federation of Television and Radio Artists; AFM is the American Federation of Musicians.

shown during a particular television show. Sometimes these sampling techniques are also used with records. The theory behind test-marketing is that it is better to fail in a single market than to go immediately to the huge expense of national marketing and promotion.

A good jingle singer must be very flexible, and also possess a certain degree of anonymity. Although actors or models on television are often identified with a product, the singers prefer to remain free of this identification. This enables them to work for many competing products. One friend of mine had ten beer commercials playing simultaneously all over the United States, some network and some local campaigns. Such singers are incredibly versatile. The qualities that make for success in the jingle business are often opposite to what makes an artist successful on records. One can generally identify a popular singer on a record almost immediately. It would be hard to confuse the sound of Mick Jagger with the sound of John Denver. In doing commercials a singer imitates dozens of styles and voices. A male singer might do a Johnny Cash-style commercial in the morning for a beer company, he might sing in a six-person jazz group in the early afternoon for an auto manufacturer, and go back and do a rock solo late in the day for a skin cream company. Basically it is the product that must be sold, not the personality of the singer.

Because of this contrast between record and jingle styles, it is difficult for recording artists to succeed in the jingle business and equally difficult for jingle singers to succeed in the record business. Self-expression is an important part of the artist's work on records, but on jingles this expression must always be filtered through such primary selling points as the name of the product and its image. If the singer gives too much personality to the performance, the agency may feel that the product image is being shortchanged. Sometimes an agency will hire a specific artist because the artist image and product image coincide. Johnny Cash selling model trains is such a successful marriage of product image and artist image. A famous recording artist has usually become successful through developing a particular recognizable style, and that artist cannot reasonably be expected to change this style for a product image. This is exactly what a good jingle singer can do. A good jingle singer is equally capable of doing solos or group singing, can read music quickly and accurately, and can also improvise in a variety of styles. Through developing stamina and good microphone techniques such singers can sing many hours each day without losing the proper vocal qualities.

People who write music for jingles demand creative fees that may vary from $500 to $10,000. Additional fees of up to $1,500 are received by the musical arranger. This creative fee is a one-time fee with no residuals. Sometimes a deal can be negotiated where the composer gets an additional payment if the same tune is used with a new set of lyrics.

A few commercials have also become hit records. This is an extra bonanza for the sponsor because most listeners will fill in the product name mentally when they hear the song, even though that name has been removed from the hit recording. Anyone who heard the hit song "I'd Like to Teach the World to Sing" would have been likely to be thinking about Coca-Cola while the record was playing.

To break into singing on commercials singers usually make demo tapes consisting of a group of jingles they have recorded or which they make up for the tape. Jingles where the singer has sung multiple parts are useful to show the singer's versatility and range. If songs are included, they should only be fragments that are done in a jingle context. If the singer wishes to do both solo and group work, then examples of both should be on the tape. If a singer is interested in doing on-camera work, then pictures should be submitted with the tape. Singers in the jingle field do not generally use agents—work is gained through word of mouth in the industry and by contacting vocal contractors, independent music houses, or even the agencies themselves.

Besides drop-ins, discussed earlier, there is also considerable work recording radio station ID packages. These are jingle versions of a station's call letters. Many drop-ins and station ID packages are recorded in Dallas. These packages may pay union wages to the singers and musicians, but many people in the industry believe that the producers of such packages do not pay reuse fees.

Unfortunately, in local markets many singers and musicians are willing to do commercials for under union scale. Such performers are cheating themselves out of a great deal of money. Unlike recordings, commercials represent more of a craft than a form of emotional expression, and it is difficult for me to understand why anyone outside a rank beginner would want to do such work without receiving proper payment.

I spent about ten years in the New York area working as a studio musician. During this time I worked on many commercials. One of the people I worked for was Mitch Leigh, who wrote the music for *Man of La Mancha,* and also operated a successful jingle house called Music Makers. One day I played on a Gleem commercial that Mitch had written. I was playing twelve string guitar, and there was an orchestra of some ten or twelve pieces. Mitch had written a beautiful melody, with a soprano sax and an oboe playing in a sort of rhythmic counter-point against the rhythm section. We recorded a few takes of the song, and then Mitch disappeared into the control room for about forty minutes. Just before the hour ended and we would have had to go into overtime the contractor appeared and told us that the session was over, but that he'd be calling us again soon.

None of us could figure out exactly what had gone wrong. The tune and the orchestration were excellent; they were even enjoyable for the musicians to play. About a week later the same basic crew of people went back and recorded four of the most unimaginative commercials I have ever heard for Gleem. Apparently the agency liked them because a couple of them were used for over a year. The conclusion that I drew from this experience was that when one works on commercials artistic validity may not be synonymous with the way a client or an advertising agency conceives the image of a product.

13 | Music Trade Papers

The lifeline of communication in the music industry is the music trade paper. Almost everyone active in the music business reads some or all of these papers. The most popular trade papers are *Billboard, Cashbox, Record World,* and *Variety.* All of the trades come out weekly. Each of them has certain special features but all contain stories on industry trends, executive job changes, the formation of new companies, articles on the sales, manufacturing, and distribution of records, and, most important of all, the charts. Charts are listings of the current top recordings, placed in different categories. The single most important chart is the chart of current pop records, which includes 100 singles and the top 200 albums. The *Billboard* chart of top albums and singles is the one that is most universally studied by record people. Rack jobbers and various distributors govern a great deal of their buying by the chart position of a record. Trade paper charts reflect the records that are selling best and getting the most national air play. In addition to the pop chart the trades publish listings for the top records in jazz, soul, disco, classical, middle-of-the-road music, and gospel music. There are also surveys of the records selling abroad, especially in Western Europe.

Sometimes a record may be fairly high on the charts, but the sales are not commensurate with the amount of air play the record receives. Such a song is called a *turntable hit.* On the other hand, strong regional sales may cause the trades to place a record in a higher position on the chart than it may actually deserve.

Each trade paper has a different way of compiling its own charts, but they all rely on sales reported by the various record distributors and rack jobbers, radio station chart activity, and sales reports from retail stores. There is usually little difference in the chart positions of the top ten singles or albums in the various trade papers, but as you get lower in the charts you will notice more variation. Included with the charts is the name of the artist, the record label, and whether the record is available on tape, cassette, or 8-track tape. With its hot 100 singles chart *Billboard* also includes the names of the producer, the songwriter, and the publisher of each of these records. Strong sales activity is reflected on the various charts by stars or bullets representing particularly hot records.

The record companies all have people whose job it is to be liaison persons to the trade papers. Naturally they spend a good deal of time hyping the trades on the wonderful sales and air play that their companies' records are showing. Chart position is very important to the record companies in order to help convince rack jobbers to stock their records. It is also the way many individual stores order their records.

The trades also review new records, and of course the record companies seek to have their product reviewed favorably. This accounts for some of the numerous full-page ads in the trade papers from the record companies. The record company assumes that by virtue of advertising in the trade paper the magazine will be apt to treat a new recording more seriously and perhaps more favorably than if no advertising takes place. Other ads celebrate gold records, anniversaries in recording, and other special events or promotions.

The main differences between the trade papers are more matters of style than substance. *Billboard* tends to be a bit more conservative than the others, while *Record World* and *Cashbox* enjoy airing controversial views by industry personalities. For the last several years *Record World* has featured a series of in-depth interviews with important industry figures giving their views on a variety of trade practices. *Cashbox* has more detailed reports on radio air play than the other trades, and *Record World* has a special feature with programming suggestions for stations in different markets with various formats. All of the trades have gossip columns from New York, Nashville, and Los Angeles. These columns discuss new records, people out of work, various agents and managers, and other matters of interest to industry readers.

Variety is somewhat different from the other papers in that it focuses on movies, theatre, and radio and television, with only slight coverage of records. The *Variety* chart only contains the top fifty albums and singles. *Variety* is vital reading for Broadway and Hollywood people because it includes the actual box office grosses of movies and plans for new Broadway shows. It also has many more reviews of live performances than do the other trades. A daily version of *Variety* is published in Hollywood.

Any chart activity or favorable reviews are used by record people in their ads in the other trades and in their visits to radio stations. Trades are sold on the newsstands in the music industry cities and in a few other major cities; otherwise they are available only by subscription. All of the trades cost close to $2 each at present, except for *Variety,* which sells for 85 cents a copy.

Other specialized trade publications deal with music retailing, radio station programming, advertising, specific musical instruments, classical music performances, jazz, and every other imaginable kind of music. *Rolling Stone* and *Crawdaddy* are consumer magazines that are read by people in the business as well as by consumers. They do not chart records, but favorable reviews, especially in *Rolling Stone,* are often quoted in record company advertisements in other consumer publications.

14 | The American Federation of Musicians

This chapter will deal with unions in a general sense but will focus on the musicians' union, the American Federation of Musicians (AFM). Toward the end of the chapter I will discuss some of the other music-related unions—AFTRA, SAG, AGVA (the American Guild of Variety Artists), and AGMA (American Guild of Musical Artists).

Why do we have unions in the music business? Basically for the same reasons that auto workers or garbage collectors or teachers have them—to regulate wages and working conditions and provide some degree of job security. The typical American union worker works in one job at a single location, but a musician may play a wedding, a funeral, a record date, a television commercial, and a dance all during the same week. If the musician had to negotiate the wage scales for all of these separate jobs there wouldn't be much time left for practicing, not to mention the legal fees that might accompany the preparation of various necessary contracts and the bill-collecting chores that would follow each job.

Many young musicians ask if they have to join the union. In other words, what does the union do for them other than collect dues and initiation fees? The union regulates wages and working conditions at two different levels—nationally and locally. The national union sets up wage scales and working conditions for recordings, television, commercials, and film work.

These scales can be fairly complex or fairly simple to understand, varying with the circumstances of the recording and the use that will be made of it. As of November 1978 the minimum wage scale set by the AFM for nonsymphonic recording is $127.05 per three-hour session for each sideman and double for the leader or contractor. A contractor is required on any sessions that use twelve or more musicians. The contractor may be a playing musician—one of the twelve or more on the date. For symphonic* recording the scale is slightly higher, $134.67 per three-hour session, with a higher scale for four-hour sessions. These figures are the minimums that an employer can pay whether the musician is employed for the full three-hour session or if the musician plays a thirty-second solo and leaves the studio after ten minutes of recording. This may actually happen on certain occasions. All of the major recording companies are signators to the AFM code, which stipulates these wages and also specifies when and how the money is to be paid. No more than four songs or fifteen minutes of music may be recorded at any single recording session, or else more money must be paid to the musicians. Provisions are made for additional payments for recordings of reuses in other media such as a movie album sound track, or other multiple-use situations. In the Appendix appear some other national wage scales.

All of this may be complicated by overtime payments of time and a half after the first three hours, by the playing of additional instruments (called doubling) which requires additional payments of differing amounts for the various media, and premium time for recording on holidays or late-night recording. It would be literally impossible for each musician to negotiate all of these payments individually. The current AFM phonograph labor agreement is fifty-two pages long, and there are separate agreements for movies and commercials. We have already discussed the problem of reuse fees for commercials. These would be virtually impossible for the individual musician to monitor.

There are hundreds of locals of the AFM in the United States and Canada. Each local has its own specific territory. For example, Local 802 in New York City is a large and powerful local, but there are other locals in New Jersey, Westchester County north of the city, and in Connecticut. Each has its own circumscribed territory. Each local union sets minimum wage

---

* Symphonic recording means recordings by a symphony orchestra.

scales at clubs and theatres in its own jurisdiction. The theory is that people who live in the area know the operating conditions better than the national union would. The scale for a million-dollar nightclub is quite a bit higher than the scale for a local piano bar. In my opinion there are too many locals of the union in North America, and some of the smaller locals really should be absorbed by larger surrounding locals. Boulder, Colorado, is twenty-five miles north of Denver, but it has its own local and sets its own dues and initiation fees. The dues and initiation fee of each local are subject to the approval of the national federation.

The initiation fees for the AFM range from as little as $10 to as much as $150. This is the initial amount required to get into the union. In addition to this, members pay quarterly dues. In the larger locals these dues may run as high as $20 a quarter. The smaller locals are invariably cheaper to join, but once you have a card in a specific local, if you work in another jurisdiction you must pay traveling tax, and you are not allowed to work a steady job in another territory unless you join that local or transfer to it. Since you may spend a year or two at a steady job in a new territory and then go back home, you may end up with several membership cards, two sets of initiation fees, and two sets of dues to pay. If you plan to make a permanent move from one jurisdiction to another you may transfer your membership. Unfortunately, this usually requires you to wait six months before you are permitted to work a steady job. If you are a nightclub musician this procedure makes it difficult to survive. The system of local jurisdiction is rather antiquated. It was designed to protect the local musician from excessive competition, but it is probably more of a nuisance than a help to anyone.

All musicians must pay work dues when they work a union job. These work dues are a small percentage of scale wages, usually 1.5 to 2 percent. This applies to symphony players and barroom pianists alike. Some locals set a maximum amount of work dues, such as $25 a year, and collect it in a lump sum in advance.

The union does more on a job than regulate scale wages. You are free to negotiate wages above scale, you simply may not work for less money than scale. On the job the union specifies rest periods between sets in a nightclub or after each hour of a recording session. This is important for your health and well-being, particularly if you play a brass instrument. Some instruments cannot be played indefinitely without rest periods. The union also has an unfair list and a national defaulter's list, which are designed to protect members against employers who have not fulfilled contracts. It is illegal for a union member to work for an employer on these lists. You also may not work for employers who have not signed union contracts. The union contract not only protects the musician, but it can protect the employer against musicians who do not show up or are capriciously unable to perform. Each local has a trial board, which deals with disputed contracts.

If enough pension credits are built up over the years, a musician receives a pension from the local to which he or she belongs. In the case of studio musicians this can mount up to quite a bit of money.

Under the Music Performance Trust Fund (MPTF) record companies that are signators to the AFM agreements must pay about ½ of 1 percent of their gross annual profits to the MPTF, and an additional ½ of 1 percent to the Special Payments Fund. Half of this money goes through the Special Payments Fund back to the musicians who make recordings, based on their earnings from recording. The other half goes to the MPTF. Each local union receives an allocation of some of this money and hires musicians to do school concerts, hospital performances, and other live music jobs. Some concerts are funded by the MPTF alone and some include matching funds from local schools or charities. These concerts are always free to the public and constitute one of the most intelligent and progressive activities of the musicians' union.

Unions do not usually get jobs for their members, but they do function on behalf of the working membership. Many locals of the union do assist their members in getting jobs through an availability list. This list states the type of music the musician plays, whether the musician reads music, and whether the musician is free to travel. If you join the union, you should be sure to ask the secretary of your local about this list. The qualities of one union local may be quite different from the way another local functions. Some of the larger locals are quite impersonal; others are informal. In twelve years of membership in the New York local I never worked an MPTF job, nor did I ever get a job directly through the union. In the four years I have been a member of the Denver local I have gotten quite a few jobs through the union, including some MPTF concerts. It is up to you to make it clear to the secretary of the local what you can do. If your union officers are not responsive to your needs, then you should vote against them in the local elections. Many locals publish a directory of members stating what instruments they play, and including addresses and phone numbers. Make sure that your listing in the directory is correct. In New York members gather on the union floor itself three times a week seeking club dates in the city and in nearby resort areas. Contacts are made and announcements are made over the public address system.

Other benefits of union membership include special discounts, group health insurance, credit unions, life insurance plans, and educational workshops. Benefits of this kind are available in most unions.

If you are planning to pursue a successful career as a professional musician you will eventually have to join the musicians' union. When should you join? It is difficult to answer this question for another person, but here are some guidelines. Most people start out by playing occasional professional jobs while going to school or working in another field. In most cases this is not the right time to join the union. Many small clubs or coffee houses don't hire union musicians because they cannot afford to pay the union minimums. Once you are a member of the union there are a number of regulations that you must follow or you may be fined or expelled from the union. You may not play professionally with nonunion musicians or work without a union contract. In some cases, such as a benefit concert involving school musicians as well as professionals, a union local may choose to give permission for the professionals to play, or it may simply ignore the rules. It is best to seek permission if you get into this type of situation or the union may press charges against you. This could lead to fines and/or expulsion.

In my judgment the time to join the union is when you have decided to be a full-time professional musician and when you have some reasonable basis to assume that you are going to be able to support yourself as a musician. If you get an opportunity for a regular symphony job, a recording date, or a job offer from a working band, then the decision will be made for you. Don't join in your hometown if you know you are going to move to Nashville next week. It is best to hold off and join in your new location rather than put up with the complexities of transferring your card. There may be a minimum residency requirement in your new local, but you may be able to overcome that with the help of a manager, record company, or a friend who is a member of the local that you wish to join.

Let's consider some problem areas involving union rules. Many of the union rules were set up in the twenties or thirties and are unrealistic today. For example, a few years ago the union raised the commission rate that it permitted to personal managers from 5 to 10 percent. Maybe that made sense in the big band era, but no competent manager would work for 10 percent today. Because of this, many of the best personal managers don't bother with union franchises.

Many union officials cut their musical teeth as horn players in the big band era of the thirties. They often have little understanding or appreciation of the complexities of playing in an electronically oriented rock band, with its huge amounts of equipment. Suppose an auto accident caused you to be delayed in setting up for a job. Although you may have arrived well before the starting time, the complexity of setting up might have caused your group to start late. If the club owner then fired you, it would be important for a union official to understand why your group needs several hours of setup time.

In recent years the AFM has shown some signs of becoming more responsive to its membership. In New York City Local 802 has begun to study the possibility of setting up a special scale for Latin music at the request of some of the Latin musicians. Denver recently set up such a scale for Country & Western musicians. The AFM has finally legalized demo records. Although the demo scales are still somewhat unrealistic, at least the union has acknowledged the existence of the problem. Some locals have reduced initiation fees in an attempt to get more younger members, and other locals will allow you to pay your initiation fee on the installment plan, so that you can pay the money off while you are working.

Many aspects of the union's operations need reconsideration. The small club owner may not be able to afford union minimums. There are several hundred small record companies in North America that press 500 to 1,000 records at a time. They obviously cannot afford to pay the national scales. Similarly a small-town grocery store may not be able to pay residuals for a local commercial. The union must move into the modern age, consolidate some of its relatively inactive locals, and establish reasonable scales for special situations.

Other Unions

AFTRA represents singers and radio and television talent. It has forty-three locals in the United States and in many of the smaller towns, the media operate nonunion. Dues are based on annual earnings, and vary from $24 to several hundred dollars a year. The initiation fee varies from local to local—in New York it is $300. AFTRA has a bonus agreement with the record companies which provides that heavy sales of an album result in bonuses for the background singers. This is an intelligent concept reflecting an acknowledgment of the value of studio singers to the finished record.

SAG has an initiation fee of $500. In order to join you must have been a working member of AFTRA, Actors' Equity, AGMA, or AGVA for at least a year, or you must have a promise of employment as a player (not an extra) in a film or a commercial on film. Dues are based on earnings.

AGMA is the union for performers in opera, ballet, concerts, recitals, and oratorios. AGMA negotiates for Metropolitan Opera singers and for touring opera companies. Dues are based on income and the initiation fee is $100 or $200, depending upon the fee received in your initial contract.

AGVA (American Guild of Variety Artists) represents comics, jugglers, magicians, variety acts, and nightclub singers. In recent years it has not been a significant factor in the music industry.

It is unfortunate that many performers have to join three or four different unions in the entertainment field. AFTRA, Actors' Equity, AGMA, and AGVA have a loose affiliation agreement. Members of these unions pay reduced dues and initiation fees when they join the other unions. The AFM does not participate in this agreement.

All of these unions hire numerous full-time employees on a national and local level. This is particularly true of the AFM. On a national level there are attorneys, recording representatives, and a variety of officials who are elected at the national conventions of the various unions. The larger locals also have their own attorneys and specialists in such areas as Broadway show scales, recording scales, commercials, and other media. The AFM employs many business agents at the local level who enforce union rules and recruit new members. As a union member of the various unions you are required to carry your membership card at all times. Nonpayment of dues eventually leads to expulsion from any of the music unions.

15 | Radio

The owner of a radio station may set policy in a general way, but the general manager of the station is responsible for the day-to-day operation and management of the station. Below the general manager is the operations manager. She must have a good general concept of both the business and creative ends of radio. The operations manager hires the program director, who may also be the music director on a music-format station, or the music director may be another person.

There are several departments in a radio station. The programming director is responsible for the on-the-air operation of the station. The traffic department handles the time that is available for commercials and attempts to keep commercials for competing products at least ten minutes apart. The sales department sells commercials in the community, and the continuity department writes script and public service announcements. The people in continuity may rewrite commercials to conform with the station's image and standards, and they also write public service announcements and make sure that the radio station log is kept. The log is a minute-by-minute description of what goes on the air, and is required by the FCC (Federal Communications Commission). The FCC licenses radio stations, and these licenses must be renewed every three years. The station is required to devote 10 percent of its air time to public service programming. This programming may include news and public service announcements (PSA). In large cities there is a separate PSA department, and it may have quite a large staff that represents different groups in the community.

The air personnel in radio include news and announcing personnel and disc jockeys. In larger markets the disc jockeys work with engineers whose job is to cue the records, monitor the sound, punch in the correct commercials (usually on cartridges), and make sure that the station signal is operating correctly. In smaller stations one person may be a disc jockey, an announcer, and an engineer. Similarly the program director and the music director of a small station may be the same person, and may also have a shift on the air as a disc jockey. Many stations do some sort of production for local commercials. This production may include voice-overs, announcements by disc jockeys, and sound collages. In the larger markets disc jockeys make a good percentage of their income from voice-overs. On the smaller stations the disc jockeys may also do their own production. Sales departments at radio stations get paid on a commission basis. In some of the large stations they make more money than anyone at the station.

Disc jockeys in the largest cities may make upwards of $1,000 a week. They can also make additional money by doing record hops, disco appearances, and commercials. In New York and Los Angeles some disc jockeys earn more from commercials than they do from their radio jobs. FM disc jockeys generally make less money than their AM counterparts because the stations have smaller audiences and bring in less money.

Radio station offices are often in the downtown section of a city, but the transmitter and antennae are usually located in the suburbs. The signal is transmitted from the offices to the transmitter on specially leased telephone lines or radio circuit cables running from the studio to the transmitter. In 1977 there were some 4,400 AM and 3,400 FM stations in the United States, according to Claude and Barbara Hall in their book *This Business of Radio Programming*. NBC was the first radio network. It was founded in 1926, and CBS followed in 1927. ABC was formed when the government broke up the two separate divisions of NBC in the late thirties.

Radio stations today generally operate under tightly controlled formats. There are formats for virtually every kind of music, from free-form to Country & Western, soul, classical music, jazz, album-oriented rock, "beautiful music," and, of course, Top 40. The start of the Top 40 format as we know it today occurred in a bar in Omaha, Nebraska, in 1955. Todd

Storz and Bill Stewart were sitting in a bar for several hours, and they noticed the same record getting a great deal of play. Just before closing time they saw a waitress take a quarter of her own money and play the same song three more times. From this experience Storz developed the concept that people liked to hear the same records over and over. In a Top 40 format the station has a play list of forty songs, which are played in rotation throughout the day and night. On some stations four to seventeen records are rotated every one or two hours; on others there is somewhat less repetition. Occasional golden oldies are played, and sometimes a new record is added as an extra. If there is a good listener reaction to the extra, and if the stores start to report sales, the record then gets charted for the next week and is played on a regular rotation basis.

The Top 40 format makes records popular faster than older programming formats because of the intensity of the exposure. It also tends to shorten the life span of the record. When a record is rotated every hour it is necessary to turn to other records to keep the format exciting. Disc jockeys on the Top 40 stations are trained to talk over the introductions and endings of the records, and their general speaking tone varies from excitement to hysteria. Bill Drake, who programs radio stations in various formats, pioneered in reducing disc jockey chatter, simplifying radio station ID's and contests, and in general making Top 40 as slick and fast-moving as possible.

FM radio tends to be a bit lower key than AM, and it is beginning to command a greater share of the total radio market. The Associated Council of the Arts Bulletin of December 1977 reports an Arbitron survey from September 1975 giving FM radio a 36.4 percent of the market in New York City. In Los Angeles the figure was 35.3 percent and in Chicago 31.6 percent. KMPX-FM in San Francisco pioneered a free-form format in the early sixties by playing tapes of unreleased albums, long cuts on other albums, and by playing records released by very small record companies. This broke down some of the Top 40 emphasis in radio and led to some looser programming in a number of cities, especially on FM. The free-form format itself began to stagnate, and today many stations masquerading as free-form feature a play list of albums, albeit a longer one than a Top 40 station would use. Even classical and jazz stations tend to use formats and to stay away from more adventurous music.

There is a growing tendency for radio stations to go to an automated format. The programming is provided on tape from one of a number of automation services, such as TM in Dallas or Drake-Chennault in Los Angeles. A local announcer usually adds the local news and weather live on the air. Automation saves quite a bit of money in station salaries, and once the format is decided all programming is done by the service. Many stations that are not automated use certain syndicated shows, such as a weekly Top 40 countdown. The reason for buying a syndicated show is that a local station could not provide the expertise or production slickness that is evident in syndicated shows. Some of the syndicated shows also feature interviews with celebrities who would not be available to a local station.

Before Top 40 took over the air waves many disc jockeys used to do a great deal of their own programming. In 1960 the FCC discovered the existence of payola. Some disc jockeys were receiving money and expensive gifts, and sometimes a cut of the publishing on a record, in return for playing records on the radio. Several jocks, notably Alan Freed, were indicted and in effect driven off the radio. Stations began to take programming out of the hands of the jocks, and the music director decided on what records were to be played. In some cases the jocks are allowed to choose which records they play from a group of several records, classified by category. For example, there may be a list of six golden oldies from which the jock's third record is selected. The next record may be a novelty record from another list. Industry gossip accepts the existence of some payola, but it is presumed to be less common than during the early rock days. It is common knowledge that stations catering to the black audience ("soul stations") pay less money to their employees than the Top 40 stations do, and it is often hinted in the trade papers that such stations are more vulnerable to payoffs. Sometimes disc jockeys take odd measures in reaction to current records or programming practices. Al "Jazzbo" Collins once programmed Art Mooney's "I'm Looking Over a Four-Leaf Clover" for three and a half hours on a radio station in Salt Lake City. The interest that he created turned a record that Collins played as a joke into a national hit.

The FCC regulates station policies by insisting upon a number of standards in hiring, programming, and free use of the air. When a station editorializes it must offer free time to people with opposing ideas. There must be someone working at the station who is a licensed engineer or a disc jockey with a first-class FCC license must be employed. In order for a disc jockey to run his own equipment he must have a third-class FCC license. Licenses are granted to those who pass the FCC examination, and some schools specialize in preparing students for these examinations. Many disc jockeys are able to pass the examinations through studying the manuals without outside assistance.

The monetary heart of radio beats to the sale of commercials. The rates for these spots are set largely through the Arbitron ratings. There are four rating periods a year. These ratings pinpoint the station's share of the market and the age group that listens to the station. During rating periods stations often hold contests, but the FCC rules specify that the contests must start before the beginning of the rating period. The prizes include money, trips, cars, records, or concert tickets. Many of the stations get the prizes through trade-outs. The station trades free commercials in return for the prizes. This is supposed to benefit the listener, the advertiser, and, of course, the station. The Arbitron ratings are done by fifteen-minute periods, and any five-minute section within a fifteen-minute period is considered to be a separate segment. The station tries to get people to listen from 4:10 to 4:20, for example. This ranks as two segments. Arbitron relies on diaries to get its results. These diaries are kept by a small population sample chosen by the rating service from the general population. When the ratings go up, so do the prices of a station's one-minute spots. In several cases program directors have been caught buying the diaries and filling in fake listening data.

There are seven FCC commissioners, appointed by the President of the United States and approved by the Senate. No more than four of them may be from one political party. The FCC has a staff of nearly 2,000 people and an annual budget of $20 million. It regulates price fixing, monitors inequality in rate cards (no special rates for preferred customers), kickbacks to advertising agencies, obscenity on the air, prohibits trading in radio station licenses, and acts in the community interest. In some instances people have petitioned the FCC to prevent a format change in a market where the old format was unique in serving the community but the new format was already represented by the programming of another station. This has been quite effective, because few stations want to undergo an extensive FCC investigation. In forty years the FCC has only lifted one radio station license for something said on the air, but on a number of occasions the FCC has provisionally approved a license renewal, contingent upon the performance of a station within a specified time period. The FCC grants some stations authority to broadcast twenty-four hours a day, and others receive authority to broadcast from sunrise to sundown. The commission has also ruled that by May 1979 all FM and AM radio stations will be limited to 25 percent duplicate programming. This is an attempt to encourage the independent development of FM radio.

Radio has its own trade papers dealing with radio station charts, programming, and licensing matters. *Radio and Records* is a weekly magazine that reports radio station programming and station response from listeners. It does not deal with store sales of records. There are numerous weekly tip sheets for radio stations, notably the *Bill Gavin Report*. Bill Gavin surveys a number of radio stations that are called Gavin reporters. They report additions of new records to their play list, and unusual listener responses to new records. Record company people avidly follow the *Gavin Report,* and they take the information that is favorable to their records to other stations in hopes of getting more air play. Gavin has many competitors, but he is generally regarded as being particularly honest and consistent in his lists.

Top 40 radio is a potent tool for exposing and selling records. At the same time it limits the number of records that are available to the radio listener. The sound of FM radio is generally acoustically superior to that of AM stations. FM stations usually broadcast in stereo, while AM stations still generally broadcast monaural sound. In its early stages FM radio was more experimental than AM because advertising revenues and station salaries were low. As FM has become increasingly popular, it has begun to sound more and more like AM radio. It would be refreshing to hear more daring programming on the part of program and music directors, and more courage on the part of advertisers in support of experimental stations. There is a market for any kind of music in this country, and that market must include consumers of all sorts of products.

I have avoided the subject of television in this book, but I would like to recommend Bob Shanks's book *The Cool Fire* as a good survey of the medium and the jobs available in it. Very little television work is specifically related to the music industry, although there are music composers, arrangers, and studio musicians who make their living doing music for television.

PART TWO

Careers in Music

16 Studio Work and Engineering

One of the most lucrative professions in the music industry is free-lance studio work. A free-lance player is one who works for a number of people in the recording of movies, television shows, commercials, or records. Most studio musicians do relatively little public performing, spending the majority of their working life in recording studios. Although all kinds of recording sessions take place in all the music industry centers, New York does the bulk of radio and television commercials, Hollywood does the great majority of film scores and television shows, and Nashville and Los Angeles do the most records. Lesser amounts of studio work are available in such cities as Toronto, Chicago, Montreal, and Miami.

Breaking into studio work is difficult because studio musicians guard their jobs very carefully and because the people who hire studio musicians have a very low tolerance for musical mistakes. Generally the vehicle for breaking in is sponsorship by an older musician or singer. This sponsorship is a delicate thing. Technically a new person is brought in only when he possesses a skill that does not replace one of the working players or singers. Usually this is not literally possible. What happens is that a musician is brought in who has a particular kind of expertise that is undeniable. A young keyboard player might break in on synthesizer or a guitar player might enter the circle through playing special effects for rock records. While these skills might be competitive to the talents of existing players, employing them is less abrasive than say bringing in a young high-note trumpet player to replace an older musician whose skills are declining.

A studio person needs to be a completely reliable person. Sessions are very tightly scheduled because of the high pay scales and the expensive studio rentals. The player is usually expected to be a good sight reader, able to pick up a piece of music and perform it almost perfectly without any rehearsal. The union does not permit rehearsals for studio jobs unless they are paid at the same rate as the actual job. The player is also expected to be able to improvise freely in any style required. He should also have an even temperament and not get upset at any changes made in the music, whether they are cuts or additions. Too much concern about one's own abilities can be harmful because the decisions made on whether to use a particular piece of music or a solo may not be at all relevant to the work of an individual player. These decisions may relate to a future cut in a commercial or film, a change of mind by the producer, or some other factor not apparent at the time of recording. The player must have the ability to shift gears rapidly without apparent effort. The key of a song may be changed to accommodate a singer, an improvised section may be thrown in to fill in for a solo that is thought to be inappropriate, or any number of things may result in a modification of the music.

The player is also expected to be able to double on various instruments. A guitar player should be able to play mandolin or banjo, sax players should also play flute, clarinet, the recorder family, and even the oboe, and brass and string players should have some doubling facility as well. Players receive extra fees for doubling, but it is still cheaper to hire a doubler than to pay an additional player for some slight passage. Singers are often expected to sing in styles or vocal ranges that are unfamiliar to the average singer.

The bulk of the hiring for studio work is done by contractors. They are paid double scale for this service, and also usually play on the session. They are responsible for calling rest periods, for making sure that the sessions are reported to the union, and that proper payments are made. In Hollywood there are some fifteen or twenty major film contractors, according to Robert R. Faulkner in his fascinating book *Hollywood Studio Musicians*. Each contractor has a first-call list. These are the people the contractor prefers to work with. If they are unavailable the contractor resorts to a second- or third-call person. One of the ways that people break into studio work is when no one that a contractor knows is available, and he takes a chance and calls an unfamiliar person. This is a nervous situation for both the contractor and the musician. If the musician flubs the job, the particular composer or arranger may not use that contractor again, and you can be sure that the contractor will never hire that musician again. Sometimes people get the opportunity to do studio work too early in their careers; they blow the chance and are in effect forever blacklisted, even though at a later date they might well have played the same part perfectly.

I have a good friend, Dan Fox, who is an arranger and composer and also a jazz guitarist. While he was a student at the Manhattan School of Music he got a call to play six-string bass guitar. This is a rather awkward instrument (it was used in the early James Bond movies), and music for it is written in the bass clef. Dan went to the date and sight-read the part without a mistake. It was a fairly difficult part, written in the key of G flat (6 flats) in the bass clef. Most guitar players have trouble reading in the bass clef, so this was a reasonably difficult reading assignment for a young guitarist. During the next few days Dan got four or five calls for studio dates, although he had done scarcely any studio work at the time. On one of these dates he had to play a style of rhythm guitar that used a rhythm pattern called a shuffle beat. Dan hadn't ever done anything like that, and he flubbed the part. He did not receive any further calls for several months, and never again on a regular basis.

Let me review what happened to Dan in the light of my previous observations about studio work. He was probably called as a sub for some unavailable player on the first date. When he did an exceptional job with a difficult part, it was assumed that he was as good and as versatile as any of the leading studio players. Therefore he got the other calls. When he betrayed his lack of experience the same grapevine that had worked for him turned against him—and contractors don't like to take chances. There is nothing especially unique about this situation. What is peculiar is that the whole process takes place without the musician's really understanding what is going on and without anyone trying to explain it.

The market for studio singers, particularly in regard to the performance of radio and television commercials is even more restricted because the financial rewards are so great and the competition is so fierce. Nevertheless the business must hire new people in order to continue to grow. It is important to be honest with the people who hire you. Some kinds of studio work are available to people who do not read music, for example. Glen

Campbell was making $100,000 a year, supposedly, as a studio guitarist in Los Angeles before he became a successful singer. He did not read music, but he could play country music and some other things better than the studio guitarists who were available in Hollywood. Similarly, soloists are hired to sing on commercials and specialists are hired to do guitar solos on rock records who read little or no music. Generally, doing studio work gives the musician some incentive to learn how to read better, and he ends up studying music. In Nashville most basic sessions are done without any written music at all. Sometimes there are chord charts using the number system. In this system a chord number is written with slashes for beats. A C-chord would be I in the key of C, or IV in the key of G. The players follow the numbers and improvise the solos based on these chord patterns. Some of the Nashville studio players also read music, but reading isn't required in order to work.

In order to make a good living in studio work it is necessary to work for a number of contractors. This can be awkward if you get several calls for the same time period. Often a musician is not told what is being recorded. Occasionally a contractor will ask a musician to try to get out of a previous call. Whether a musician will do this depends upon how much work the contractor gives the musician and what the relationship is between the musician and the other contractor. If you ask favors too many times the contractor will probably stop calling you. Similarly, many studio players and singers do not take any real vacations, or they take vacations for very brief periods of time. There is a certain paranoia in studio work. If you are away and the contractor calls someone else, he may stop using you. In the major recording centers many musicians and singers use answering services. When one of these services makes a mistake on a time or date of a session the contractor will not always believe the musician's explanation and may not hire him again.

In Faulkner's study of studio musicians he found that most string players were frustrated recitalists. They never had any desire to play in the symphony but wanted to do solo recitals. Since the market for such recitalists is small, they drifted into studio work as a remunerative alternative to the symphony. For these string players anything less than a solo career was musically insignificant, and studio work paid better and was more varied than symphonic work, so they went that way. Brass and woodwind players usually find studio work more challenging. Their parts are usually more interesting and more demanding than the string parts on today's rock records or in most of the current movies. Some ex-jazz players became arrangers and composers through diligent study. A few of them, such as Quincy Jones and Lalo Schifrin, are now successful film composers.

Some studio players continue to play music in their spare time that is closer to their own personal preferences. Some play in chamber groups, community orchestras, jazz bands, or compose and conduct. Except for some record dates, the bulk of recording sessions are done during the day, so it is possible to perform other music at night. As musicians get older it becomes a question of how much energy and love they have for playing music. After working all day do they really want to play at night? One excellent studio percussion player in New York once told me that he doesn't have a musical instrument in his house and hasn't practiced in twenty years.

Studio work pays quite well. Faulkner found that the income of the musicians he surveyed in 1965 ranged from $7,000 to $62,000, with the median point at $27,800. I suspect that the current figure would be more like $20,000–$100,000, with the median around $45,000. Singers command even higher wages. Whether one should go after a career in studio work depends upon whether you have the right personality, talent, and contacts. For the first time musicians are beginning to work in the studios who have actually sought such a career in their college programs. Most of the people in studio work today got there by accident rather than intention.

There really is no one way for musicians to break into the studio scene. Singers can make tapes and give them to contractors, but musicians do not get hired this way. A positive approach is to use any opportunity to get into any recording situation. When you are starting out, do local commercials, demos for songwriters, work in a studio at your college if you can. Once you get to one of the recording centers try to meet as many musicians as possible. Some of the musicians will become arrangers and composers, and they will tend to hire people that they know. Take any opportunity to play that will bring you to the attention of composers, arrangers, and contractors. If you continue to study your instrument to perfect your skills, study with someone who has been or is a studio player. He may be able to help you meet some of the people who do the hiring. Think in terms of developing versatility. Take up other instruments if you can, and in your practice sessions work on your weaknesses rather than your strengths. Have patience and keep practicing so that when the work comes you are ready for it.

Engineering

In the last twenty years the technical aspects of recording have become increasingly complex. A multitrack recording studio looks like something out of a science fiction film. Often two engineers sit at the giant control panel. One operates the tape machine and the other does the actual recording. The tape machine operator may be an apprentice engineer, and may also set up microphones in the studio under the engineer's direction.

Many of the best engineers in the business have started out as apprentices. Gradually they worked their way up to doing small sessions, and eventually larger sessions. A good engineer has an almost unlimited reserve of patience and tact. Many hours must be spent in the studio. Much time is wasted on following the whims of the producers or musicians, but there is a great deal of gratification, too. Larger studios also employ maintenance engineers. Many recording engineers don't have a great deal of technical knowledge of the equipment. Maintenance engineers are responsible for maintaining and repairing the equipment, and they usually do little recording work. Mastering engineers work in mastering studios and spend their time converting tapes to disc. There are many such studios in the leading music centers.

A number of colleges have their own recording studios. Studying at such a school is one way to learn how to operate the equipment. The RIA (Recording Institute of America) offers courses in a number of cities designed to give the student familiarity with multitrack engineering techniques, with some emphasis on production as well.* Another way to get into engineering is to apprentice yourself to a studio for little or no pay. Over a period of time you will become familiar with the equipment and end up doing some recording sessions. It is increasingly difficult to get this kind of training in New York or Los Angeles because there are too many people who want it. You might be better off starting in your hometown or the town where you are going to college. When you do come to a music center you will then have a basic grasp of the equipment and have a better chance of getting a job. If you study engineering in college, you should also take some basic music courses. This will help you to work with musicians and arrangers. Some business

---

* See Appendix.

courses can help if you harbor any thoughts of owning and operating your own studio someday.

There are studios all over North America now that have reasonably contemporary equipment. Hit records have been cut in Miami, Florida; Muscle Shoals, Alabama; Aspen, Colorado; and Omaha, Nebraska. Local commercials and industrial films are recorded anywhere that studio facilities and a large market exist. Some engineers are even beginning to get production points on records, as do producers. In Los Angeles, Nashville, and New York, some engineers free-lance in the same way that producers do, not working for one studio but working for specific clients. For a successful engineer this is one way out of the exhausting routine of recording hour after hour.

ɔne in the studio. Applewood Studios (a division of AMI), Golden, Colorado. *Photo cour-
y AMI, Denver, Colorado*

ɛen-track recorder and console, Applewood Studios (a division of AMI), now a 24-track
io, Golden, Colorado. *Photo courtesy AMI, Denver, Colorado*

Photos on this and following two pages are by Diane Deschanel

Graphic equalizer and patch bay at Woodstock Recording, Woodstock, New York.

Eight-track recording console at Woodstock Recording, Woodstock, New York.

Artie Traum, relaxing after a recording session at Woodstock Recording, Woodstock, New York.

West Forty-eighth Street music stores in New York City.

Manny's, West Forty-eighth Street, New York City.

Used guitars at Manny's in New York City.

Music display, Rockley Music, Lakewood, Colorado.

Rockley Music, Lakewood, Colorado.

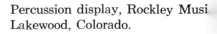

Percussion display, Rockley Music, Lakewood, Colorado.

17 | Careers in Records and Radio

Since I have covered the scope of the record business in some detail you should have a good overview of what jobs are available at record companies. How does one prepare for these jobs? If you are planning to go to college there are quite a few schools offering degree programs, or at least courses, in the music industry.* If your orientation is toward the creative side of the business, such as producing records, it is helpful to have a fairly comprehensive music background, some knowledge of engineering, and a business background. If the college of your choice does not offer all of these options, take some courses at another college and arrange for the credits to be transferred. Any work in a studio will build familiarity with the equipment and give you a chance to experiment with various sounds and instruments.

If your direction is in the business area of records, including promotion, sales, or accounting work, you will probably want to get a degree in business administration. Take as many music courses as you can, particularly a few basic theory courses and a history of popular music and jazz. Try to take some courses in copywriting and advertising, if they are available. Show busi-

---

* See Chapter 22 and the list of colleges offering music business programs in the Appendix.

ness law is another business area that is available to the law
student. Vanderbilt University has a course in show business
law, and some other schools offer seminars from time to time.
The most practical way to get started in show business law is to
get your degree and to find a law firm in one of the music
capitals that specializes in entertainment law. Books like *This
Business of Music* will give you a general introduction to music
industry procedures, but it is necessary to get some practical
experience with a firm that handles many industry clients.

Do you have to go to college to pursue a career in the
record business? Not necessarily. Particularly in the creative
area, it is possible for musicians to develop production skills
through extensive work in recording studios. In my opinion at
least a couple of years of college will definitely be helpful in
developing your skills and expanding your general knowledge.
As the business expands degrees will probably become more of a
prerequisite to getting good jobs and advancing up the corporate ladder, particularly with the larger companies. Be sure if
you are going to school that there is some relationship between
what you are studying and what you want to do after
graduation.

Radio

Program directors and air personalities should choose a
communications major in college. Histories of popular music,
jazz, folk, and country music are useful to an air personality in
order to build a broad understanding of the roots of American
music. Unfortunately, most colleges offer limited surveys of
American popular music, if they offer any such courses at all.
Sometimes it is possible to take such classes through the exten-
sion departments of a local college or university. Local schools
that advertise on the radio and in the newspaper promising you
careers in radio or television should be carefully investigated.
Who is doing the teaching, and what happened to graduates of
the programs? Be skeptical about any extravagant promises
offered by such schools. They may be able to help you pass the
FCC engineering license examinations, however.

In their day-to-day work disc jockeys may have to cue their
own records, operate a control board, do live commercials from
prewritten copy, prepare copy for commercials, do some production work for commercials, set up microphones, answer the tele-
phones, do public service announcements, weather, and sports,
and offer occasional or frequent bits of humor. The morning disc

jockeys tend to talk more than those on the air later in the day. In the larger markets the engineering work may be done by an engineer, but on a small radio station the disc jockey is a one-person team. Many disc jockeys get their start on college radio. The vehicle for progressing is an audition tape called an *air check*. An air check is a tape of the jockey, featuring disc jockey patter, introductions to records, weather, and other talk, interspersed with only fragments of the actual records.

There is a great deal of turnover in on-the-air personalities because of changes in station ownership or format. Formats may change because of poor ratings, sale of the radio station, a revamping of station policy, or arbitrary decisions on the part of the station management. Personality is a key factor in getting a job as a disc jockey, and it is important that the personality of the jock be compatible with the format of the station. Disc jockeys are expected to do their homework. They should read the music trade papers and be able to provide some background on the records they air. Some jocks keep a notebook where they write down thoughts or bits of humor. Some do quite a bit of home preparation before they come to the station and some are masters of improvisation. They are often involved in public service community activities, such as fund-raising events for charities.

A salesperson in a radio station is more apt to come from a business background, with a college degree in business or no degree at all. Salespeople need to develop an intimate knowledge of a community's structure and its business life. They need to be able to match a station's ratings and demographics to the needs of a particular business, and they must have the type of personality that enjoys selling. Sometimes they may prepare sample copy for commercials for prospective clients.

The operations department of the station must referee any disputes between sales and programming. Sometimes these departments have opposing orientations. A commercial should not be at odds with the music format of the station. Certain disc jockeys may do particularly good commercials for products which go along with their own image. The operations manager must know what the station does and where it is going.

Station managers come out of a sales or programming background, as do many general managers. Some radio station people have turned to syndication as a more lucrative source of income, and some program directors have turned to consultation services or are involved in the production of station jingle packages or comedy packages for radio stations.

18 Composing, Arranging, and Film Music

A composer writes original music. An arranger is someone who orchestrates music by himself or by other writers. Some composers are also arrangers, but the two skills are somewhat different. Irving Berlin is a composer; he writes melodies and lyrics. He has little formal knowledge of music and does not arrange his own songs. Nelson Riddle has arranged quite a few songs for recording sessions, songs that were written by other people. Lalo Schifrin is a composer and arranger who writes film scores. Some people would not consider Berlin to be a composer but would describe him only as a songwriter. This is their attempt to differentiate him from Beethoven or Bartók.

Composers and arrangers usually have music school backgrounds, with years of study in theory, orchestration, and composition. Some successful composer-arrangers have extensive playing backgrounds, and pursued their interests in arranging and composing through private studies with a master teacher.

Very few musicians can make a reasonable living composing music for orchestra. Contemporary serious music does not sell well on records, and contemporary music is not widely performed by symphonies, so composer royalties are small. The copying of parts for symphonic works is incredibly expensive because of the large number of pages and parts involved. Many composers survive by teaching at colleges. Their works are performed by college orchestras or chamber groups, and graduate students are enlisted to copy parts. This can be a somewhat frustrating existence because the student orchestras are usually mediocre and because the composer may prefer to spend all her time writing, not teaching beginning music theory courses. Quite a few composers, such as Martin Mailman at the North Texas State University, seem to be able to compose a considerable body of work while teaching at a college.

Lucrative careers are available to composer-arrangers in the composition and scoring of commercials, television shows, nightclub acts, Broadway shows, and movies. This sort of work requires a broad understanding of jazz and popular music. Most colleges have some sort of jazz or marching band, and writing for such groups is an invaluable experience in the training of a composer-arranger. Certain colleges, such as the Berklee College of Music in Boston or North Texas State University in Denton, Texas, specialize in training their students in the performance and writing of contemporary music. Some schools also offer courses in writing for film.

Film Music

Composing for the film is one of the most challenging possibilities available for the contemporary composer. There are many drawbacks, but also quite a few aesthetic challenges. Generally the composer must work quickly, with little notice and tight deadlines. Often film-editing decisions are delayed, and so the music deadlines get tighter. In writing music to picture, the composer watches a rough cut of the film and is provided with cue sheets, which describe the action on the screen and give timings expressed in terms of feet of film. Using a conversion chart the composer converts these footages to minutes and seconds. Many film composers have a Moviola in their home. A Moviola is a machine with a small glass window through which the film may be viewed. It also has small speakers for the sound of dialogue. It can be used like a tape recorder, rewound, pushed forward, or replayed.

In the 1930s many of the film composers were really songwriters, and they could not do their own orchestrations. Today the same person may arrange, compose, and conduct all of the music. If time problems develop, an orchestrator may be hired, but usually the composer will at least sketch out the arrangements. When a rock band "scores" a film they work in a different way. Usually they will write a series of songs around the action of the picture. Someone else may then do background

instrumental music as required or the group may do it themselves. Whether a rock group's music will work with a film
better or worse than a more formal score depends upon the
subject matter of the movie and what the director is trying to
achieve. Film music can be quite subtle, expressing unconscious
motivations, setting time and place, helping to develop a character, and even expressing contradictions in a characterization.
Some serious music composers, such as Aaron Copland, Virgil
Thomson, and Irwin Bazelon have composed quite a bit of film
music.

It is usually the director of a film who decides on the person
to write a film score and who makes the final decisions on what
music will be used and what gets cut from the film. This is a sore
point with composers, who often feel that their music is muti-
lated in the process, just as the cinematographers may well feel
that their work has been butchered in the editing room. In the
final dubbing process all of the music and other sounds in the
film are synched with the picture. These other sounds include
dialogue and natural sounds, such as thunderstorms. The director is the one who decides on the final mix, and the composer is
usually not even present at this session.

There is a great deal of pressure placed upon the film composer to come up with a hit song to help promote a movie. A hit
song is undoubtedly a potent promotional tool in selling the
movie to the public, and a hit sound-track album can produce
further revenue for the studio, and for the composer. Many film
companies, among them Warner Brothers and United Artists,
have strong music publishing companies. Usually the film company keeps the publishing rights to the music of a film. A
particularly hot composer may be able to retain half of the
publishing rights for himself.

The fee for composing a feature film score is usually
$15,000–$25,000, although it may be more or less depending on
the total budget of the film and the reputation of the composer.
Certain songwriters, such as Sammy Cahn, are brought in to
write a hit song for a film. This is usually the title song, and it
will be performed at the beginning and/or end of the film. Such
a songwriter will demand as much as $15,000 for this sort of
assignment, and of course there is no guarantee that the song
will become a hit. Some film composers, such as Henry Mancini,
have been quite successful in coming up with hit songs or instrumental themes for films.

When film scores are written outside of Los Angeles the
composer must often provide his own timing and cue sheets.

Jobs available in the composing and arranging field include composing and arranging for films, music copying, music supervision for a film studio, music librarians, vocal arrangers, lyricists, composers and arrangers for Broadway shows, and people to do the cue and timing sheets for movies.

The challenge of doing film music is in the variety of subjects that a film may cover. Each subject may necessitate research and experimentation in the music of various cultures or historical periods.

19 | Concert Promotion and Careers in Publicity

To be a good concert promoter one must have the heart of a gambler and the brain of a computer. Concert promotion begins with the choice of an act to promote. The promoter should check on record sales, air play, and the attendance at any previous concerts that a group has done in the immediate area. If the act has appeared nearby the promoter will want to know if the group is reliable, and whether the concert appearances were a financial success. Most promoters concentrate on a single city or a small area that may include several cities. Occasionally a promoter will try something more ambitious, such as Bill Graham's nationwide tours of Bob Dylan and George Harrison. Most local promoters will resent such invasions of their territory, and few promoters try such tactics.

The price of an act is usually set by the act's booking agency. Often that agency will have a strong relationship with certain local promoters, and they will discourage a new person from entering the business. Some promoters start their careers while attending college. This gives them the luxury of operating without risking their own money, since most college concerts are financed by student activity fees.

To keep up with the current music scene a promoter must read the trade papers. She may also read such papers as the *Village Voice, Rolling Stone,* the *New York Times,* and the weekend sections of the *San Francisco Chronicle* and the *Los*

Angeles Times. These papers will keep her informed on what new acts are appearing in the major cities and what reviewers think of them.

In determining how to promote a particular concert it is important to know exactly what age group the act will draw. This will govern the type of advertising that a promoter will do. If you are promoting a country music act it would be natural to advertise on the local country music radio stations and to concentrate on newspapers and magazines that you think country music fans might read. The timing of a concert must be carefully considered. If you are planning to draw from a college-age audience and the college is in finals week or out of session you may be in trouble. Certain holidays may cause people to stay home, while others may draw them out to celebrate. If a concert is held outdoors, attendance will be affected by the weather, and you may also need to arrange an alternate site or a rain date.

Most of the more successful acts today demand a percentage of the gross receipts of the concert. This percentage may vary from 60 to 90 percent of the gross. If an act has been overexposed through frequent concert appearances, you may not be able to create sufficient excitement to sell many tickets. If the act is virtually unknown in your area, it is going to be necessary to do an all-out promotion job so that people will be enticed to the performance. Similarly, these factors should affect the setting of the ticket prices. A relatively unknown act will not sell out if the ticket prices are set too high. In the late fifties and early sixties percentage deals were less common, and a promoter could hire acts by paying a flat fee.

Promotional help may be available from the artist's record company. They may be willing to sponsor newspaper or radio ads advertising the group's current record, and also mentioning the concert. These ads may be bought by the record company, or the costs may be shared with the promoter. The record can also help with posters, giveaways, radio interviews, window displays, and by reservicing the local radio stations and record stores with large quantities of the group's records.

Once a price is agreed upon and a signed contract is received preparations for the concert should go full speed ahead. The campaign really gets under way some 6 to 8 weeks before the actual concert. Tickets must be printed and ticket distribution outlets arranged. If the group does not provide its own light and sound equipment, arrangements must be made for rentals. Newspapers and magazines should be contacted with press releases, pictures, and other promotional materials. Enough lead time should be given so that the newspapers don't print their stories after the concert is over.

Posters should be printed and distributed in neighboring towns as well as in the city where the concert is to take place. The initial posters should go out well in advance and should be placed in important locations, such as college bookstores, record stores, important intersections, and in any retail stores that cater to the age group that you think will attend the concert. The promoter often inserts a rider in the contract stating that the group may not perform within a certain radius of the concert for a number of months before and after this particular concert. This is to protect the promoter from any overexposure of the group in a particular market.

Advertising must be planned with great care. The promoter may set a minimal advertising budget and hold a reserve fund for extra newspaper and radio ads if ticket sales are slow. It is important to advertise in media that match the demographics of the group's audience. Free radio publicity can be obtained through community bulletin board features. College newspaper rates are cheap compared to the rates of commercial newspapers. There may be local entertainment magazines and tourist-oriented weeklies that will be happy to include details of the concert without charge. Sometimes a promoter presents a series of concerts and offers discounts for season tickets. The same brochure may be used for the concerts of an entire season. This requires committing funds and getting signed contracts in advance.

As the actual date of the concert approaches the promoter should send out mailings to her own mailing list. Press releases should be followed up by phone calls and invitations to the press to attend the performance.

If the concert appears to be in trouble a week or two before the date certain remedial measures can be taken. More money could be spent on advertising, and discounts can be offered to such groups as hospital patients, handicapped people, charity groups, or others. Any revenue is better than an empty hall. Flyers can be handed out on the streets if necessary and even placed on the seats at other concerts that precede yours and might appeal to the same general audience. If an act is planning to arrive several days before the show, it may be possible to arrange interviews with any media people of influence in your city.

The promotion of classical music is somewhat more dignified, but it assumes the same general forms. Critical praise by

prestigious reviewers should play a prominent part in any publicity releases. It is also easier to focus on the demographics of a
classical or jazz audience. It is fairly obvious where to advertise,
and what music critics would be especially interested in such an
event. The demand for classical artists is more of a long-term
demand, so that it is possible to book concerts in advance with
some measure of security. The demand for an artist like Isaac
Stern will change little from year to year. In popular music an
artist who has a hot record may no longer be hot by the time of
the actual concert. Even in classical music artists occasionally
may be in great demand because of winning an international
contest or making a best-selling record.

One of the worst features of concert promotion is the riders
that appear at the end of contracts with so many of the contemporary rock acts. These riders may regulate the color of the
limousines that chauffeur the act around, or they may contain
detailed specifications on what type of food the group and its
road crew should be served. The Rolling Stones travel with a
road crew of fifty people, and their setup time includes hours of
lighting and sound checks. In the contract between the promoter and the group there should be specific information as to
what time the group intends to do a sound check and what
hours the auditorium will be available.

The promoter must arrange for security and must hire
stagehands. If the city owns the auditorium it may specify the
type of security which is required. The stagehands are usually
union members, and for a large concert the cost for hiring them
will run into thousands of dollars.

During the concert the promoter needs to check on the
light and sound throughout the show, make sure there are no
disturbances at the box office, and make sure that the show runs
on time. After it is all over it is time to assess the situation. Did
the concert make money, were the reviews good, would the
promoter want to do it again? Thank you notes and personal
calls should be made to radio people, music critics, and anyone
who helped.

The easiest way to find out how to promote concerts if you
are attending college is to get on the concert committee at your
college. This will give you the experience of working with booking agencies, talent, and the media. It will also enable you to see
what the possible risks and rewards may be before gambling
with your own money. After your college career has ended you
might consider working for a local promoter or booking agent to
give you a better feeling for the actual promotion process. At

some point you should leap in with your own promotion, taking care not to risk everything on your first venture.

Careers in Publicity

A publicist or press agent needs to know how to write in an informative and entertaining style, and to understand image-making and the promotion of images. Some publicists work on record company staffs. They are involved in the promotion of record acts, and naturally their work centers on the recording career of the artist. The publicist needs to spend as much time with the artist as possible, finding out interesting sidelights of his life, and any hobbies or unusual talents that an artist may possess. Many newspapers will print stories ghosted by publicists if the stories are sufficiently entertaining.

Independent publicists are hired by the artist or his manager. They are paid a monthly fee, and there may be a contract guaranteeing a number of months of work. In selling a pop group through the media the image of the group is as important as the music. A good publicist may have all sorts of ideas for creating or promoting the image of a group. These ideas may relate to costumes, stage gestures, attitude presented to the media, and the type of photographs that the group uses as promotional pictures. Certain photographers might be perfect for a specific kind of action shot, but not as good for another type of pose.

The publicist needs to coordinate the overall campaign of creating an image. It is most important that the act, the record company, the personal manager, and the publicist agree on what the image of the group is. Images can vary from serious artistry (Paul Simon) to glitter (David Bowie) to put-on (Alice Cooper). The goal is to get the attention of the public, and it really isn't necessary that the artist be what the public thinks an artist is. Once the attention of the public is captured, an act is on the way toward building an audience.

20 | Careers in Music Performance

There are many long roads to travel for a young musician who decides to pursue a career in music performance. Your initial goal should be to get performing experience wherever it may be available. Singers or players should start to participate in school musical activities as soon as they can find such outlets. For most schools this means singing in the choir or playing in the band. Most schools have several scheduled performances by such groups during the school year. These may be in the school itself, in other schools, or for various community organizations. Churches have choral groups that provide good early training for singers, and most communities also have amateur bands and choral groups that are constantly seeking new members.

Pianists and string players generally start to take lessons by the age of five or six, but woodwind and brass players start between the ages of ten and twelve, depending on their physical development. It is difficult for parents or for a young child to know exactly what musical direction they wish to go in, but as a child gets older he should be sure that the music that he is studying will be useful in his eventual music career. A jazz pianist, for example, will do quite well taking some lessons from a classical teacher, but after several years the lessons should include some theory and harmony. Many classical teachers simply teach reading and technique because that is the way they were taught. A jazz-oriented player must receive training in

chord structure and music theory. The actual playing techniques in the performance of different styles may also differ. If
your playing habits are too deeply entrenched in one kind of
technique it may be difficult to master another method of playing. Such questions as what constitutes a good sound on an
instrument may have different answers in the context of different musical styles. Anyone that is studying a musical instrument should get some training in music theory and learn how to
sight-read music. It is possible that you will not require these
skills because you will primarily perform your own music, but
reading and writing music are efficient ways of communicating
with other musicians.

By the time you enter your teens you need to use some
common sense in determining whether to continue with the
same teacher or to find another one. If you are headed for a
chair in a symphony orchestra it is advisable to study, if possible, with a first-chair player in the local symphony. Studying
with a solo recitalist will not prepare you for a career in symphonic work, which concentrates on ensemble playing rather
than solo work. If you are aiming toward a free-lance career
doing studio singing in New York, you should not devote all of
your attention to operatic vocal production because that is not
what will be required of you. If you have any intention of doing
studio work, be sure you are studying with a teacher who can
improvise as well as read music. The more musical styles you
have at your command, the more studio dates you will be eligi-
ble to play. The first-chair player in the symphony or an outstanding studio player will also be able to introduce you to
people who will offer you opportunities to work, and they will
be able to explain the music business to you in a way that
someone who has not had these experiences could never
understand.

No matter what kind of work you intend to pursue there
are certain jobs that are staples for musicians and singers every-
where. Club dates are available in every large city, and in many
small towns and resort areas. These are one-night jobs where a
band or group is hired to provide dance or background music,
depending upon the occasion. In New York such club dates are
actually contracted on the floor of the union (Local 802, AFM),
and your own union local may be able to help by giving you the
names of leaders who contract club dates. Other one-night or
one-day jobs are weddings, parties, and meetings of clubs or
organizations. If these are small affairs union membership may
not be necessary. If you are not in the union make sure that

there is some sort of written agreement between the leader of the group and the employer stating the wages and hours of the performance. One protective feature that the union offers is that such details appear on the union contract, leaving little room for misunderstanding about when the band is supposed to play.

It is possible to solicit such small club dates by advertising in local newspapers, by putting posters or cards up in music stores, and by contacting local restaurant owners and caterers. Restaurant people are often asked to recommend bands for banquets or private parties. In the club date field versatility of any kind is useful. The larger your repertoire, the more jobs you will be able to play. If you can play more than one instrument this makes you a more desirable employee for a leader, and it also enables you to play a lengthy job without becoming too bored. If you are weaker on one of your instruments, this will give you a chance to practice in a relatively unpressured situation. Musicians that can sing or singers that can play also do better in the club date field. Multiple skills reduce the necessary size of the band and increase the amount of money for each musician or singer. If you are comfortable fronting a group and selling a band to people, there is no reason why you can't put together a band yourself and earn a bigger share of the take. The leader of a band in union contracts gets double scale, or twice what the "sidemen," or other players, are paid.* The leader of a club date group may not be the best musician in the band, but he is almost always the best salesperson in the group.

Churches provide another source of supplementary income for singers and keyboard players. Pianists and organists often play for church services, funerals, or weddings, and singers may also be hired for such occasions. There are full-time opportunities for choral conductors and organists at the larger churches, but for the free-lancer these jobs provide a steady flow of extra income.

To work in a small club it is customary to audition for the owner or manager, sometimes in front of a live audience. The union may control any auditions at larger clubs to eliminate unfair competition, but we are talking now about neighborhood bars. Generally, such clubs provide a forum for performers who are seeking to work out the kinks in their style. It should be a temporary step because the pay is bad and the hours are long—

---

* Under certain conditions the leader gets one and one half times scale.

often from 9:00 P.M. to 1:00 or 2:00 A.M. Sometimes these jobs are available six nights a week, sometimes on weekends only. Quite a few clubs hire singer-pianists or singer-guitarists for the cocktail hour, from 4:00 to 6:00 P.M. or thereabouts. These jobs are generally available five days a week and will provide a basic living, leaving the performer free to concentrate on songwriting, rehearsing with a band, or studying music.

Some clubs have what they call showcases or open stages. On these nights performers are invited to come in and sing for fifteen to twenty minutes. Performers are not paid but may be hired in the future by the club owner. In fact artists seldom get work in this way, but sometimes the exposure before a live audience is useful. As mentioned previously a few select clubs are frequented by a number of industry people, and a few performers actually started successful careers at these showcases. Other opportunities to perform free are available through hospitals, charity groups, mental hospitals, homes for the aged, and other such organizations.

If you play or sing and are looking for other people to form a group you might check on the Musicians' Referral Services that advertise in *Rolling Stone* and in local newspapers. Other ways of finding musicians are by checking the bulletin boards at music schools and music stores, by hanging out at showcase nights in clubs, and by placing your own ads or signs in newspapers or on school bulletin boards. If you are friendly with the owner of a local music store he may help you to meet other musicians with the same goals. The musicians' union is another place to find people looking to put together a musical group. If your local is small enough, talk to some of the people that work there and put a notice on their bulletin board.

Many colleges have performing ensembles that play at school dances, football rallies, or do jazz or symphonic concerts. Such playing experience gives you practice in reading music and following a conductor, and is another source of contacts that might lead to your own group. Many college students are able to get part-time work while going to school by playing dances and parties on the weekend. Check with the local college fraternities and student activity boards to find out about such jobs.

Many singers and musicians, particularly if they have moved to a large city from their hometown, are forced to find some other kind of employment until they can build up some contacts to get jobs in music. Try to find a job that is sufficiently flexible so that you can pursue job opportunities in the music business. Office temporary groups may have jobs that are on a day-to-day or week-to-week basis. Jobs as waitresses or waiters also leave enough free time for practicing and doing auditions, or even playing jobs. Try to find a job that will leave you some free time and is not so exhausting that you can't devote any time to music.

I have not spoken about agents or managers in this chapter because there really is no need for them at this stage of your career. If you have playing experience and you or your group are ready to find a record deal, then it is certainly time to find some representation.

Classical Music Performance

In building a career in classical music the nature of your early training is very important. High-grade teachers will not want to give you lessons unless you have had good early training in technique. If you are trying for a career as a recitalist, you should try to study with a player who is or was a famous soloist. When you and the teacher decide you are ready to take the risk, you then must do some sort of debut concert in New York City. This is usually done at Carnegie Recital Hall, or a similar smaller auditorium. The student rents the hall, and makes sure that agents and critics are invited to the recital. There are certain managers in New York, like Norman Seaman, who specialize in presenting such recital debuts. The promoter handles such arrangements as the renting of the hall and printing the program, placing small ads in the newspapers, and will try to urge music critics to attend. A good review of the concert, particularly one in the *New York Times* will spark some interest from one of the classical agent-manager groups, such as Columbia Artists Management. They may take the young recitalist under their wing and ship her off to community concerts all over the United States. Such concerts do not pay big money but will give the artist a good deal of performing experience, and some more reviews. The next level of the artist's career could include appearances with some lesser-known symphony orchestras, higher-level concerts, and perhaps some recordings. The summit of a recital career includes frequent recordings, solo recitals in major halls, and guest appearances with major symphonies throughout the Western world.

The career of a classical recitalist presents an attractive picture, but it is a vista open to only a handful of musicians in the world. Think of the number of piano and violin soloists that you can name—even worse, think of the number of solo flute or oboe players that come to mind. The odds against a successful solo career are very heavy. There are a number of international competitions, especially for pianists and violinists, that can provide the winners with the entrée to a successful career. Victory in such a contest, especially a European contest, will almost surely bring the opportunity to do recordings and invitations to play with good symphony orchestras. I really can't think of a music career that is harder to achieve than that of the solo recitalist. Alvin Toffler, writing in *The Culture Consumers* in 1973, reported that there were only 500 people making a living in the United States as recitalists.

There are numerous contests for operatic singers. The prizes usually are a scholarship or a chance to apprentice with an outstanding opera company. There are very few permanent opera companies in the United States, but roles are available for younger performers in the choruses or in bit parts. Some opera singers go abroad and get their experiences in one of the many European opera companies. There are some touring companies in the United States, and some opportunities in acting roles in musical comedies that may require particularly strong voices. During the past such roles were not uncommon in movies as well, but today there really is no one that corresponds to the light-opera singers of the past like Nelson Eddy or Jeanette MacDonald.

Studying voice with a renowned performer or ex-performer is a valuable calling card, and the contacts that your teacher has developed over the years may help you to meet the proper agents, managers, and promoters. The demand for opera in the United States is still relatively small when compared to that for other kinds of serious music. It is possible that government art subsidies in the future may help to form new opera companies in cities that do not have such companies now.

Jobs for symphonic players are available through playing auditions. These auditions are conducted whenever vacancies occur and are advertised in the American Symphony League's magazine and in the *International Musician,* the monthly publication of the American Federation of Musicians. The prospective player must send a résumé to the personnel manager of the orchestra. Lessons with a distinguished teacher are part of a good résumé that may help you to survive this screening procedure. If you pass the initial application you will be invited to an audition with a number of other players who are competing for the job. For the first audition the player must always pay his own expenses, a disturbing part of the procedure for a young player since the audition can involve considerable travel expenses. There may be any number of other players at the audition, as many as 120 in some cases. Some orchestras hold their auditions behind a screen to avoid any charges of sex or race discrimination. Usually a personnel committee of the first-chair players of the orchestra will hear the initial auditions, with or without the permanent conductor. Out of this large group a very small number of players are called back to a second audition. In the larger orchestras the expenses will be paid by the orchestra on this second trial. The audition is judged again, and the conductor is almost always the final judge.

Sight-reading and familiarity with the symphonic repertoire are important in a large orchestra because there are only a limited number of rehearsals set by union regulations. There might be three two-and-one-half-hour rehearsals for a single concert performance of three or four works. This is one reason why conductors are reluctant to program new and difficult music. There simply is not enough rehearsal time available.

Before the auditions are conducted the orchestra has usually informed the contestants that there are certain specific pieces that they will be expected to play. The players are judged on such criteria as tone, sight-reading, expression, technique, concept of style, rhythm, and even general attitude. While ensemble playing and sight-reading may not be important in a solo career, they are essential for a good symphony player. This is why it is necessary to be so careful in selecting a teacher. Teachers who are preparing a student for a career as a soloist often concentrate in taking a few pieces and polishing them over and over. Soloists never really have to be concerned with ensemble playing because the ensemble is usually playing behind them. Because the presence of a screen makes the audition procedure so impersonal there are some who feel that is not a feasible way of judging applicants.

The top five symphony orchestras in the United States are the Boston, Chicago, Cleveland, New York, and Philadelphia symphony orchestras. They all guarantee the musicians a fifty-two week season, and their minimum pay scales at present are in the neighborhood of $500 a week, with extensive fringe benefits, and some money guaranteed from recording sessions. At the moment there are some 2,500 full-time symphonic musicians employed in the United States.*

---

* American Music Center, *Careers in Music*.

Usually a young symphony player starts his career with a local community orchestra and works his way through a small orchestra with a short season—say, twenty weeks—in a medium-sized town. The player then tries to gain a job in a major orchestra as a "back chair" player, meaning the fourth French horn or one of the many violin and viola players that sit in the rear of the orchestra. The ultimate goal is to play first chair in a major orchestra. First-chair players get paid well above union minimums, they get extra fees for recording, do some solo work with the symphony, and are able to teach a small group of select students at very high fees. For a brass or woodwind player the first-chair position is particularly rewarding because the solo opportunities for such players are so limited.

Many of the community or regional orchestras have shorter seasons and lower pay scales. An orchestra member working in a town where there is a twenty-week season must pursue other job opportunities. He will often teach at a local college, give private lessons, or try to get summer playing jobs in another town. Some players prefer such diversified careers to full-time work with the same orchestra.

Chamber music ensembles must usually teach college as well in order to earn a satisfactory living. These groups may combine their concertizing and recording with these teaching posts. There is a very small demand for touring chamber music ensembles in this country.

Jazz Performance

Opportunities for jazz players and singers vary according to how much interest there is in jazz at any particular time. At the moment there is something of a flowering of demand for jazz, and quite a few clubs are flourishing in some of the major cities. To pursue a jazz career without making any commercial compromises a musician has to anticipate a lifetime of playing in bars, interspersed with occasional concerts and recordings. Some jazz musicians end up teaching school or doing studio work. These jobs require versatility and technical ability rather than a brilliant individual improvisational style, so that a jazz talent is not always compatible with these careers. Someone like John Coltrane or Charlie Parker had too identifiable a sound to make him a valuable commodity in the anonymous world of the television commerical. The jazz life has also typically encouraged rootlessness and instability, also qualities incompatible with studio work. The newest jazz always seems to be somewhat ahead of its audience, in the same way that modern classical music of the twentieth century has a difficult time holding its audience. Some opportunities are available for jazz players in various cities to back up traveling singers who come into town with a conductor and/or piano player and hire a local band. Reading ability and reliability are the prime requisites for a player seeking such work. Other examples of such work are ice shows and circuses. These shows also generally hire sizeable bands in every town, besides traveling with their own rhythm section and one or two soloists.

Some of the younger jazz players have broken through to the market for popular music by recording rock tunes or using heavy studio electronics. Whether a player is comfortable in such a role is a matter of individual choice. The audience for rock music is a different audience from the relatively placid listeners at jazz clubs. They also are usually intent on having the musicians reproduce the sound of their records, something a real jazz player is not excited about doing. George Benson, Miles Davis, Donald Byrd, and Grover Washington, Jr., are some of the jazz musicians who have achieved commercial success in the past few years.

Different kinds of music are popular in different parts of the country and with a variety of audiences. There is still a solid audience for folksingers in coffee houses and small folklore centers in different parts of the United States, and such varieties of music as Cajun music, polka bands, gospel groups, or dozens of other musical styles may be found in different clubs and locations. Performing careers in popular music were badly hurt by the disco craze, but this finally seems to be slowing down. Live musicians have the advantage of being flexible, unpredictable, and versatile.

Many people combine part-time music careers with other full-time jobs. Club dates are the most common jobs for such players. Many cities also are convention centers, and local groups may exist that play conventions and annual meetings. These shows are generally patterned after Las Vegas variety shows. The music is a sprinkling of different styles, with the emphasis on humor and entertainment rather than musical expertise. Some jobs that can take musicians abroad are USO tours and cruise ship jobs. The USO goes wherever the United States army may be. Cruise ships generally are busiest in the winter months, going to warm climates. Other foreign jobs that are available are tours for the State Department. In these tours a group is selected to represent some particular aspect of American music to people in another culture.

21 | Songwriting as a Career

Before Bob Dylan came along, the rules for writing songs were cut-and-dried. There were the good music "standards" of the thirties and forties and the rock songs of the fifties. Standards had an introductory melody followed by a verse and chorus. Sometimes there was a reprise of the verse, but the music was slightly different the second time. Chorus and verse melodies were different from one another. Rock 'n' roll songs often used the same melodies for the verse and chorus, and the form of the song became simply verse-chorus. The chorus was a repeating part and usually contained the title of the song and some sort of musical hook that the listener was supposed to remember. "Poison Ivy," by Leiber and Stoller, is a good example of the fifties rock song. The unusual title is sung in every chorus, and there are lots of choruses. Songs were expected to be under three minutes in length to get more radio play, and many of the songs were under two and a half minutes long.

The hit songs of the thirties were performed by the big stars of the day, such as Al Jolson. Many of the hits came from Broadway shows, written by such sophisticated musicians as Richard Rodgers, Jerome Kern, or George Gershwin. Lyricists like Lorenz Hart were equally clever. There was another kind of songwriter of the day, the Tin Pan Alley songwriter exemplified by Irving Berlin. He was an untrained musician with a natural talent for writing catchy tunes and simple, direct lyrics that captured the ear of the American public. Most of the popular songs of the thirties and forties were nostalgic love songs. They were miniature fantasies describing a world that didn't exist. Love in the sand, never leave me, I'll love you always, it had to be you. Once in a while a song like "Strange Fruit," about a lynching, or "Brother, Can You Spare a Dime?" about the depression, interrupted America's reverie over faraway places and nonexistent times.

The rock composers of the fifties were not suave, but they were smart and they really shook up the apple cart. Many of their songs were based on black slang or teenage colloquialisms. Some of the songs were bizarre epics about people dying in car wrecks and being kissed by their lovers as they expired, but others had a note of reality and the spark of humor. If anything the composers of the fifties were, of course, more conscious of radio air play than the earlier writers, and everything seemed to get done in about two minutes. Most of the records had extremely broad hooks, and they were repeated many times in the record. Later the *fade hook* was developed, where the ending of the song was repeated endlessly. "Hey, Jude," by the Beatles, was probably the ultimate example of the fade—the ending was longer than the rest of the song.

Then along came Dylan. His songs were not usually about one thing. Even when they did have a focus, like "Blowin' in the Wind," the songs seemed to fragment out in all directions from the central point. When Dylan added electricity to his sound in 1964 the forms of his songs became even stranger in terms of the existing pop songs. Dylan enjoyed a sort of surrealist blues, like "Positively 4th Street" and "Highway 61." When there was a hook, as in "Like a Rolling Stone," it was presented in an almost parody form. There were no set times for Dylan's songs; some were three minutes long, some six or seven, and "Sad-Eyed Lady of the Lowlands" took up one whole side of an LP.

There is no question that Dylan changed the course of pop songwriting. Some of the earlier writers tried to match his artistry, but found they really couldn't write outside of the familiar formulas. Younger writers, like Neil Young or Joni Mitchell and later Bruce Springsteen, were free to express themselves as they wished. Often these songs were not performed by other artists. The songs tended to be personal and obscure at the same time. The artist usually recorded the song first, and other artists might have trouble relating to the songs or even understanding them. It's difficult to imagine Eddie Fisher or Tony Bennett singing "Masters of War." Many of these songs had no hooks;

they were about feelings rather than specific events.

When you read books that are supposed to teach you how to write songs keep all of the things described above in mind. Most of these instruction books ignore the Dylan revolution, as though its influence might disappear if it is not acknowledged. They tell you to use hooks, find catchy rhythms, experiment with chord progressions, come up with catchy titles, and to use a notebook to write down titles or song ideas. There is nothing wrong with doing any or all of these things, nor is there anything bad about using a rhyming dictionary to come up with difficult rhymes. It's just that none of it seems very relevant anymore. The formulas have broken down, but the doctors are still selling the same prescriptions.

Songs can be written about anything. They can concern the writer's experiences, his fantasies, the experiences of friends, they can be about love, or hate, or society, an individual, or whatever you want them to be about. You can write them with any melodies you wish, but if you use much more than an octave and a half most singers and most listeners will have trouble performing them. Some people write the words first; others write the music first. Some writers do them both at the same time. Cole Porter supposedly wrote the rhythms of his songs first, then the words, and the music last. If you stop to think about a song like "Begin the Beguine," it makes more sense than you might initially think. Some people come up with an idea for a song first. This gets them started, and the words and music both flow from the concept. Many songs are written quickly, but a writer should not get discouraged if one part lags behind the rest of a song. Most writers have an easier time writing either the words or the music, so some work with a collaborator to do what they find hardest.

Studying poetry is helpful, particularly if your songs rhyme. It will help to give you some feeling for the flow of lyrics, and for the rhythms of syllables. A good deal of nonsense has been written about the poetry of popular music. In fact many of the lyrics don't stand up without the melodies. The music often needs a particular arrangement or performance to sound complete. Songs are at their best when words, music, arrangement, and performance work together. The whole is greater than the sum of its parts. Many contemporary songwriters write all of their melodies while playing guitar or piano, and their melodies seem more a function of chords than tunes that stand on their own. If this seems to be happening to your songs, try writing the melody in your head away from your instrument.

Songwriters who do not perform their own songs must be prepared for many rejections before their music becomes performed. Sometimes an artist or a producer simply cannot hear a song beyond the arrangement on a demo record. To sell a song you need to cast it, which means that you and your publisher need to determine what artist might be suitable for the song. Many songs get recorded because the artist and the songwriter are friendly, and in the course of their normal relationship the songwriter sings a few of his songs for the artist. Many songs that ended up being major hits were turned down a dozen or more times by famous artists and producers.

In making a demo the publisher usually wants the demo singer to convey the style of a song. If the singer imitates the style of a specific artist too closely then it may be difficult to submit the song to other artists—especially if the original target doesn't like the song.

Many songwriters run up against the problem of dry periods when they simply cannot write. One way to combat such periods is to try a new approach. Try writing melodies away from your instrument. If most of your songs are about personal experiences, experiment with subjects that are far from your own experiences. Try writing a country tune or a novelty song, if these are things you haven't done before. BMI and ASCAP both have workshops for songwriters, and BMI has a weekly songwriter's showcase at The Improvisation in Los Angeles. Going to such a showcase or to the workshops gives you a chance to meet writers and publishers and to get some feedback on your work.

When you write a song you should try to record it as soon as possible on a cheap cassette recorder. This will save you the trouble of writing a lead sheet immediately, and yet enable you to have a copy of the song to refer to later. For a typical lead sheet see the Appendix of this book. In the larger cities some writers do their lead sheets on onion skins, a thin paper. The lead sheets are then duplicated on a special machine. This process is called *deshon* or *ozalid*. Engineers use this process to duplicate blueprints. Xerox machines provide easy duplication of ordinary lead sheets, but the deshon process gives cleaner reproductions.

Although it is advantageous for a songwriter to be able to perform his own songs, there will probably always be artists who are primarily singers, like Natalie Cole or Glen Campbell. These people provide the basic market for the prospective writer. Sometimes a songwriter may collaborate with a recording artist. Robert Hunter is the lyricist for The Grateful Dead. Their successful recordings are an immediate outlet for his work.

The American Songs Festival is an annual event that offers prizes to writers. Songs are submitted on tape, and the songwriters are divided into professional and amateur categories. There are large money prizes, but the odds are always against winning such a contest. Someone has to win, though, and you might be the one. Getting your songs recorded by artists that you know personally is probably the single most effective way to succeed in the business of songwriting.

Magazines about songwriting, such as *Songwriter's Review.* can give you tips about writing and addresses of publishers. Most of all it is a matter of perfecting your craft and making contacts with people who are making records. If you are able to write a hit song for someone else, there is a good chance that you will be able to get a recording contract for yourself, even if your career plans don't focus on a career as a performer. If nothing else, such a record will give you a great tool for exposing your own songs at someone else's expense.

22 College: Getting the Education You Need

A number of schools (listed in the Appendix of this book) offer degree programs of courses in the music industry. From one year to the next different schools enter the field and others drop certain courses. Be sure to write to the schools of your choice requesting a current catalog. Some colleges have high-level, professional-quality recording studios and electronic music facilities, some offer extensive courses in music merchandising, some offer courses in such subjects as copyright protection, musical instrument repair, and songwriting. Attending a college with a music industry program gives you a chance to experience the various facets of the industry. Many schools offer internships in actual jobs. In these programs the student works for a company that is in the music business, learns their procedures, and does the same kind of work that actual employees of the company are expected to do. Such internships can be arranged with music publishers, record companies, music stores, radio stations, music instrument builders or restorers, recording studios, or whatever is available to the school. In her academic work the student is generally required to take a number of courses in various disciplines. Music history and theory are usually required, along with basic business and accounting courses.

The question of whether such a program will be useful for you is one that only you can decide. There are certain guidelines which I can offer to help you in deciding whether a particular music industry program will be advantageous to you in pursing your career. Who is doing the teaching? Have the teachers in the program had much practical experience in the music business, or are they mostly teaching people to do something they themselves have never done? How recent is the teacher's experience? The music industry changes constantly, and you will want to feel that your instructors are in touch with current practices. How large are the classes? If you are studying engineering and you are promised the use of the school's 16-track studio, how many hours a week will you get to use the studio, and will you have to share that use with other students? In some schools the equipment itself may be fine, but there are so many people using it, including faculty members doing some of their own projects, that you might get only one or two hours a week of studio time. This is really not enough to be of much use. How personalized is the instruction? Is it oriented for the beginner, and is there someone around to answer your questions, or are the classes too large and the teachers too busy or uninterested to devote any time to working out your individual problems? Be sure to talk to the teachers in the program so you can begin to develop a feeling for them as people. That feeling may in itself answer many of your questions.

If you get vague answers to your questions, then perhaps more questions are in order. How many students are there in the program, and how many teachers are there? Are the people teaching the business courses familiar with the music industry or do they simply have a general business background? Are studio and practice facilities open at night and on weekends so that you can work on some of your own projects? Is there a maintenance engineer for the recording studio to repair the equipment when something goes wrong? Are the teachers sympathetic to the type of music that you expect to play? Even today many of the people teaching music in the colleges are ignorant of or hostile to country and rock music. If you are taking music arranging and history classes there should not be artificial limitations placed on the type of music studied. You should be working with as many different kinds of music as possible in order to get the experience that you will need in the real world of the music business.

What kind of internships are available in the program? Ask to see a list of internships that students have done in the past several years. Does the music department at the school seem to have enough contacts to get you an internship in the area of your choice? Try talking to students already in the program to find out what the good and bad points of the program have been for them.

Most students do not realize how much power they possess in the colleges today. Private colleges are in almost desperate need of students, and most state universities are funded based on the number of students that are registered. Colleges are more eager to attract students today than they have been since the days of the great depression. If the college you are interested in attending doesn't offer everything you want, see if they can arrange independent study programs to fill in the blanks in their academic offerings. Is there someone on the staff who can teach you songwriting on a one-to-one basis? Sometimes individual studies programs can be more useful than a formal class situation. How far will the school go in helping you to work out a program? Will the college allow you to take summer courses for credit at another school, or will they give you credit for study-related work experiences, such as an apprenticeship at a recording studio?

If you find that a college emphasizes requirements for graduation more than it seems to want to deal with what the student wants to learn, my advice is to avoid that college. There are so many career possibilities in the music industry today that it would be foolish to lock yourself into a limited curriculum. You may not think of yourself as a future music critic, but a music criticism course might be highly beneficial for you. It might help your perspectives on music performance and could also be useful in helping you to develop a writing style. If you are a communications major headed for a career in radio you should choose a college that has a radio station. You should also plan to take some courses in music theory, and in the history of jazz and popular music. If the school you are dealing with doesn't offer such courses, insist that they allow you to take the courses elsewhere. The more inflexible a school is, the less likely it is to train you for a diversified industry like the music business.

Business courses may sound grim to you, but in reading this book you should have realized by now just how important the business part of a career can be. If your records are not merchandised and promoted properly your career will never get off the ground. An artist should develop a good general grounding in business to protect himself and to work more efficiently with the people whose prime responsibility is to merchandise his career.

If your orientation is toward the performing end of music,

take a good look at what kinds of ensembles and instrumental instruction the school offers. A typical college today has the usual choral groups, a jazz-rock stage band that does occasional concerts, and in the larger schools a marching band for football and pep rallies. Have you heard these ensembles? Who writes the arrangements? Will membership in such a playing group help you to grasp a broad variety of musical styles or is the music limited to one idiom? If none of the school ensembles plays any music that interests you, there is a good chance that you shouldn't attend that school. If you are studying arranging and composition, listen to some of the work that your prospective teachers have done. The fact that they can write music well doesn't necessarily mean that they will be great teachers, but if you hate their music there may be good reason to question whether you are going to be able to learn much of value from them.

If you are taking private lessons in a particular instrument, and you consider this to be an important part of your education, find out who teaches your instrument at the college. Is the teacher a versatile player? Will she understand what you are trying to do, and help you to reach your playing goals, or will you be molded into some shape that is not relevant to your goals? If a teacher is good in one area but not another, can you take additional lessons for credit from another teacher? Is there someone your teacher can recommend, if you don't know such a teacher? Many jazz players do not have a good legitimate classical technique of their instruments, and many classical players can't play jazz. Virtually no college music teachers have a clear understanding of how to play country music, or soul, or even contemporary popular music.

What I am trying to say is that your education should be tailored to your own needs and goals. If you are seventeen you may not have a complete picture of what you need to do to get into the music industry or how you stay there once you have gotten in the door. Opposite is a list of subjects that might be offered in an ideal music industry program. Consider how many of these courses are available at a college, and if they are not whether the school will assist you in finding such course offerings elsewhere or in setting up independent study programs. Be sure you get college credit for anything that you are studying that relates to the music industry program.

All that stands between you and getting the kind of music industry education that you want is your willingness to aggressively pursue the things that you need to make such a

MUSIC INDUSTRY COURSE AREAS

CREATIVE AREAS	GENERAL MUSIC COURSES	BUSINESS COURSES
Composing and arranging	Music theory and history	Introduction to music business
Record production	Jazz and popular music	General business and accounting courses
Songwriting	Music criticism	Music merchandising, instrument manufacturing, instrument repair, wholesaling
All styles on the instrument of your choice	Non-Western music	Retail music store operation
Electronic music	Music therapy	Music publishing
Film music	Music education and private music teaching	Sales and promotion (records, instruments, etc.)
Commercials	Music librarian careers	Advertising and copywriting
Music ensembles of all kinds—vocals and instrumental		Copyright and legal aspects of the business
		Music in print—editing, engraving, etc.
		Arts management
		Concert promotion
		Radio and television courses

program work for you as an individual, rather than as one of 180 students at a large university. The broader the background you have received in your college education the more industry jobs you will be able to undertake. Ten years from now your career direction may be quite different from your present orientation. The more you learn today, the more you can use tomorrow.

23 | Careers in Music Education and Private Teaching

The training offered in music education in American music schools and colleges is somewhat standardized. There are required courses in music theory and history, ear training and sight singing, conducting and piano. There are some electives in music offered, a major instrument is required, and there are requirements to perform in vocal and instrumental ensembles. Other courses are required in education and psychology, and liberal arts electives must be selected from a large number of courses. During the last year practice teaching in the classroom is required.

There are many books available about music education, and it is not my intention to duplicate this information, but I do want to provide a brief survey of the careers in this area. Over the last ten years or so a number of music education systems have been introduced to this country that reflect fresh approaches to music education. Zoltán Kodály was a famous Hungarian composer who believed in teaching music in the schools by concentrating on the national heritage of the student, her nation's folk music. The Kodály system strongly emphasizes the development of music skills through sight singing. The Orff system was created by the German composer Carl Orff. It uses special instruments that are available for use with the Orff music. They are xylophones with limited scales, and a large number of percussion instruments and simple wind instruments.

The music taught to the younger children starts with very simple scales, leading to a considerable amount of music using the pentatonic (five-note) scale. The Dalcroze system is called eurythmics. It seeks to involve the student with music and dance simultaneously. The Suzuki system has created a great stir in music circles because it starts to teach children at a preschool age, on smaller-sized instruments. Suzuki even believes in introducing music to the baby's crib, and claims success at getting the child to recognize and sing selections of classical works by the ages of two or three.

In practice teaching the student goes into a classroom and teaches children under the supervision of a music teacher. It is here that a student can discover whether he has a feeling for teaching, and what methods seem to work in the classroom. The teacher is responsible for evaluating the work of the student.

For the last few years the school-age population has been declining in proportion to the total population of this country, and it shows signs of continuing to do so. This means that music education jobs are going to be in short supply relative to the number of available teachers. In the junior high schools and high schools music teachers usually specialize in either band or chorus. The band teacher is generally a specialist in string, brass, or woodwind instruments who has had some basic methods courses in other instruments. The band teacher is expected to put together a band, and even to offer basic instruction on all of the instruments. Band teachers feel inadequate in any family of instruments with which they have had little experience. Both band and choral teachers are expected to be able to conduct their ensembles and give school performances. In a small school the same person may teach band and chorus. Large school districts employ music supervisors and administrators. They generally have masters degrees and sometimes doctorates in music. In a very large city the music supervisor may formulate music programs for the music departments of dozens of schools, and supervise the hiring of music teachers for these schools. This also requires keeping up to date on the latest music education literature and instrumental method books.

College music teaching also suffers from an oversupply of teachers and an undersupply of jobs. College theory and music history teachers usually have doctorates. Teachers of specific musical instruments have at least a performance degree in their instruments, and often a masters degree as well. There are many specialized fields of music study, such as music industry or ethnomusicology. At the present moment there are no advanced degree programs available in music industry in this country. Ethnomusicologists may study at a half-dozen graduate schools that specialize in this subject, such as UCLA, the University of Michigan, and the University of Indiana. Professors in ethnomusicology generally have Ph.D.'s or at least masters degrees, and have done research in the field. In college teaching it is sometimes possible, especially in private colleges, to substitute practical experience or published works for a degree. A composer might be employed by a college who has a limited number of degrees but who has a number of performances by leading ensembles to her credit. Cecil Effinger, who teaches composition at the University of Colorado, has a B.A. in mathematics. Other credits that might substitute for advanced degrees are an outstanding career as a solo performer or the publication of books about music.

There is an increasing emphasis on jazz and rock in the school bands. Some experience composing and arranging for such ensembles may be useful in getting a teaching job. Many schools are now offering class instruction in guitar in response to wide student interest. The ability to play and teach guitar is another saleable skill for the prospective teacher.

Each state has its own specific teaching requirements. There is some reciprocity, but often a teacher moving from state to state will find it necessary to take some additional courses to meet the requirements in the new state. Some colleges maintain personnel offices that help their graduates find employment. It is worthwhile to check with state employment services, and there are some private employment agencies that specialize in securing jobs for teachers.

Private Teaching

Private teaching can be done in the teacher's home, the student's home, or at a music store or studio. Many stores have teaching facilities as a way of promoting the sale of instruments and sheet music. Many schoolteachers, symphony players, and free-lancers also teach part-time as a way of adding some extra income. A good private teaching practice is usually built up by word of mouth. This is a process that may take some time. A teacher generally builds up a reputation in a town, and other teachers, students, or music store owners begin to recommend him to inquiring students or parents.

Private teaching can be enjoyable, but it can also be a frustrating profession if the teacher is counting on it as his major source of income. Cancellations, sickness, people forgetting lessons, late-paying clients, and people unwilling to practice are among the various frustrations that someone running his own private music studio must handle. Some teachers prefer to work in a music studio run by a retail store because the store can then set cancellation policies. It is best for a private teacher to clearly limit the number of conditions under which lessons can be cancelled, and to insist on makeup lessons. Even doctors and dentists have problems with cancellations, so it is no wonder that in a nonessential luxury profession like music the reliability of the students can be a problem. Private students pay anywhere from $5 to $25 an hour and even more, depending upon the city and the reputation of the teacher.

24 | Careers Related to Music in Print: The Writing, Publication, and Sale of Written Music

Scarcely more than a dozen music publishers produce the majority of sheet music and music folios that are published in the United States. New York is still the headquarters for this part of the business, but over the last ten years there has been a gradual dispersal of print publishers.* There are now two large publishers in Los Angeles, and others in Miami, Philadelphia, St. Louis, and Milwaukee.

Printed music is distributed in the same general way that records are sold and promoted. The print company actually prints the music and owns the music books. It then sells directly to stores, utilizing its own sales personnel and making many telephone calls, or the publisher may sell to a music *jobber*. A jobber is a wholesaler who carries music books of all leading publishers—in other words, the equivalent in music publishing to the one-stop in the record business. There are also rack jobbers who will completely stock a location for a store owner. These rack jobbers are important because they distribute music books to locations that do not have sufficient traffic to justify the necessary paperwork or telephone calls to order books from

---

* I am using the term music publisher in this section to mean a company that prints and sells written music, as opposed to its use in the section on music publishing.

the individual publishers. At the present moment the music jobbing system is in a transitional state because of the recent bankruptcy of one of the country's major music jobbers. Music publishers do not have local branches in the way that record companies do because the dollar volume of the print business cannot support such overhead. Music is also sold through the mail by some companies that prepare catalogs and develop large mailing lists of consumers interested in music. Some music teachers also sell music to their students because it is convenient and profitable to do so.

Many of the major music publishers started out as one-person businesses, with a single author who was determined to distribute his own book. Such an operation is Mel Bay, with an office in a suburb of St. Louis, Missouri. Over a thirty-year period the Mel Bay operation expanded from Bay's own famous guitar method to dozens of books. Although he still specializes in guitar instruction books, Mel Bay has expanded his activities to include method books and studies for many other instruments by numerous authors.

There are many styles and formats in the publications of the various music publishers. The major popular music hits are still published individually in sheet music form. The sheet music includes a basic piano arrangement with guitar chords diagramed above the lyrics. There are also entire songbooks featuring the songs of specific artists. These collections capitalize on the popularity of a specific artist, including songs, pictures, and some biographical material about the artist. Sometimes such books contain the songs on an artist's latest record, or the songbook may be a collection that includes songs selected from a number of record albums. The artist, who is always featured on the cover of the songbook, may or may not be a songwriter. If the songs have been written by other writers, permission must be received from the appropriate song publishers to print the songs, and royalties must be paid to the various publishers represented in the book. They in turn pay the writers.

The royalty paid for songbooks is generally 10 percent of the retail selling price of the book. If several writers and publishers are involved the royalty is split proportionally. If the artist has not written any of the songs, some sort of agreement must be worked out where the artist whose name and picture decorate the front cover of the book also gets a royalty. This may lead to a total royalty of as much as 15 percent of the retail selling price. In some instances the music publisher leases the songs for a flat fee rather than paying royalties for them. Some artists even own their own music print companies in an effort to diversify their earnings and investment opportunities. In general publishers try to keep the total costs of music folios down to 20 percent of the retail selling price of the book.

Some other works that music publishers might print include method books for various instruments, educational arrangements for stage bands and choral groups, and general collections of music that are merchandised not on the basis of an artist's name but because of interest in a particular style of music. Such a book might be entitled *100 Great Jazz Tunes,* or *100 Best Hits for Easy Guitar.* There are also general collections called *fakebooks,* which are intended for bands and pickup groups that work one-night jobs. Fakebooks include the melody line, lyrics, and chords of a song. For many years these books were sold illegally under the counter and used by professional musicians all over the country. The reason that fakebooks were illegal was that they did not obtain permission to use the songs, nor did their publishers pay royalties to publishers or writers. Today a number of the larger music publishers have put together their own legal fakebooks by leasing material from many different publishers. Some of these books contain as many as a thousand songs and sell for as much as $20 or $25. The royalties on the songs are divided between the various publishers and writers. No one gets rich this way, but at least the creators share in the profits.

The author of a music instruction book should get a royalty of 10 percent of the retail selling price of the book, plus an advance. The advance may vary from nothing to as much as a thousand dollars. Some publishers pay half the advance on receiving a signed contract, and the other half upon completion of the manuscript. Some pay the entire sum on completion, or upon reaching contractual agreement. Some publishers try to pay the author a smaller royalty, or to reduce the royalty when the publisher offers high discounts to jobbers or for special promotions. Under normal circumstances I do not feel that the author should accept a royalty of less than 10 percent. Whether a smaller royalty is acceptable for specially discounted books depends upon your relationship with the publisher, and whether you have confidence that a higher discount structure will lead to sufficient sales so that your overall royalties will not suffer. Some publishers may seek the rights to your next manuscript or even your next two manuscripts. This is not unusual in the book publishing business, but is unnecessarily strict for a music publisher. Some publishers try to charge off the advances of one book to the royalties of another book. This is a poor deal for the author, unless the books are part of a series which logically falls into such an agreement. The publisher will probably pay only 50 percent of royalties for foreign sales, for the same reasons that this is done with records. If the publisher owns his own foreign affiliate the artist should seek more than a 50 percent share of the foreign royalties. Some music publishers are taking a leaf from the record industry and attempting to charge some of the costs of a book against the author's royalties. The author should attempt to revise such provisions. The author is usually given a specified number of free books and is permitted to purchase additional copies at discounts equivalent to, or greater than, the discounts afforded retail stores. Some publishers pay royalties every three months, some pay every six months, and some once a year. There is even one music publisher, who shall remain nameless to protect me from potential libel suits, who is rumored not to bother paying royalties at all. In all fairness I should report that in my experience music publishers pay royalties more quickly and more consistently than do record companies.

If you do a collection of solos for an instrument that includes some songs owned by other publishers and written by other writers, those writers and publishers will share in your royalties, unless your publisher is able to lease the songs for a flat fee. This is why so many method books consist entirely of new compositions by the author or works in the public domain. These are works published more than seventy-five years ago whose copyright protection has expired, so that the original writer and publisher no longer receive royalties.* Sometimes a publisher hires a music arranger to do arrangements of classical works or works in the public domain. Often the publisher will try to hire the arranger by paying a flat fee instead of royalties. The arranger should resist this temptation because it is very difficult to predict how much royalties of a book will bring in over a number of years.

Let's go through the creation of a music book from conception to distribution. To sell such a book to a music publisher the author should have completed a table of contents, a rough outline of the book, and perhaps one sample chapter. It is unwise to submit a complete manuscript because the publisher

---

* New works are protected for the life of the last surviving author and an additional fifty years.

may want you to make certain changes in your style or presentation, or even use some music that you hadn't included in your rough draft. The book should be submitted to the director of publications or editor in chief at one of the music publishing companies listed in our Appendix. Once you have written some successful books you may be able to make a sale without a complete presentation of this nature, but as a beginning writer you need to submit some of your work to establish to the editor that you are capable of delivering a legible finished manuscript that is intelligently constructed.

Once you have reached an agreement with the publisher, the editor will work with you on your manuscript. She will make suggestions and correct mistakes. Music books are bound in groups of eight pages, so that it is wise to make your total number of pages divisible by that number. In many cases printing sixteen pages costs little more than printing eight, so that a large number of books are forty-eight or sixty-four pages long. When you are preparing your book you must figure in space for any necessary photos, drawings, or diagrams. The music publisher has a production manager who is responsible for working on the physical content of your book. A typeface must be chosen, and the book must be precisely laid out with spaces between the lines. This is skilled work and requires considerable experience. The production manager then sends the book out to a music engraver.* Engravers are experienced in working with written music; in fact the more experience they have, the more useful they will be to you. An engraver may find mistakes that you or your editor have overlooked. Some typical mistakes might include note stems written in the wrong direction, wrong number of beats in a bar, omission of rests, or wrong notes or chord symbols. Many music engravers are also musicians and can detect such mistakes. The engraver returns a copy of the engraved manuscript to the publisher, where the author and/or a proofreader check it over. Proofreading requires great patience, and it is very easy for an author to miss her own mistakes without realizing it. A good proofreader can even uncover conceptual errors, passages that are not technically incorrect but are not explained properly. The manuscript is then returned

---

* All music today is prepared by music typing, but the term music engraver is used to describe the work. This dates back to the time when the engraving process was actually used.

to the engraver for correction. The engraver makes the necessary corrections, and then passes the manuscript on to a printer. The printer meanwhile receives the cover and any necessary artwork or photography. Some music publishers have their own art departments; others use free-lance artists. The printer shoots each page with a camera and prepares blueprints of the book. These are returned to the publisher for a final check by the author and/or editor. The printer then makes plates and prints the book. After printing, the book is collated and bound and shipped to the publisher's warehouse.

Jobs in Music Publishing

Music publishing companies often have a copyright department manager, whose job is to lease songs from other publishers for print rights. Anyone negotiating copyrights needs a thorough knowledge of the copyright law. This may be obtained through college courses, consultation with lawyers, or by on-the-job training procedures. Leasing foreign songs may be particularly complicated. Sometimes some negotiating skills are necessary, because the publisher of a current hit will seek outrageous guarantees, or attempt to restrict the printing of a hit to one or two books. The copyright law does not force the publisher to lease the print rights for a song as it does the recording rights.

The sales department of the music publisher takes the new book and introduces it to music educators, retail stores, jobbers, and whatever markets may exist for a particular piece of music. The educational market can be reached through advertising in the national or regional music educators' journals, and the consumer can be reached through ads in popular publications such as *Guitar Player* or by in-store displays. Music stores can be contacted through press releases and brochures, catalogs and personal visits by the sales staff. Some of the publishers have their own staffs to write copy for ads and brochures. The sales staff will visit their major accounts once or twice a year. Often the salespeople may cover a huge territory, such as the entire western United States from New Mexico to Washington and Oregon. Many salespeople are ex-musicians because it is easier to sell something that you understand, and many of the music store owners or managers are or were musicians.

Many music publishers send their authors out as clinicians and lecturers. The authors give seminars, sometimes called clinics, for music teachers at conventions or do demonstrations at large music stores to attract customers and sales. Clinicians are paid fees and expenses, but the goal for the clinician as well as for the publisher is to increase sales. A successful clinic will affect book sales in the same way that a successful concert will stimulate record sales in a market.

25 Music Criticism

Newspaper reviewing is the most readily available source of employment for the music critic. The trend in newspaper ownership today is consolidation. There are fewer newspapers almost every year as some go out of business and others join forces with other existing papers. Consequently there are fewer newspaper jobs available now than in previous years. On the other hand, there are some additional opportunities available for popular music critics because of the increase in the number of popular music concerts and records.

The newspaper music critic on a large paper usually has some sort of training in music history, performance, or in composition. Critics who review classical music concerts seldom write about jazz and almost never cover popular music. The Newspaper Guild is a union for newspaper employees. It sets salary minimums for papers in which it bargains for the employees. Non-Guild papers also usually set some sort of minimum salaries for their writers. Part-time newspaper writers are called stringers and are paid per article. Often the stringers are hired by the regular music critic when that critic doesn't feel qualified to review a particular concert or when there are several competing concerts taking place on the same day at the same time.

The critic for a morning newspaper must be able to write quickly because a typical concert might end at 10:30 P.M. and the final deadline for the morning paper is around 11:00 or

11:15 P.M. The critic may call in at intermission to find out how much space the editor has left vacant for the night's review. When a concert takes place at a location far from the offices of the newspaper the critic will have to leave the concert early or phone in his review. Obviously in this sort of situation there is no time for careful rewriting and the copy editor may omit a key sentence or rephrase a sentence in such a way that the original thought is lost or distorted. Not everyone who is capable of writing well can turn out an acceptable review in thirty or forty minutes. A slower stylist might prefer to work for an afternoon paper, which generally has a deadline of 7 or 8 A.M. the next morning.

The critic is expected to know quite a bit about music, and also is supposed to know how to write. The critic for a small-town paper may also review films, plays, art exhibits, and be a sportswriter when necessary. No human being is going to be able to perform all of these duties with equal facility. On such a paper there is not enough money or not enough work to support a full-time music critic.

On Sundays the regular critic usually writes a column in which she discusses some musical event or issue at length. This is a welcome change from the pressure of the nightly deadlines for the thoughtful critic. Occasionally a music critic may inter-view an important figure who is passing through town or giving a special performance.

When the critic has a good musical background, reviewing concerts in the symphonic repertoire is not as difficult as it might seem. She has usually heard the work performed before because the symphonic repertoire as played by most orchestras is not very daring. New music presents more difficult problems. Sometimes she will try to get a copy of the musical score and read through it in advance or follow it as the orchestra plays. One of the problems in reviewing new music is that many pieces need to be heard more than once, but in the case of a new work the critic does not have that luxury. It is difficult for a critic to be totally objective—in fact, it is probably impossible. The critic must be aware of the specific performance problems as well as general aesthetic standards. A student symphony is not really comparable to a nationally known orchestra. When reviewing amateur or semiprofessional groups the critic tries to strike a balance between being supportive and being objective. It is im-portant for the critic to encourage the development of perform-ing organizations in her city, and yet there is a responsibility to the reader not to praise a poor performance. The critic must also take into account the intelligence level and reading ability of her particular newspaper, which may be higher or lower than that of another publication.

Many critics have additional jobs besides their newspaper work. They may teach at a college or do a local radio show. Some critics write magazine articles or books about music. These books may be collections of their newspaper or magazine articles or they may be other works of music criticism or history.

Reviewing popular music is more difficult in some ways than writing about classical music. There are no universally supported standards for popular music performances, and many popular music critics have little or no musical training. The critic should be able to provide a historical context for the reader that will be helpful in understanding the roots and development of musical styles. To understand the early music of the Rolling Stones, it is really necessary for the reader to be familiar with Chicago blues and its development from the Mississippi delta blues styles of the rural black man. Unfortunately many pop music critics lack a broad historical background in music, and the reviews may degenerate into a review of the audience rather than a review of the concert. A popular music critic should do homework before attending a concert in the same fashion that we have described this process in classical music. How does the present performance or record compare with previous ones? Are there any changes in musical style? Is the artist attempting to grow and to expand his musical horizons? One seldom sees a popular music review that comments on the harmonic or rhythmic structure of the music.

There are many regional and national popular music journals that can provide opportunities for writing reviews. Critics may even be offered payola in the form of free trips or extra records in return for reviewing concerts or records. Record companies may offer employment to critics to write album notes for records, and if a record company feels that a critic has a readable writing style the critic may end up on staff as a record company publicist.

There is a great shortage and an expanding market for critics who are knowledgeable about folk music, blues, jazz, and soul music. Some of the better popular music critics, like the late Ralph J. Gleason, have even opened up new markets for musical styles by lending them credibility through informed reviews. The critic must continue to think, study, and listen throughout her career in order to be receptive to new musical experiences and to help introduce these experiences to new audiences.

There is no formal training available at this time for music critics, but the Music Critics Association does sponsor occasional seminars and meetings. This is a good way of meeting people active in the field. Such personal contacts may even lead to potential employment.

26 | Music Library Careers

Music librarians work for large university libraries or for libraries in large cities that maintain sizeable music collections. Degrees in library science and musicology are recommended for someone attempting entrance into this field. Many libraries also maintain circulating or special collections of records, so that the contemporary music librarian must be knowledgeable about records as well as the written word or music score. A knowledge of foreign languages is useful, depending upon the nature of a specific library and its collection and the ethnic composition of a particular city.

Another possible employment opportunity is working as a librarian for a symphony orchestra. The symphony librarian must order parts from publishers, check to make sure that all the correct parts are received and distributed to the orchestra, and collect the music for return to the symphony's library or, if the music is rented, for return to the publisher. An orchestra librarian will find the ability to read and write music crucial to the performance of such duties.

Some libraries have particularly strong collections in certain specialties, such as folk music, jazz, or popular music. A knowledge of these areas of music would prove helpful in working for such a library. When applying for a job the applicant should be aware of the areas of music that a library might specialize in. Courses may be available at a local college that will provide specific information about the history and music of a specific ethnic group or musical style.

Radio and television stations have large record libraries, and some stations employ a record librarian. The type of music that a station plays will govern their concept of an expert music librarian. To be a music librarian at a radio station does not necessarily require academic expertise, but it does require the music librarian to be current on what records are available to the station, and what is in the station library. At some stations a music librarian may assist the programming director in music programming decisions.

Since many musicological publications are relatively obscure, it is important that the music librarian have an extensive bibliographical knowledge of music. This can be attained through academic study and by reading the many critical journals that deal with different musical styles and instruments.

In smaller libraries there may be no music specialist, but the same person might be in charge of an entire arts department, requiring a strong background in other art subjects such as painting, drama, and film. Some libraries offer concerts and film programs, and the music librarian may need to be a producer or consultant for such events.

One of the most difficult areas in music library work and in running a sheet music department at a music retail store is being cognizant of various musical editions of the same work, and being able to recommend and describe the different qualities of the various editions. In some libraries it is the music librarian who will be ordering the specific editions of a work that the library purchases. Naturally a performing knowledge of music is a prerequisite when the librarian is confronted with this kind of decision.

Some library training is useful to a person working in the sheet music department of a well-stocked music store such as Sherman Clay in San Francisco or Schirmer's in New York. Such an employee may even be able to recommend new or obscure repertoire to the concert artist.

Because training in music library work is not given in a single coordinated college program, a music librarian should have at least one degree in each of the two disciplines. To be a music librarian in a major library, both of these degrees should be at least on the masters level.

27 Musical Instrument Manufacturing

In 1976 music industry sales reached nearly $2 billion.* This figure includes the sale of sheet music, musical instruments, and accessories. The sales were just short of record company sales for the same period. However, record companies and music stores both figure their sales on list price, and when you consider that in most parts of the country records are discounted more heavily than musical instruments, it is actually possible that the sales of music stores exceeded the sales of record stores. The most popular instrument in the United States is the piano, with 17,800,000 amateur players. Second in popularity is the guitar, with 10,600,000 players, and third is the organ, with 5,700,000. There are 23,777 concert bands and 25,312 choral groups in the schools in this country. Other musical ensembles in the schools include marching and stage bands and various orchestral and vocal combos. The market for educational music and band instruments is suffering slightly because there is a population decline of school-age children. This decline is expected to continue until at least the mid-1980s.

Many of the musical instrument manufacturers headquarter in the Midwest, especially around Chicago, in such towns as Elkhart, Indiana. There is a trend to purchase the manufac-

---

* *Music USA 1977: Review of the Music Industry and Amateur Music Participation,* published by the American Music Conference.

turers by conglomerates and a decline of family-owned businesses as is true for so many products in this country. CBS owns Fender Guitars, Gibson Guitars are part of a conglomerate called Norlin, and the Selmer Company, which makes brass instruments, is a division of Magnavox. Fifty years ago there were some 500 piano manufacturers in the United States—now there are less than a dozen. Although there have been some inroads made by foreign manufacturers, particularly in the market for cheap acoustic guitars, for the first time in the nine-year period that the American Music Conference has kept such records, the United States exported more musical instruments in 1976 than it imported.

Many of the jobs in musical instrument manufacturing require a business background, and music skills are useful but not required. This is particularly true in the financial areas of a company—the people who deal with credit ratings, accounting procedures—and of personnel directors. In the actual making of musical instruments many handcraftsmen are still employed, but many of the production workers, such as tool and die makers, do not need any sort of musical skills.

Manufacturers of any kind are concerned with the development of new technical processes. This may involve the invention of new musical instruments or new designs or modifications of older instruments. Engineers are employed to work out the technical problems, and product managers are employed to come up with new ideas. Engineering skills are particularly useful in the design of synthesizers or amplifiers. Musicians may be hired as consultants on new design ideas. When the prototype instruments are produced, they are given to musicians to test whether the experiment has worked. Some of the engineers in the research labs have some musical training or background. Manufacturers also have a repair and service division. This department is maintained to service instruments that are damaged while covered by manufacturers' guarantees, or as the result of accident or wear. Some playing ability is helpful for the repair people in order to deal with customer complaints or to be able to test an instrument after it has been repaired.

The sales department is organized much like that of record companies, with a national manager and regional people. There are periodic regional and even national sales meetings, where sales personnel exchange experiences of value, provide feedback to the company on consumer reaction to new products, and discuss competing products. Many musical instrument salespeople have had some formal musical training, or at least can play some of the instruments that they sell. This is particularly important in trying to interest a school district in the purchase of band instruments. The salesperson must be able to speak the language of the music educator in order to have any sort of dialogue.

To stimulate sales and promotion and to establish good public relations many companies have an educational services manager. This person is usually an experienced music educator and is responsible for hiring educational clinicians. These player-teachers give free concerts and demonstrations at the music educators' national, regional, and even state meetings. Sometimes they give free performances at large music stores, where there is sufficient interest in an instrument to attract a sizeable audience. Some of the instrument manufacturers also seek to get endorsements from top players in various styles. The endorsement by a top player can be of great value, if that player is known as a significant stylist on the instrument. Sometimes a musician may actually design musical instruments for the company, as Les Paul has done for the Gibson Guitar Company. In other instances the company might design the instrument after conferring with a musician about possible innovations in appearance or design. If a musician has actually designed a musical instrument, particularly if the model is named after the musician, the company may pay her a royalty on each instrument sold. Famous musicians may receive fees, free instruments, or large discounts and special services from the manufacturer in return for endorsements. The musicians also get additional free publicity from posters, magazine ads, and brochures featuring pictures of the musician playing the instrument. Occasionally musicians will make special records for the manufacturer demonstrating technique, with descriptive material on the jacket about the instrument.

Some of the instrument manufacturers act as distributors for foreign-made instruments in this country. An alternative is for an American manufacturer to buy a foreign company because they cannot manufacture a comparably cheap instrument in this country.

As the population shifts to an older age group and the school-age population declines, musical instrument manufacturers may have to adopt new measures in order to reach the adult population. Marching-band instruments will decrease in demand if this trend continues, but the piano, organ, and guitar would appear to be able to maintain their popularity without any great difficulties.

28 | Music Retailing and Wholesaling

There are 6,000 retail music stores in the United States at the present time. Some of them are full-service stores stocking band instruments, keyboard instruments, fretted instruments, percussion, sheet music, amplifiers, and records. Some are specialty stores carrying only pianos and organs or guitars and other fretted instruments. Some 42.6 percent of retail stores are located in cities of under 50,000 people, 32.2 percent are in cities of 50,000–250,000 population, 23.2 percent are in cities of over 250,000, and 18.1 percent are in suburbs of large cities.*

To operate a successful music store the owner must have a good location, a knowledge of music, good relationships with the music educators in the community, and some business ability. Sales personnel in music stores may be paid a salary, a salary plus a commission, or they may work on a straight commission basis. When the salesperson gets a salary plus commission, the commission is usually based on sales over a certain amount of money. Because the retail price of pianos and organs is so high a commission deal can be very lucrative.

There are some colleges that specialize in degree programs in music merchandising. They include Bradley University, the

---

* *Music USA 1977,* American Music Conference. The percentages add up to over 100 percent because many stores have one or more branches.

University of Indiana at Evansville, the University of Miami, Foothills College in Los Altos Hills, California, and the University of Wisconsin at Oshkosh. In these programs the student serves an internship while attending school. Such internships often lead to job offers when the student graduates.

A retail music store owner should have a variety of business skills mixed in with his music background. New editions of music and new instruments must be evaluated from an aesthetic and sales viewpoint, repair personnel and salespeople hired, and financing deals must be arranged. Many instruments are purchased on time payment plans. It is wise for the owner to have the bank finance these plans. If the store owner does the financing, he may find himself in a cash bind where a number of instruments have been sold, but no cash is available to replace them with new instruments. Without any retail stock the owner cannot possibly survive.

Some music stores supply instruments to public or private schools on a contract basis. This requires working closely with school administrators, and sometimes written bids must be submitted in competition with other stores. A school may buy or rent instruments, depending on the needs of the school district. Naturally the owner must be able to evaluate the school's needs and to select suitable instruments that are sturdy but playable.

Specialty music store operators often are ex-musicians who have a good working knowledge of how to play their instrument and possess considerable knowledge of who will buy such instruments. If the market in a particular area is sufficiently concentrated, such a shop can be quite successful. The most common specialty music stores sell pianos and/or organs and guitars.

Many music store owners operate teaching studios, hiring teachers from the colleges or high schools or music students from the colleges. The teaching is done after school and in the evenings and on Saturdays. Some store owners make tie-ins with instrument sales, giving several free lessons with the purchase of a new instrument. It is presumed that when a student comes to a studio inside the store or close to it, further sales will be made of instrumental accessories and music, and eventually a replacement instrument will be purchased as the student becomes more advanced. The teacher is paid most of the lesson fee, and the owner keeps a percentage—usually around 20 percent for providing the studio space and booking the student.

Whether or not the owner operates a music studio, he will try to make contact with local music teachers. Teachers are offered a professional discount, ranging from 10 to 20 percent.

The store will seek to stock music books or even the instruments that the teacher recommends to her students. This represents a convenience for the teacher and a profit-making opportunity for the store owner.

The larger music stores maintain their own musical instrument repair services. There is a shortage of competent instrument repair personnel of almost every kind, and also a need for amplifier repair people. Instrument repair can be a good business in itself, but it is also valuable because it brings traffic into the store, results in trade-ins and the subsequent sale of used instruments, and offers service to the consumer. Repair personnel may be paid a salary, or they may be paid in the same fashion as teachers in the owner's music studios, with the owner taking a small percentage of the bill. If a store does not have a repair service or if a new instrument has some defect in it the store owner must sublet the work to another repair service or send the instrument back to the factory. This is time consuming and will often irritate the customer.

In New York and Los Angeles and in some other large cities there are discount music stores. These stores sell to the public at steep discounts, relying on a large volume of business to produce some profit. In New York there is a concentration of some ten music stores on one block of West 48th Street. When so many stores are close to one another, discounting is inevitable. Discount stores often do not offer repair services, or they offer service on only the most minor repairs.

Wholesaling

The wholesaler buys large quantities of instruments and some sheet music and accessories from many manufacturers and offers a one-stop service to the smaller music store. The larger wholesalers have salesmen that cover numerous states and specialize in servicing the small retail store. Wholesalers may also import instruments directly. In recent years acoustic guitars from Japan, Korea, and Formosa have been heavy import items. Wholesale salespeople have to have some knowledge of the instruments which they sell, and playing experience is helpful. To the small music store the wholesaler offers the convenience of ordering all of their merchandise from one or two sources instead of having to deal with dozens of manufacturers.

29 | Music Therapy

Degree programs in music therapy are available at a number of colleges.* The majority of hours are taken in music, with some special music therapy courses, psychology, sociology, anthropology, and general electives. An internship in one of eighty approved institutions is required to complete a music therapy degree. Seven schools offer additional training for the masters degree. This training includes clinical experience.

Music therapy is used for physical and mental disorders. Playing wind instruments can be helpful in restoring proper breathing, and problems of speech and vocal articulation can be aided by music therapy. Paralysis and heart patients are also treated as a form of physical therapy. Motor coordination and skills can be improved through the playing of musical instruments.

In a mental hospital situation music therapy can be used for soothing purposes, for purposes of drawing out the patient, or for general recreation and socialization procedures. Sometimes a particular song or style of music has associative value to the patient and may bring a flood of memories that can be helpful in treating the patient. Some amazing instances have been reported where patients who were regarded as hopeless

---

* See Appendix.

incurables reacted so strongly to the work of a musical therapist that eventually the patient was discharged from the hospital.

Historically music has been used in a therapeutic way. Medicine men used singing as part of the healing process in many primitive societies. The Arabs have been reported to use flutes with mental patients, and the ancient Greeks and Chinese attached much philosophical value to music as a means of balancing the universe.

Music therapy can be done in a one-to-one situation with a patient, it can be practiced in small groups, or it may be used with large groups of patients. The intensity of the treatment may vary according to the patient's situation and the availability of the therapist. Music must be tailored to the needs of each patient. Some patients may respond to soothing music; others are attracted by dissonant music. Some exceedingly restless psychotic children have been observed concentrating in music lessons for periods of over an hour. Certain chords or musical intervals can produce measurable changes of respiration in patients.

The music therapist should be able to play the piano and also a more portable stringed instrument, such as the guitar. The ability to play other musical instruments may also prove helpful in performance or instruction. The broader the therapist's knowledge of music is, the better. A patient may have some secret locked in him which a particular piece of music will reach. A music therapist must be able to read music fluently, and should also be able to improvise freely. In playing a particular piece of music the therapist may find that the patient has a reaction to it. In such cases the therapist should be able to elaborate on the theme while observing the patient as closely as possible. It is valuable for the treatment facility to have an extensive collection of records and tapes of all styles of music because a patient's response to different styles of music can be so unpredictable. In working with geriatric patients music can bring life and purpose to the generally depressed world of the patient.

At the present time opportunities in music therapy are somewhat ambiguous. The field is growing conceptually, but as the budgets of state facilities continue to be cut experimental programs are not looked upon with favor. A student who is in doubt about her career might consider volunteering in a treatment facility to get a taste of what a music therapy career offers. A part-time job might be another way of testing the waters before making a more serious commitment.

Another academic possibility is a psychology major with a music therapy minor. The student could then do some music therapy work as an adjunct to her normal clinical work. Such a degree program might provide a good background for a job at a typical state mental hospital. Check with your local treatment facilities and see if they employ any full-time music therapists or if they have any plans to institute a music therapy program.

Job opportunities for music therapists exist in mental hospitals, in geriatric treatment facilities, mental health centers, day care centers, schools for the retarded, special education facilities, and hospitals for the physically disabled. Teaching opportunities are available on the college level.

30 | Piano Tuning, Instrument Repair, Music in the Armed Forces, Church Music, and Careers in Law

Piano Tuning

A considerable number of jobs are available for piano tuners. The piano tuner serves an apprenticeship, usually about two years. During this period she learns technical skills. Some piano tuners are in business for themselves; some are on staff with schools or music stores. Self-employed tuners may have part-time contracts to tune pianos for particular schools, concert halls, or recording studios. Although there is no legal regulation of piano tuners at this time, there is a Piano Technicians Guild, which gives an examination as a prerequisite for membership. Guild members charge fees of $25 and up for a tuning, while nonmembers may charge lower fees. To maintain a normal piano it should be tuned twice a year, but pianos used in recording studios or at the concert hall must be tuned more frequently. Many performers specify in their contracts with a nightclub or a concert hall that the piano must be tuned before they perform.

Some piano tuners work part-time, and there is an increasing opportunity for women in the field. Clients are usually gained through word of mouth, and by advertising in the Yellow Pages of the telephone book. Some piano tuners also do repair and restoration work, but in larger cities such craftsmen have sufficient work so that they need not spend their time tuning pianos. In smaller cities tuners may have to make or adapt parts if replacement parts are unavailable.

Instrument Repair and Building

There is a great shortage of instrument repair personnel in almost every family of instruments. Some schools, such as Washington State Community College in Spokane, offer courses in string and fretted instrument repair. Some of the music merchandising programs offer repair courses in various families of instruments. The repair of high-quality instruments is a highly paid and skilled job available wherever these instruments are owned. Repair people may own their own businesses, or work for a music store on a salary or commission basis. Some instrument manufacturers endorse specific shops to do their guarantee work. Such an endorsement provides prestige and some assured income for the repair person.

There are a number of people who build instruments and sell them directly to the consumer or through consignments at local music stores. A successful instrument maker often has customers in excess of his ability to make instruments. Advertisements for courses or apprenticeships in instrument making may be found in the journals of the various instruments.

Music in the Armed Forces

All of the branches of the armed services have some full-time music organizations. This includes some playing opportunities for women. To enter an armed service band an audition is required. If the applicant passes, the service requires a three- or four-year term of enlistment. Several thousand jobs are available in the armed services. Some of the bands are stationed in the United States, some at American installations abroad. There is some rotation of personnel, but this can sometimes be avoided by the better players. Positions are available on almost every instrument, and there are symphonic and marching bands, string ensembles, and even vocal groups and small combos. Some jobs are available for arrangers and music librarians. There is an armed services music school at Little Creek, Virginia. It provides an opportunity to receive formal music instruction at government expense. All of the services except the Marine Corps require basic training as a condition for membership in the bands. Some of the bands do tours in addition to their regular service. Medical benefits and thirty days of paid vacation are part of the contract with the armed services.

Careful consideration should be given to a military career before signing the contract because the full term of enlistment must be served. Information about military music careers is available from your local military recruiting service.

Church Music

Full- and part-time careers are available in church music. The salary and duties of the job will vary with the size of the church. Large urban churches may have a full-time music director, who conducts the choir, writes some music for services, and is responsible for planning a concert series. Smaller churches may employ a part-time choir director or organist. Composers of church music submit new music to a committee of the church for approval, and sometimes the committee commissions new works. Additional part-time work is available at weddings and funerals for vocalists and keyboard musicians.

A job in a large church may be sought by numerous applicants. The music director may need to have a Ph.D. degree with extensive study in music literature and history. Sometimes the church music director is also responsible for working with dramatics and dancing, so that acquiring such skills may also be useful. Church music organizations hold music workshops and offer courses in church music at regional meetings or denominational colleges.

Music Law

Los Angeles, New York, and Nashville are the cities most likely to employ music business attorneys. In smaller cities part-time opportunities may be available to a lawyer in general practice. At the present time there are no music industry specialty programs offered, although Vanderbilt University does have a course in show business law. The usual way to break into this field would be to work as a young lawyer in a firm that specializes in the entertainment business or to get a job as a staff attorney for a major record company. Music business lawyers charge high fees, ranging as high as $200 an hour. Some work for clients on a percentage basis, taking a portion of the client's gross, or on retainer for a monthly fee. Some music business attorneys act as business advisors for their clients, doing investment and tax work for additional fees. Many music business lawyers have numerous personal contacts in the industry and may undertake functions usually performed by personal managers, such as selling an act to a record or music publishing company. A few music lawyers have gone on to become personal managers or record company executives.

31 Arts Management

Arts management specialists must have a background in business procedures together with a deep love and knowledge of the arts. The large number of symphony orchestras and the size of these orchestras makes a job with a symphony one of the more obvious career possibilities for an arts management specialist. Other opportunities exist with federal and state arts commissions, opera companies, and in jobs related to the other arts, such as working with theatre groups or ballet companies, or working at an art museum. A number of colleges offer degree and advanced degree programs in arts management.*

The large symphony orchestras employ a number of people in their offices. There is a general manager, who has a title as president or vice-president of the orchestra, there is an orchestra manager, and a director of development. The orchestra manager deals with contracts for the orchestra members, and must negotiate with the musician's union and with the first-chair players, the conductor, guest conductors, or soloists. The personnel manager is responsible for sending out notices of vacancies in the orchestra, screening applicants for these positions, and setting up auditions. The director of development coordinates fund-raising activities and attempts to expand the audience for

---

* See Appendix.

the orchestra. As the larger orchestras have gone to fifty-two-week seasons, new concert series are developed in adjoining communities, residencies are undertaken in colleges, and tours are set up. Tours in neighboring towns, ghetto communities, playing for hospitals, and outdoor concerts are some other activities that symphonies are beginning to pursue. Many of these performances are financed by grants from state arts councils, city governments, or private foundations. Some of these grants call for matching funds by the group applying, and the development director must also do a considerable amount of paperwork in preparing the grant applications. Fund-raising is an important activity for arts organizations because most of them run at a deficit even if their performances have 100 percent attendance.

Arts management personnel must have a thorough knowledge of their community. The audience for performances should be thoroughly researched and the arts manager should seek to reach an increasing number of community members. With the board of trustees the head of the arts management team must select new conductors, and with the help of the conductor of the orchestra guest conductors and soloists must be selected. These guests are generally contracted at least two years in advance, so that considerable scheduling is involved. Many orchestras have symphony guilds. Guild members are often wives of prominent community leaders. Through their enthusiasm, attendance at events can be improved and the financial support of corporate leaders and community business people can be obtained. The trustees themselves can constitute an important source of funds, and an active trustee group is of inestimable aid in fund-raising activities. Familiarity with the symphonic repertoire is useful because it gives the manager a clear idea of what budgetary problems may arise in the scheduling of a particular piece. Public speaking skills and the ability to write press releases or brochures are helpful in the fulfillment of arts management jobs. Many of the arts management programs include internships, and these are also sometimes available to high school students with some interest in arts management careers.

The highest salaries in the field run in excess of $50,000, but the beginner is apt to find employment in a small orchestra where the salary may start at about $10,000. In a small orchestra the arts management team may consist of one or two people who handle all of the responsibilities outlined in the preceding paragraphs. The American Symphony Orchestra League lists job openings in orchestra management in its newsletter, and the Associated Council of the Arts also lists vacancies in its publication. Some regional arts organizations, such as the Western States Arts Foundation, may have additional listings for their particular regions in their publications.

Since 1965 the National Endowment for the Arts has funded state arts councils and artists through grants procedures. Many jobs are available working for the state councils or the national endowment. Responsibilities and salaries will vary with the size of the organization. The New York State Council of the Arts is a large organization with a major budget, but some state councils are very small operations.

32 | Grants

Some form of grant is available today for doing almost anything. There are even people making a living teaching others how to write grant proposals. Grants are available from state and regional arts councils all over the United States, from the National Endowment for the Arts (NEA), and through numerous other federal programs. Most grants require some sort of matching funds and are made only to nonprofit groups. There are some grant programs and some foundation support available for the individual artist, but the bulk of grant support demands a good deal of paperwork and is channeled through organizations. The concept of matching funds is that the government is not in the giveaway business, and it is considered to be the responsibility of the applicant to come up with some community support from a nonprofit organization that will match the government grant. The crux of the problem is that many of the artists who need grant support do not have the public relations skills to find such a sponsor, or the clerical ability to complete the grant proposal. The majority of the applications are rejected because there simply isn't enough money to fund them.

National funding in the arts dates from 1965.* The amount of funding has grown from $2.7 million in 1967 to $82 million in

---

* Except for temporary WPA programs in the thirties.

1976. The state arts councils were mostly founded in order to take advantage of matching funds granted to the states by the NEA. There are two levels of members of the state commissions—the professional full-time staff and the unpaid appointees. The appointees are selected by the governor, and the full-time staff are people with some arts management background, general knowledge or background in the arts, or some administrative experience. New York State started its Art Council in 1961 and is the largest state council, spending $33.9 million in grants in 1974–75. The organization of this council is quite large in itself, and the staff is divided up into panels that deal with requests in the various arts. State and national councils can only act on applications—they are not authorized to plan specific programs. This procedure is followed to minimize any sort of favoritism.

Grant forms include descriptions of the grant proposal and complete budgetary data as to where and how the money will be spent. Sometimes the matching funds may be provided in services, such as office services by the staff of the sponsoring organization, but the councils prefer that all or most of the matching funds be in cash. After the grant form is filled out, it is read by one of the full-time staff. Notes and recommendations are made and the proposal is passed on to the appointed staff. A recommended project will not necessarily be funded, but one that is passed on with negative recommendations will usually die unless one or more of the appointees champions the project at the grants meetings. The appointees are a combination of artists, business patrons of the arts, and political supporters of the governor who for some reason wished to receive the honor of a council appointment. Some effort will probably be made to represent different regions of the state, and there is usually at least token minority group representation on the council.

At this point we come to some knotty matters of policy. What is the function of grants? Should they support established excellence in the arts through working with a proven group, such as the Metropolitan Opera, or should they be expansion-oriented programs seeking to bring the arts to ghetto areas or rural areas where people have relatively little contact with the arts? Should grants concentrate on teaching experiences, such as artists in residence in the public schools, or should they be general cultural programs designed to bring high-level arts professionals into the community? Should dollars be spent on new and untried programs, or should existing programs of value be supported? Are amateur groups worthy of funding? Should grants be particularly generous to young professionals to provide them with income and experience, or should they be given to proven practitioners to continue careers which are already in motion? Should the focus be on large institutional groups such as a symphony orchestra or on the work of individual artists? Should jazz or folk arts be supported, or should the traditional classical art forms such as the opera and ballet predominate?

I feel that it is necessary to bring up these issues not in order to express my own point of view but because when you write a grants proposal the context in which it will be read will have a strong influence upon whether or not your program will be funded. No two state councils, or for that matter two readers, will have exactly the same views. Before writing a grants proposal it might be useful to check with the NEA or your state arts council* to see what proposals they have funded in the last five years. The particular proposal that you have in mind may have already been funded or rejected. Or you may discover that your state council simply is not interested in funding a jazz performance in a rural area, to give a remote example. The NEA does give individual grants to composers and artists in specific art forms. These are usually for the completion of a specific work and do not require matching funds. This type of grant is relatively small, and a comparatively small number of individual grants are given.

CETA (Comprehensive Employment and Training Act) currently employs 10,000 people in its arts program. They receive annual salaries of $7,500–$10,000, with an average of $8,500. These grants are intended for unemployed artists, and eligibility is based on unemployment or earnings of less than 70 percent of federal subsistence standards for the area in which the artist lives. This program is a significant addition to grants funding in the arts, but it has some odd provisions. For example, someone else may be funded for a program which you have designed.

Other funding is available through corporate support. Dick Nitzer points out in his book *The Subsidized Muse* that in effect the federal government participates in this support, because it allows generous tax deductions for corporate giving to the arts, while European countries, which give more government dollars directly to the arts, do not allow such tax credits. Corporate support for the arts has grown from $27 million in 1967 to $221

---

* Usually headquartered in the capital city of the state.

million in 1977. The National Endowment for the Humanities, the sister organization to the NEA also has funds available for theoretical, historical, and critical works on the arts.

San Francisco has its own city arts funding, financed by a city hotel tax. Funding of $2.5 million was distributed in 1977 to various arts groups throughout the city. The Music Performance Trust Fund (MPTF) of the American Federation of Musicians also offers grants for free concerts in locals throughout the country. A small number of individual fellowships, scholarships, and grants are given by private foundations or organizations.

Several other sources of funding are available through the federal government, particularly projects that relate to arts education. These are funded through various educational titles passed by the U.S. Congress. The emphasis in these programs is on measurable criteria for the improvement of education in specific subject areas. This type of grant may be most difficult for artists to conceive and execute because art and music by their very nature may not provide specific testable data to the researcher.

Several private organizations, such as Young Audiences and Affiliate Artists, provide performances or residencies in the schools or communities for performers. Young Audiences has forty-seven chapters in thirty-four states. Its programs pay union scale, and can provide a supplementary source of income to the musician or singer. Groups perform in every medium from chamber music to folk music. To become accredited an audition and some paperwork, including a comprehensive program outline, are required. Affiliate Artists provides eight-week residencies in various communities. It pays the artists $7,000, and there are approximately fifty appointments a year at present. Both Young Audiences and Affiliate Artists get their funding from a variety of sources, including the government, corporations, and the musicians' union.

Your outlook for receiving a grant is dependent upon careful planning and thought in the preparation of the grant proposal. If you do your homework on the history of the issuing agency, and if you prepare your proposal with care and receive proper references and recommendations, with some luck you may receive the grant. I recommend patience and a sense of humor as a corrective to dealing with the bureaucratic structure that necessarily governs the issuance of such funds. Try to get some help from people who have already gotten grants from the organization you are applying to or from people who have had experiences with similar organizations.

33 Minorities in the Music Business

The Position of Women

At the present time men occupy almost all of the major positions of responsibility and power in the music business. In the last ten years women have begun to make inroads in middle-range executive positions. Many aspects of the business have a "macho" air surrounding them. Aggressiveness is valued as a prime trait, for example, in the case of record promotion. Since aggression has been customarily identified as a masculine trait, a woman is caught in the "Catch 22" routine. If a woman is not aggressive then she must not be an industry heavyweight, which means she doesn't have to be taken seriously. If she is aggressive there must be something wrong with her. Either she is hostile, a lesbian, or a misfit. Generally speaking, a job in the music business requires that you project a positive self-image, and also that you be aware of when being positive creates such a strong image of self-confidence that you may be threatening to others. To the extent that it is feasible a prospective employer should be interviewed in the same way that he or she is examining you. Anyone who is a continual hassle to work for or with may be better left alone, unless you have absolutely no options.

This is a good time for women to seek jobs in the music industry. Most companies are aware that they have discriminated against women in the past and are quite ready to make amends, if only at a fairly basic level. In the case of the broad-cast media, the FCC has compelled radio and television stations to become equal opportunity employers, and women and other minority group members are finding jobs as air personalities, and in sales, promotion, and technical areas that were partially or totally closed to them in the past.

It needs to be said that part of the enthusiasm for hiring women or other minority group members is that they generally offer a cheap labor supply. Women must demand wage in-creases, job promotions, and added responsibilities in order to advance beyond the roles of secretaries. It is not an inevitable condition for women to be treated as sex objects. Some record company and music publishing executives have hired exotic-looking women as promotion people, but what is going to hap-pen to these people when they no longer look young or attrac-tive? Women should not have to behave according to the preconceptions or prejudices of men. Many men are unaware of their prejudices but may be willing to listen if you choose the proper time and place to express your feelings.

There are numerous male prejudices against women involv-ing flightiness, irresponsibility, inability to function under pres-sure, inefficiency, etc. These charges can be equated with portrayals of men as being overly aggressive, insensitive, boorish, or always delegating their work to others. Clearly there are men and women whose limitations are described by the above clichés, and those who in no way relate to the stereotypes. When people can relate to one another with their minds re-leased from stereotypes real cooperation, friendship and a suc-cessful business relationship can evolve. At the present time men and women on the job are not treated as equals, but this state of affairs is improving.

Perhaps it is time for corporations to make use of some of the special qualities of women. Women seem to have a talent for teamwork, and an ability to consider the feelings of their co-workers in pressure situations. Efficiency is often dependent on the ability to work with others rather than the use of manipula-tive power. In more and more cities there are conferences and workshops on the special problems of women in business. Con-sult your local college, newspaper, or chapter of NOW (Na-tional Organization for Women) for more information. If you feel you are being denied job opportunities because of sex dis-crimination NOW or the ACLU (American Civil Liberties Un-ion) can offer advice or even legal aid.

When I first began working in the music business in the late

1950s the most prestigious jobs available to women were as executive secretaries to top-ranking male officials. Gradually women have eased into middle-management roles. In looking at job announcements and promotions in the music industry trade papers I find women starting to appear in such jobs as product manager for a major record company, local promotion representative, marketing and media coordinator, press representative, national publicity director, production manager for a music publishing company, disc jockey, or on the staff of the trade papers. Some women have moved into jobs in record production, engineering positions in records or radio, and radio station managerial positions. Women have also appeared as sales and promotion people in radio, as air personalities on television, and they are becoming increasingly visible as performers in all areas of music, including conducting. There are twenty to twenty-five women who are program directors of radio stations * and even a few female music business lawyers. In general this has been happening at a slower rate of speed than the acceptance of women in high-level jobs in the advertising and book publishing industries. There is not one woman in the record business who is as powerful a figure as Mary Wells, of Wells, Rich, Greene advertising. Some of the more important women in the music industry are Theresa Sterne, head of Nonesuch Records, Susanne de Passe, vice-president of creative services at Motown Records, and Marcia Day, personal manager of Seals and Crofts. The presidents of all the major record companies continue to be males.

Careers in music performance have been open to women for some time. In the thirties and through the fifties such performers as the Andrews Sisters, Doris Day, Peggy Lee, Jo Stafford, and Margaret Whiting were quite popular, as were such classical musicians as Wanda Landowska, Margaret Dessoff, and the famous teacher and composer Nadia Boulanger. Today we have a greater representation of female musicians. In the pop music area Joan Baez, Toni Brown, Natalie Cole, Judy Collins, Roberta Flack, Aretha Franklin, Terry Garthwaite, Emmy Lou Harris, Carole King, Loretta Lynn, Joni Mitchell, Dolly Parton, Linda Ronstadt, Diana Ross, Carly Simon, Grace Slick, and Tammy Wynette immediately come to mind. It is true that male stars still dominate, especially in rock groups, but more and more women artists are achieving success. The image of the

---

* Claude and Barbara Hall, *This Business of Radio Programming.*

present-day female performer is also on a higher level. Many of these performers are clearly intelligent and creative people.

An ever-increasing number of women are establishing careers as symphony orchestra players.* Women in the symphonies seem to concentrate in the string, harp, and woodwind sections. This concentration on particular instruments has much to do with the traditions of who plays what instruments. As these barriers begin to fall we can anticipate more women as brass or percussion players. In jazz women have traditionally been accepted as piano players. Barbara Carroll, Marion McPartland, and Mary Lou Williams are examples. Only a few women, such as Carla Bley, Melba Liston, and Mary Lou Williams have received recognition as composers and arrangers. Broadway has also begun to feel the presence of such composing talents as Gretchen Cryer and Nancy Ford, Carolyn Leigh and Elizabeth Swados.

There are some women making significant strides at the conducting level of the classical music establishment. Sarah Caldwell, artistic director, conductor, and producer for the Opera Company of Boston, Eve Queler, who conducts the Opera Orchestra of New York, and Margaret Harris, Sylvia Carduff, and Antonia Brico are among these conductors. Judy Collins and Jill Godmilow directed and produced an award-winning movie about the struggles of Antonia Brico to be accepted as a conductor.

There are some 850 women composers in the United States. These include such people as Mabel Daniels, Vivian Fine, Marian Gideon, Mary Howe, Barbara Kolb, Pauline Oliveros, and Julia Perry. Sophie Drinker's book, *Music and Women,* details the prejudice against women in music, particularly in the church and synagogue. Although this book was written in 1948 we are just now beginning to respond to the conditions described in it.

Adrienne Fried Block, writing in *High Fidelity/Musical America* for June 1975, detailed discrimination against women in music in the academic world. Although 21.4 percent of college music teachers were women, they held only 10.6 percent of the

---

* According to Barbara Jepson, writing in *You've Come a Long Way,* published by the American Symphony League in 1975, in 1964 women held 8.5% of the jobs in 33 major symphony orchestras, in 1975 the figure had risen to 24.9%. In the 5 most prestigious orchestras the number of women employed ranged from 9 to 13 out of 104–106 players.

full professorships. On the other hand, they represented 35.6 percent of employees at the instructor level, the lowest level in full-time academic employment. Since promotion in the academic field takes time, it will be interesting to survey the same situation in 1990, and see whether there was any sex discrimination in the promotion of these instructors.

In American popular music women artists have never been as popular as men. This may stem partly from the large sale of records to teenaged girls. The emphasis in the United States in the fifties and sixties was on the male culture, and the role of women was seen as taking care of the children, doing housework, and taking care of the husband. As we have moved into the present era this type of woman's role has given way to such thoughts as are presented in Carly Simon's "That's the Way I've Always Heard It Should Be," Joni Mitchell's "Little Green," or Helen Reddy's "I Am Woman." These songs assert women's independence, or at least question the traditional roles attributed to women in our culture.

Several years ago NOW challenged the Warner Brothers record group over the issue of sexist album covers. A feminist woman performer, Holly Near, established her own record company, Redwood Records, to record and distribute her work. Another group of feminist women established Olivia Records in 1973. Olivia attempts to make women's music available to the public, and to train women in all aspects of the industry, including production, promotion, engineering, graphics, sales, and other functions. Olivia has published its financial statements yearly in feminist journals. Its goal is to own a record pressing plant, mastering studios, and complete technical facilities. It also publishes songbooks and has a tape library of women's music available on request to other women.

Should there be women's record companies, pressing plants, and the like? I would hope that at a future time such alternatives would cease to be necessary, but the hard facts are that companies like RCA or Warner Brothers and the major music publishing companies are owned and operated by men. This does not prevent a major record company like Capitol from merchandising and manufacturing Helen Reddy's "I Am Woman," any more than the giant CBS corporate structure kept that company from promoting the work of Bob Dylan. The basic question involved, from a corporate standpoint, is will the record sell? If it will, the company will put it out and continue to record the artist. Principles to a large corporation are essentially defined by profit and loss statements. If women's liberation goes out of fashion, record companies will quickly lose enthusiasm for songs about it. The primary issue is money, not politics. Of course, there are some exceptions to this, but even they may be influenced by marketing factors. It is doubtful if a direct and fervent plea for racial integration would be promoted on Top 40 radio by a major record company in the southern United States. At times the air play of records has been restricted because of protests by offended groups, or because the artist has been caught engaging in some immoral activity. By and large the question remains, will the record sell?

The point that I am trying to make is that large companies support activities that produce income. Small companies like Olivia are based on ideology rather than money. Nevertheless some money must be made or the smallest company cannot survive. In the next chapter we will return in depth to the subject of alternative media.

There is no question in my mind that eventually there will be women presidents of major record companies. At the present time women can take pride in their expanding role in middle management, and as performers, conductors, arrangers, personal managers, record producers, etc. Those who wish to go further must "keep on pushing."

Black Participation in the Music Business

Discrimination against black musicians in the music business dates from their very entry into the business. In the 1920s and 1930s black music was separately classified under the category of "race records," and these records were not even distributed to most record stores. In the forties the term became an embarrassment and was replaced by the title "rhythm and blues." When rock 'n' roll became popular in the mid-fifties many of the early hits were rerecordings by white artists of rhythm and blues hits. Radio and record people felt that the originals were too hard for white teenagers to understand. Some of these rhythm and blues records did sell in white markets, but without much regularity. Black musicians were consigned to lower-priced bookings for largely black audiences. There were some exceptions, such as Nat King Cole, who was quite popular with white audiences, but the bulk of black musicians did not earn money comparable to their white compatriots.

In the 1930s many black musicians waived their writer's royalties when recording. Sometimes token payments were given for these rights, sometimes no payment at all was given.

They were also paid flat fees for recording, without subsequent royalty payments. The rights to the songs written by these artists were owned by the record companies or by the A & R men, who often copyrighted them in their own names. Sometimes these A & R men also served as the manager of the artists. Chapple and Garafalo, writing in *Rock 'n' Roll Is Here to Pay* describe how Arthur "Big Boy" Crudup had his royalties for two of Elvis Presley's biggest hits, "That's All Right, Mama" and "My Baby Left Me," ripped off by Lester Melrose, his manager. Many other black writers complained of receiving irregular royalty payments or no royalties at all.

Most of the musicians who succeeded in making big money in jazz, like Paul Whiteman, Benny Goodman, or Artie Shaw were white, even though the origins of the music and most of the really innovative players have always been black. Until the late 1930s there was no integration in jazz groups, except for a handful of recordings on which the musicians sometimes used pseudonyms.

When the folk music boom was strong in the late 1950s and early 1960s a number of the older black blues singers were rediscovered by young white blues enthusiasts and were brought up north and employed at colleges and coffee houses playing for young white audiences. When the English rock groups became popular many American disc jockeys and fans were astonished to find that the favorite entertainers of many of the English groups were the old black blues singers. Some of these rock groups recorded songs by these bluesmen and even toured with them.

Motown was the first large black-owned record company, and many of its artists achieved popularity in the broad pop market. Although there are still records that are popular only on black "soul" music radio stations, an increasing number of black popular and jazz artists, such as George Benson, Natalie Cole, Ray Charles, and others have been able to achieve universal popularity. There are even five country disc jockeys who are black, according to Claude Hall.* The employment of black executives lags behind in the large record companies, and when they are employed it is usually in production, sales, and promotion capacities that relate to black music. Black radio stations, many of which are owned by whites, pay notoriously low wages, and blacks are underrepresented in the large booking agencies, as personal managers, and in other important industry functions.

---

* Claude and Barbara Hall, *This Business of Radio Programming.*

The classical music establishment has not readily accepted black musicians either. There have been so many charges of discrimination against black symphonic musicians that some orchestras have taken to auditioning the musicians behind screens, as I mentioned in writing about symphonies. Although this may pose other problems in judging the musician's technique and attitude it is one corrective to the problem. In 1964 a number of black classical musicians founded the Symphony of the New World, an orchestra that consists largely of black musicians. There have been a number of interesting black composers and Columbia Records has issued a number of recordings. Some of these composers are contemporary, and some are historical figures. The famous ragtime composer Scott Joplin and the superb jazz and blues pianist James P. Johnson both composed serious music, but experienced great difficulty in getting their work performed. In Raoul Abdul's recent book *Blacks in Classical Music,* he reports that a recent survey of 54 symphony orchestras employing 4,640 musicians turned up only 67 players who were minority group members. This is less than 1.5 percent. As a remedy to this lack of interest in minority groups, Abdul suggests that NEA grants should be awarded only to groups that meet the needs of an entire community.

Although black musicians were somewhat shut out of lucrative studio work in the early days, this is less true today. This is partly because a number of black composers and arrangers, such as Quincy Jones and J. J. Johnson, have become quite successful. Since composers and arrangers are in charge of hiring musicians, or hire contractors to employ the musicians, this has resulted in a better representation of black players in the studio. There are also some important black executives who work in the music departments of major advertising agencies, such as Billy Davis at McCann Erickson.

Other Minority Groups

In the same fashion that black executives are hired to deal with black music, the few Spanish employees of the major companies are working primarily with Spanish music. While such practices may appear to make sense at first glance, they really do not. Enforcement of this concept would then limit Jewish and Italian executives to promoting or selling Jewish or Italian music, a position not too many music business executives would favor.

34 Power in the Arts and Alternative Media

Most of us are accustomed to thinking of art as an individual expression of an artist's deepest feelings. When you examine the ownership of the media and the concentration of power in conglomerates that operate in so many different fields, a wholly different picture emerges. Look at the power wielded by the radio and television networks.* CBS owns five television stations and five radio stations. It is in the musical instrument business through its ownership of Rogers Drums, Fender Guitars, and Steinway Pianos. Columbia and Epic Records are powerful CBS record companies, and publishing properties of CBS include Holt, Rinehart and Winston, Popular Library, Fawcett Publications, and a number of magazines including *Women's Day* and *Mechanix Illustrated*. ABC owns five television stations and twelve radio stations, ABC, Command, and Impulse Records,** a magazine group that publishes *High Fidelity* and *Modern Photography* among others, and 190 movie theatres. RCA is NBC with five television and five radio sta-

---

* Much of this information comes from James Monaco's *Media Culture*.
** At the present moment (February 1979) it appears that ABC Records will be sold to MCA Records, which is itself a large conglomerate also in the record, music publishing, and movie business.

tions, RCA Records, and a strong position in the book publishing field through ownership of Random House, which itself owns Ballantine, Alfred A. Knopf, Vintage, and Pantheon Books. All of these conglomerates also own music publishing companies and businesses in nonentertainment areas.

The concentration of power in the media provides enough material for several books, and in fact several large books have been written on the subject.* Media connections extend further through newspaper companies owning radio and television stations, and also book and magazine publishers. Music and media are big business. In 1976 the book industry grossed $4.6 billion, television grossed $7.58 billion, musical instruments and sheet music were just under $2 billion, and in 1977 the record and tape business grossed $3.5 billion. Some of these figures are based on retail list price, which in the record business is somewhat misleading, but nonetheless these are impressive amounts of money.

The significance of these figures for you as an artist is that the more you understand about the music industry and the media the more you begin to realize that unless you are working on a project that has a potential for earning large amounts of money, major companies are simply not interested in you. There are alternatives, as we will see shortly, but let's look at some other manifestations of power in the arts.

In the period 1957–73 the Ford Foundation distributed some of its money to the arts in the following fashion: to symphony orchestras $80.2 million, to theatre groups $35.5 million, to Lincoln Center (in New York City) $29.7 million, to dance groups $22.5 million and $13.8 million for the visual arts.** The Ford Foundation is located in New York City. The average age of its board members is sixty; on the board are many business people along with some women and some professionals. The policies set by the Foundation are going to reflect the age and background of the board members. Their tendency is to support traditional and safe art areas. The Rockefeller Foundation contributed $70 million to the arts and the Mellon Foundation added another $45 million in the fifteen-year period ending in 1975. Such foundations are in effect setting policy in the arts because they are providing so much financial support. Founda-

---

* See Bibliography.
** See Joan Simpson Burns, *The Awkward Embrace: The Creative Artist and the Institution in America.*

tion dollars will probably always tend to go to the old and proven forms of art rather than to new or experimental ones. Yet if art is going to grow and thrive it must be treated as an exciting and experimental area of human endeavor, not as a living museum of forms that basically represent the enthusiasm and creativity of the past. This is not to deny the validity of traditional art but simply to suggest that newer forms also have validity and deserve support.

Alternative Media

In 1976 Warner Communications and the CBS Record group accounted for 65 percent of the record and tape business in the United States through their products, merchandised on the Asylum, Atlantic, Elektra, Nonesuch, Reprise, Warner Brothers, Columbia, and Epic labels. There are also hundreds of small record labels operating in North America, many of which sell only a few thousand or fewer records. The young artist is confronted by some complicated decisions. Virtually all of the books about the music business are written with the view of how to succeed in rock 'n' roll. "Is that all there is?"—to quote the Leiber–Stoller song recorded by Peggy Lee. No, it is not. In Canada a group called String Band has actually financed its own recordings through subscriptions. These are beautiful, eclectic records well recorded in professional studios. The group retained artistic control over its own product from beginning to end and simply ignored the mass distribution network that makes and merchandises records. There are small specialty record companies that record classical music of all periods, avant-garde and traditional jazz, blues, bluegrass, and any other kind of music you can name or imagine. These companies exist all over the United States and Canada, in places like Salt Lake City, Winnipeg, New York, and San Francisco. It is these small record companies that have helped keep jazz and folk music alive when they were not profitable items. The artist should consider what constitutes intelligent goals in the performance and sale of his music. One is not compelled to be processed through the media apparatus that so much of this book has described. It really is a question of goals. Do you have music that you wish to communicate in a specific way, or are you after a large dollar return necessitating the use of the media with its various conglomerates? I am not posing this question in such a way as to presuppose your answer. I am simply suggesting that there is more than one way to approach the process of building a career. The artist who is primarily concerned with pursuing his own goals as opposed to receiving the maximum dollar return should consider dealing with alternative media.

To sustain a successful career in music it may be necessary to be able to do more than one thing. This is the point that I have tried to stress in discussing a college education. At this point in your life you may want to make records. In five years you may be more interested in producing records or writing songs without performing them. The more you can experience and learn the better chance you have of making a living in the music business without turning into the grotesque stereotype of a person that so many music and media people seem to become.

In dealing with alternative media it is important to understand what you are giving up, as well as what you can accomplish. If you publish by yourself a book of your songs, you cannot expect to walk into a music store in North Platte, Nebraska, and see a dozen copies of your book alongside *The John Denver Songbook*. If you record for a record company that presses 1,000 copies of your record it will not get on every radio station in North America. Most of the frustrated musicians that I know have a basic misapprehension of the business processes. If you record for RCA or Warner Brothers, they want to sell thousands or hundreds of thousands of records. If the initial response to your record does not produce significant sales, they will probably not continue to record you. Yes, there are occasional exceptions. There are companies that have stayed with a group that did not sell, or that have retained an artist because the artist has great prestige in the community of musicians and may lead to interest from other, more commercial artists. But the bottom line is the bottom line. No major company will continue to plow money after lost money indefinitely. This is also true in classical music or jazz. Some artists sell better than others, some classical composers have dozens of their works recorded, and some have a single record that goes out of print almost instantly.

I have a friend who has tried to produce pop records for alternative record companies. He is terribly frustrated because he records with minute budgets, and he feels that he doesn't get enough distribution or promotion. But in reality, he is in the wrong place. An alternative record company cannot compete with a major label any more than someone who makes handcrafted guitars can compete with the Gibson or Fender Guitar Company. The skills, goals, ambitions, and products are simply not comparable.

The unions that represent musicians and singers present another odd stumbling block. Unions are a business too. They have high overhead, and their leadership gets fairly high salaries. The union minimums for recordings are based on the sales of the large record companies. If the unions are going to represent artists in the 1980s, and if they don't want to make some of their own members into outlaws, different minimums must be established for small record companies. The unions need to rediscover the aesthetic procedures that are part of the performance of music and to realistically assess the business structure of the small record company.

See the periodical list in the Bibliography for appropriate magazines.

There is even an alternative to alternative media, if you wish to be in total control of your own work. This alternative is to operate your own business. I have a friend who lives in Woodstock, New York, named Happy Traum. Happy has a mail order tape business, offering instruction on banjo, guitar, fiddle, mandolin, and piano through cassette tapes. He advertises in appropriate magazines and has assembled an excellent mailing list over a period of years. Another friend, Steve Wiencrot, wrote, published, and distributed his own mandolin method. The Canadian group String Band actually sold advance subscriptions in order to raise money to make a recording. There are several people in New York City who make a living by selling music instruction books to jobbers. They act as middle men for the authors, taking a 20 percent commission for their services. The author can thereby avoid the actual selling of her own book.

Many artists write vanity books or do vanity records. These are books or records financed by the artist. There are companies that specialize in putting out such books or records; they will even provide some promotional and production assistance if the artist desires help. Before entering into an agreement to have such a company produce a book or record, be sure that you have a specific idea of what it is going to cost you.

My final bit of advice is that you try to control your artistic destiny as much as possible. Be honest about your goals. How important is money to you? How important is it that you retain control over your music? How do you balance these two factors? As you answer these questions, keep in mind that you may change your mind at a later date. Perhaps what you want right now is success. If you do achieve it, or if you don't, try to keep your options open. Consider changing the thrust of your attack on the business if you decide you do not like the people determining your destiny. It may well work in the opposite way, as you move from a desire to present your music on its own terms to the desire to make a reasonable income. Neither goal is the right one. The right goal is to do what you want to do.

My goal has been to explain the way the music business operates. The way you deal with that process is your own decision. To illustrate the idiosyncratic nature of the music business I would like to share one last story with you. I recently heard a tape of an audition that Laura Nyro did for Mercury Records in 1966. In this audition she sang "When I Die," which several years later was a tremendous hit record performed by Blood, Sweat and Tears. After this she sang several songs which were quite successful on her own recordings some years later. After Laura had gone through several of these songs the A & R men said over the studio intercom, "Laura do you sing songs by other people? Do you know 'Stardust'?" There is a moment of silence on the tape, followed by obvious despair. Laura says, yes, she can sing some songs which she hasn't written, but she doesn't really play them and hasn't worked them out. She goes through a couple of false starts, including a brief version of "Kansas City." It is clear that she is close to tears. The producers, the people who are supposed to know what's happening in the business, come back on the intercom and say, "Okay, do another of your songs." She sings one more song.

Imagine the scene. Laura must have been about eighteen at the time—young, enthusiastic, eager to perform her music. Two unsympathetic and unimaginative hacks hear her unique songs and quickly decide the songs will never sell.

People in the music business love to apply pat formulas. Don't let them oversell you on that approach.

Appendix

College Music Business Programs

Colleges Offering Music Industry Programs

Below is a list of colleges offering courses or degree programs in Music Industry. Many of these programs include internships. NARAS (see list of Music Business Organizations) is now acting as a consultant to these colleges and in some cases has inspected and approved their programs.

College	Program
Appalachian State University Boone, N.C.	B.A. in Music Merchandising
Barrington College Barrington, R.I.	B.A. in Music Business
Belmont College Nashville, Tenn.	B.A. in Business Administration, specializing in music business
Berklee College Boston, Mass.	Courses in legal protection, musical instrument repair, composing film music. Renowned as a jazz-oriented school
Bradley University Peoria, Ill.	B.S. in Music Business
Claremore Junior College Claremore, Okla.	A junior college offering an A.A. in Country & Western music

College	*Program*
College of Mount St. Joseph-on-the-Ohio Mount St. Joseph, Ohio	B.A. in Music Merchandising
College for Recording Arts San Francisco, Calif.	Gives a diploma, offers courses in engineering, production, and business of music
Colorado Women's College Denver, Colo.	B.A. in Music Industry
DePauw University Greencastle, Ind.	B.A. in Music and Business
Eastern Kentucky University Richmond, Ky.	B.A. in Retail and Wholesale Music Merchandising
Eastern Washington University Cheyney, Wash.	Offers a Radio-TV degree, with a concentration in audio engineering
Emporia Kansas State College Emporia, Kans.	B.A. in Music Merchandising
Fanshawe College London, Ontario, Canada	Diploma in Music Industry Arts
Georgia State University Atlanta, Ga.	A.A. in commercial music/recording
Heidelberg College Tiffon, Ohio	B.A. in Music Merchandising
Institute of Audio Engineering New York, N.Y.	In cooperation with NYU offers a B.S. in Music and Technology
Kansas Benedictine College Atchison, Kans.	B.A. in Music Marketing
Middle Tennessee State University Murfreesboro, Tenn.	B.S. in Music Industry, courses in marketing and promoting records
New School for Social Research New York, N. Y.	Courses in music business and audio engineering

College	*Program*
North Park College Chicago, Ill.	B.A. in Music Management
North Texas State University Denton, Tex.	Offers a major in jazz education, courses in instrument repair
Quincy College Quincy, Ill.	B.A. in music and business studies
The Recording Workshop New York, N.Y.	Gives a certificate in audio
South Plains College Levelland, Tex.	Offers a country and bluegrass music program with A.A. degree
Syracuse University Syracuse, N.Y.	Music Industry degree
University of Colorado at Denver Denver, Colo.	B.S. in Music and Media
University of Miami Miami, Fla.	Two degree programs, one in music engineering and one in music merchandising
University of South Carolina Columbia, S.C.	Bachelor of Media Arts, with courses in audio engineering
University of Tennessee at Martin Martin, Tenn.	Courses in recording techniques and music industry survey course
University of Tennessee at Nashville Nashville, Tenn.	Offers courses in songwriting
University of Wisconsin at Oshkosh Oshkosh, Wis.	B.A. in Music Merchandising
Vanderbilt University School of Law Nashville, Tenn.	The law school offers a course in music industry legal problems
Washtenaw Community College Ann Arbor, Mich.	Offers songwriting courses

Note: If your college doesn't offer a music industry degree, you may be able to create your own program. Get a catalog from one of the schools listed and try to match the courses. To do this take whatever is appropriate at your college and arrange for college credit by going to other schools or by arranging internships with local music stores, radio stations, recording studios, or whatever. Some schools call this a "contract major" or "open degree program."

Colleges Offering Music Therapy Programs

College	*Program*
Anna Maria College Paxton, Mass.	Bachelor's degree
Belmont College Nashville, Tenn.	Bachelor's degree
Catholic University of America Washington, D.C.	Bachelor's degree
College of Mount St. Joseph-on-the-Ohio Mount St. Joseph, Ohio	Bachelor's degree
College of St. Teresa Winona, Minn.	Bachelor's degree
Combs College Philadelphia, Pa.	Bachelor's degree
Dean Junior College Franklin, Mass.	Associate Arts degree
Duquesne University Pittsburgh, Pa.	Bachelor's degree

Eastern North
  Carolina
  University
Greenville, N.C.
	Bachelor's degree

Georgia College Milledgeville, Ga.	Bachelor's degree
Lincoln University Jefferson City, Mo.	Bachelor's degree
Loyola University New Orleans, La.	B.A. and M.A. degrees
Maryville College St. Louis, Mo.	Bachelor's degree

College	*Program*
Michigan State University East Lansing, Mich.	Bachelor's degree
Montclair State College Montclair, N.J.	Bachelor's degree
Oberlin College Oberlin, Ohio	Bachelor's degree
Ohio University Athens, Ohio	Bachelor's degree
Russell Sage College Troy, N.Y.	Bachelor's degree
Shenandoah College and Conservatory of Music Winchester, Va.	Associate Arts degree
Southern Methodist University (SMU) Dallas, Tex.	B.A. and M.A. degrees
Texas Women's University Denton, Tex.	Bachelor's degree
University of Evansville Evansville, Ind.	Bachelor's degree
University of Kansas Lawrence, Kans.	B.A., M.A., Ph.D.
University of the Pacific Stockton, Calif.	Bachelor's degree
University of Wisconsin at Eau Claire Eau Claire, Wis.	Bachelor's degree
University of Wisconsin at Milwaukee Milwaukee, Wis.	Bachelor's degree
University of Wisconsin at Oshkosh Oshkosh, Wis.	Bachelor's degree

College	*Program*
Virginia State College Petersburg, Va.	Bachelor's degree
Wesley College Dover, Del.	Associate Arts degree
Western Michigan University Kalamazoo, Mich.	B.A. and M.A. degrees
Xavier University of Louisiana New Orleans, La.	Bachelor's degree

Other music degree programs, such as music education programs, are listed in *The College Bluebook,* an annual publication of Macmillan Services, Macmillan Publishers, New York.

Colleges Offering Church Music Programs

Liturgical Music: Alverno College, Milwaukee, Wis., bachelor's degree in Liturgical Music

Music Ministry: Oregon Bible College, Oregon, Ill., bachelor's degree

Music and Religion: Athens College, Athens, Ala., bachelor's degree

Sacred Music: Kansas City College, Kansas City, Kans., B.A. and M.A. programs

Colleges Offering Arts Management Programs

College	*Program*
Adelphi University Garden City, N.Y.	Credit courses, degree program in preparation
American University Washington, D.C.	M.A. in Performing Arts Administration
Brooklyn College Brooklyn, N.Y.	M.F.A. in Performing Arts Management
Drexel University Philadelphia, Pa.	M.S. with concentration in Urban Arts Administration
Golden Gate University San Francisco, Calif.	M.B.A. and certificate in Arts Administration

College	Program
Indiana University Bloomington, Ind.	M.A. in Arts Administration
Lake Erie College Painesville, Ohio	B.F.A. in Arts Management
New York University New York, N.Y.	M.A. in Performing Arts Administration
Rollins College Winter Park, Fla.	M.B.A. in Performing Arts Management
Sangamon State University Springfield, Ill.	M.A. in Arts Administration
Southern Methodist University Dallas, Tex.	M.F.A. in Arts Administration
State University of New York at Binghamton Binghamton, N.Y.	M.B.A. in the Arts
UCLA Los Angeles, Calif.	M.B.A.
University of Cincinnati College–Conservatory of Music Cincinnati, Ohio	M.A. in Arts Administration
University of Texas at Austin Austin, Tex.	M.F.A. in Arts Administration
University of Wisconsin Madison, Wis.	M.A. in Arts Administration
York University Downsview, Ontario, Canada	M.B.A.

A number of internships and seminars are mentioned in the invaluable publication *A Survey of Arts Administration Training,* referred to on the ACA publications list. One of these internships is offered by the National Endowment for the Arts, Washington, D.C. 20506. Fifteen participants attend a thirteen-week program. This program is offered three times a year.

Lists of Music Business Organizations

Unions (National Headquarters)

AFM (American Federation of Musicians), 1500 Broadway, New York, N.Y. 10036

AFTRA (American Federation of Television and Radio Artists), 1350 Avenue of the Americas, New York, N.Y. 10036

AGMA (American Guild of Musical Artists), 1841 Broadway, New York, N.Y. 10023

AGVA (American Guild of Variety Artists), 1540 Broadway, New York, N.Y. 10036

SAG (Screen Actors Guild), 7750 Sunset Blvd., Hollywood, Calif. 90046

Local chapters of these unions exist in various cities, especially the AFM, which has over 600 local offices.

Performing Rights Organizations

ASCAP,   1 Lincoln Plaza, New York, N.Y. 10023

BMI,   40 West 57th St., New York, N.Y. 10019

SESAC,   10 Columbus Circle, New York, N.Y. 10019

All have additional offices in Los Angeles and Nashville, BMI and ASCAP have several other offices as well.

Other Organizations

AGAC (American Guild of Authors and Composers), 40 W. 57 St., New York, N.Y. 10019. A songwriter's protective association offering assistance in contracts, royalty collection, and other services.

Alternative Chorus, 943 Palm Ave., North Hollywood, Calif. 90069. This is the weekly BMI-sponsored Songwriters' Showcase.

American Composers Alliance, 170 W. 74th St., New York, N.Y. 10023. Maintains a music library and assists composers of serious music with copyrights, licenses, contracts, and legal matters.

American Music Center, 250 W. 57th St., New York, N.Y. 10019. Has an extensive library of serious music and assists composers in a variety of ways.

American Music Conference, 150 E. Huron, Chicago, Ill. 60611

American Songs Festival, P.O. Box 57, Hollywood, Calif. 90028. Sponsors competitions for amateur and professional songwriters.

American Symphony Orchestra League, P.O. Box 66, Vienna, Va. 22180. Organizations of symphony orchestra managers.

Associated Council for the Arts, 570 Seventh Ave., New York, N.Y. 10018. Holds seminars and issues many publications on arts management.

Composers and Lyricists Guild of America, 6565 Sunset Blvd., Los Angeles, Calif. 90028

Copyright Office, Library of Congress, Washington, D.C. 20559. Issues copyright forms.

Country Music Association, 7 Music Circle N., Nashville, Tenn. 37203

Foundation Center, 888 Seventh Ave., New York, N.Y. 10019. A clearinghouse for grants available through foundations.

Harry Fox Agency, Inc., 110 East 59th St., New York, N.Y. 10022. A royalty collection agency for publishers.

Gospel Music Association, 38 Music Sq. N., Nashville, Tenn. 37203

International Conference of Symphony and Opera Musicians, c/o current officers. Organization of symphony and opera musicians.

Music Critics Association, 6201 Tuckerman Lane, Rockville, Md. 20852. Holds workshops, publishes newsletter, and arranges critic exchanges between newspapers.

Music Educators National Conference, 1902 Association Dr., Reston, Va. 22091. The national organization of music teachers in the schools.

Music Library Association, 343 S. Main St., Ann Arbor, Mich, 48108

Music Publishers Association, 130 W. 57th St., New York, N.Y. 10019.

NAB (National Association of Broadcasters), 1771 N St. N.W., Washington, D.C. 20036. Members subscribe to a code of ethics.

NAMM (National Association of Music Merchants), 35 E. Wacker Dr., Chicago, Ill. 60601. Sponsors training seminars, distributes a cassette series on retailing.

NARAS Institute, The Institute of Recording Arts and Sciences and the Business of Music, 505 N. Lake Shore Drive, Chicago, Ill. 60611. Hold educational seminars, accredits college music industry programs, and issues Grammies. Chapters in key music industry cities.

NARM (National Association of Record Merchandisers), 1060 Kings Highway, Cherry Hill, N.J. 08034. Sponsors surveys of record buyers to determine present and future market for records.

National Association for Music Therapy, P.O. Box 610, Lawrence, Kans. 66044.

National Musical Publishers Association, 110 E. 59th St., New York, N.Y. 10022

NEA (National Endowment for the Arts), Washington, D.C. 20506. Offers many grants to individuals and organizations in the arts.

Organization of Women in Music, 229 Shupley St., San Francisco, Calif. 94107. Monthly meetings and job referrals.

Piano Technicians Guild, P.O. Box 1813, Seattle, Wash. 98111.

RIA (Recording Institute of America), 15 Columbus Circle, New York, N.Y. 10023. Sponsors courses in audio engineering at various cities in the United States. The courses are given in studios that have multitrack facilities.

RIAA (Recording Industry Association of America), 1 E. 57th St., New York, N.Y. 10022, and 9200 Sunset Blvd., Los Angeles, Calif. 90069. Certifies sales of records for industry awards of gold and platinum records.

Society for Ethnomusicology, 201 South Main St., Ann Arbor, Mich. 48108. Publishes a magazine, books, and recordings in this field.

List of Publishers of Printed Music

Below is a list of the most active publishers of printed music. Almo-Irving, Cherry Lane, Screen Gems, United Artists, and Warner Brothers are most active in the publication of hits. The other publishers concentrate on educational uses, instrumental method books, and arrangements for high school and college bands and choruses.

Alfred Music, 15335 Morrison St., Sherman Oaks, Calif. 91403

Almo-Irving Music, 1312 N. La Brea, Hollywood, Calif. 90028

Big Bells, 33 Hovey Ave., Trenton, N.J. 08610

Cherry Lane Music, P.O. Box 4724, Greenwich, Conn. 06830

Hansen Publications, 1824 West Ave., Miami Beach, Fla. 33139

Hal Leonard, 64 East 2nd St., Winona, Minn. 55987

Mel Bay Publications, 107 W. Jefferson, Kirkwood, Mo. 63122

Oak Publications, 33 W. 60th St., New York, N.Y. 10023

J. W. Pepper & Son, Valley Forge Corporate Center, Valley Forge, Pa.

Theodore Presser, Presser Bldg., Bryn Mawr, Pa. 19010

G. Schirmer, 866 Third Ave., New York, N.Y. 10022

Screen Gems Columbia Pub. Co., 6744 N.E. 4th Ave., Miami, Fla. 33132

United Artists Music, 729 7th Ave., New York, N.Y. 10019

Warner Brothers Publications, 75 Rockefeller Plaza, New York, N.Y. 10019

Union Scales

AFM   The current scale for radio and television commercials pays musicians $50 per hour when five or more musicians play, $54 for two to four musicians. The leader of the session gets double scale. Cartage is paid for carrying extra instruments and amplifiers. Reuse fees must be paid after the initial thirteen-week period. For each new thirteen-week cycle the fee is $35.50 per spot.. There are also rules that govern multiple uses or conversions from one media to another. When commercials are made for one market only, there is a scale of $25 per hour, subject to approval of each local of the union.

The scale for recording movies is based on the size of the band and the budget of the film. As of August 1979, the scale for movies under a $350,000 budget will be $111.07; for movies above that figure the fee is $119.36. Playing one extra instrument pays 50 percent more, plus 20 percent for each additional double. This is the highest doubling rate for any media. The current record-date scale is $127.05 for a three-hour popular music session, $134.67 for symphonic recording.

The minimum fees change as contracts expire and new contracts are renegotiated. There are also minimums set for arranging and copying music.

AFTRA   Soloist minimum for AFTRA is $90. For group singers the rate is $35.50 per hour or per side, whichever is greater. Group singers receive a minimum payment of $71 for any recording. When albums sell 160,000 copies group singers must be paid a 50 percent bonus fee. Additional 50 percent bonuses are given as sales pass 300,000, 450,000, and 600,000 copies. Sessions fees for commercials are comparable to recording, but the reuse fees are quite high. The formula for paying them is complex because payments vary according to national, local, or regional uses.

AGMA   AGMA enforces a four-year limitation on management contracts and limits the amount of money that a manager may spend on behalf of an artist without permission. In the first year of an AGMA management contract the artist must earn six times her regular fee or she can get out of the contract.

SAG The comments made about AFTRA payments on commercials also apply to SAG payments.

Schirmer Brochure for Piano
Howard Kasschau Piano Course

NEWLY REVISED
HOWARD KASSCHAU
PIANO COURSE

The *Howard Kasschau Piano Course* covers the entire range of piano study from the young beginner to the college preparatory level. The beginner is introduced to the new musical experiences of notation, technic, and repertoire in interesting, entertaining and gradually progressive steps. Each new musical experience is approached in four ways to insure complete understanding: by Reading; by Writing; by Reading Music; by Playing Music. As the course progresses, there is a gradual expansion of technical ability, performance and recital repertoire, knowledge of musical forms, musical history and harmonic understanding.

```
....Teach Me to Play (2336) ...............1.50
....First Book (2347) ......................2.25
....Second Book (2348) ...................2.25
....Third Book (2395) ......................2.25
....Fourth Book (2404) ....................2.25
....Fifth Book (2405) ......................2.25
```

SUPPLEMENTARY MATERIAL

```
....Ensemble Book (to be used with "Teach
   Me To Play") 1 Piano, 4 hands or 2 pianos,
   4 hands (2349) .........................75
....First Grade Pedal Book (2350) ..........85
....Note Speller (2381) ...................1.50
```

The next three collections are the latest compositions by Mr. Kasschau. Each collection is designed as a group for the beginning, early and intermediate grades. They may be used singly as teaching pieces or in conjunction with the Howard Kasschau Piano Course.

```
....Five Beginner's Pieces (2973) ..........1.50
....Six Easy Pieces—Recital Music for
   the Early Grades (2966) .................1.75
....Seven Recital Pieces     .
   for the Intermediate Grades (2965) .......2.00
```

```
....73 Favorite Pieces For Piano (with Guitar
   chords)—Arranged by Howard Kasschau.
```
A marvelous new collection of familiar tunes ranging from Aura Lee, Ciribiribin, Glow Worm and Joy to the World to Country Gardens, Greensleeves, Londonderry Air and Pomp and Circumstance. A real value
```
(2917) ...................................2.50
....Keyboard Interpretation (2592) ..........1.50
....Reading Through Intervals (2735) ........3.00
```
SCHIRMER'S SELECT PIANO MUSIC SERIES
Compiled from Best Sellers by Howard Kasschau
```
....For Early Grades (2343) ................2.00
....For Intermediate Grades (2344) ........2.00
....For Advanced Grades (2345) ...........3.00
```
106 GREATEST PIANO STUDIES
Compiled and Edited by Howard Kasschau
```
....Vol. I (No.'s 1-62) (2429) ...............2.50
....Vol. II (No.'s 63-106) (2430) ...........2.50
```

```
....25 VENTURES IN ROCK, WESTERN
   & BLUES (3054) ........................2.50
```
Please send copies as indicated beside each title.

Name _____

Address _____

City _____

State _____ Zip _____

Printed by permission of G. Schirmer, Inc.

Schirmer Brochure for Rock Guitar

The Great New Rock Book Has Arrived!

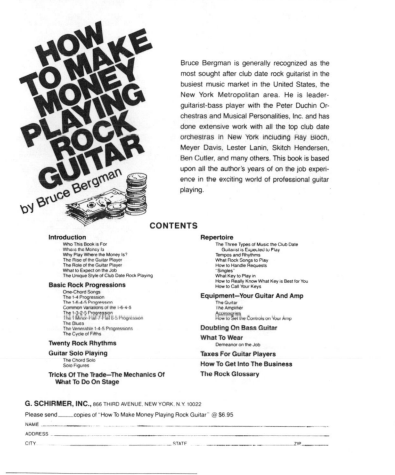

Bruce Bergman is generally recognized as the most sought after club date rock guitarist in the busiest music market in the United States, the New York Metropolitan area. He is leader-guitarist-bass player with the Peter Duchin Orchestras and Musical Personalities, Inc. and has done extensive work with all the top club date orchestras in New York including Ray Bloch, Meyer Davis, Lester Lanin, Skitch Henderson, Ben Cutler, and many others. This book is based upon all the author's years of on the job experience in the exciting world of professional guitar playing.

CONTENTS

Introduction
Who This Book is For
Where the Money Is
Why Play Where the Money Is?
The Rise of the Guitar Player
The Role of the Guitar Player
What to Expect on the Job
The Unique Style of Club Date Rock Playing

Basic Rock Progressions
One-Chord Songs
The 1-4 Progression
The 1-6-4-5 Progression
Common Variations of the 1-6-4-5
The 1-3-2-5 Progression
The 1 Minor-Flat-7-Flat 6-5 Progression
The Blues
The Venerable 1-4-5 Progressions
The Cycle of Fifths

Twenty Rock Rhythms

Guitar Solo Playing
The Chord Solo
Solo Figures

Tricks Of The Trade—The Mechanics Of What To Do On Stage

Repertoire
The Three Types of Music the Club Date
    Guitarist is Expected to Play
Tempos and Rhythms
What Rock Songs to Play
How to Handle Requests
"Singles"
What Key to Play in
How to Really Know What Key is Best for You
How to Call Your Keys

Equipment—Your Guitar And Amp
The Guitar
The Amplifier
Accessories
How to Set the Controls on Your Amp

Doubling On Bass Guitar

What To Wear
Demeanor on the Job

Taxes For Guitar Players

How To Get Into The Business

The Rock Glossary

G. SCHIRMER, INC., 866 THIRD AVENUE, NEW YORK, N.Y. 10022

Please send _____ copies of "How To Make Money Playing Rock Guitar" @ $6.95

NAME _____

ADDRESS _____

CITY _____ STATE _____ ZIP _____

Printed by permission of G. Schirmer, Inc.

Note the contrast between these two sales brochures, both printed by the same publisher. The emphasis in the Kasschau piano books is strictly academic, while the Bergman book is intended to sell to the working musician. The graphics are straight and serious for the piano book, eye-catching and a bit playful for the rock guitar book. These are judgments that the publisher has made about the audience for the two books. The Bergman book, by the way, is an excellent guide to the performance of rock music, useful to other musicians as well as guitarists.

Sample Lead Sheet

© 1974 by Padmi Publishing Co., used by permission.

When a song is registered for ASCAP, BMI, or SESAC, the name of the proper performing rights association also appears after the credit for the publishing company. For example, Padmi Publishing Co. ASCAP.

Glossary of Music Business Terms

Agent Someone who gets work for singers or musicians. Also called a booking agent.

Aircheck Tape of a disc jockey's show used for audition purposes.

ASCAP See **Performing rights.**

Bed Instrumental background for a vocal commercial.

BMI See **Performing rights.**

C&W Country and Western.

Chart A musical arrangement; Top 40 chart (a list of hits).

Click track A click fed through headphones to musicians in a recording studio in order to provide a perfect tempo.

Contractor The person that hires musicians. Usually a musician, but may not play on the session he is booking.

Control room The area where an engineer and a producer monitor the sound from a recording session.

Co-publishing When the publishing rights to a copyright are shared by more than one publisher.

Crossover record A record that starts to achieve popularity in one area of music, and then crosses over to become popular in another idiom.

Cutout   A record that is discontinued from the catalog and remaindered at a heavy discount.

DBX   A system for noise reduction used in recording.

Demo   A demonstration record. It is a sample of the finished product used to sell an artist or a song.

Demographics   Population breakdown by age, sex, or other factors.

Direct to disc   Recording directly to a master record without the use of tape.

Dolby   Another system for noise reduction.

Donut   A music bed used as a background for narration in a commercial.

Fakebook   A collection of tunes by many authors and different publishers.

Head arrangement   An arrangement done with little or no written music. It is usually worked out in the recording studio.

Hook   A repetitive phrase designed to hook the listener's attention. Can be a lyric or an instrumental phrase.

Jingle   A commercial for radio or television.

Jobber   A wholesaler that sells music books of many publishers.

Lead sheet   The words, music, and chords of a song. Lead sheets are required for copyright purposes.

Lip sync   When a singer mouths to words of a song to match a record without actually singing the song.

Logging   Literally means writing down in a radio log. Also used to indicate a way of keeping track of air play by performing rights societies.

Master   A finished product that can be turned into a record.

Mechanical license   The license that a record company applies for from a publisher to legally issue a song on a record.

Mix   To take a multitrack master and reduce it to a finished product.

Modulation   Changing the key of a song in the middle of the song.

MOR   Middle-of-the-road—noncontroversial music. Sometimes called easy-listening or beautiful music.

Noise reduction   Systems to reduce tape hiss. See DBX and Dolby.

One-stop   A wholesaler that carries records of many companies.

Overdub   To add parts on a multichannel recording—technically this process is called sel synchronization.

Payola Illegal payments to radio station personnel to get them to give extra play to records. In a general sense any kind of illegal payments for favors.

Performing rights Composer rights for play on radio and television. These rights are governed by ASCAP, BMI, and SESAC.

Personal manager A career guide for the artist.

R&B Rhythm and blues.

Push record A record that a record company is particularly anxious for its promotion staff to push.

R&B Rhythm and blues.

Record producer The person who puts together a record, corresponds to the director of a movie. A producer may hire the musicians, rent a studio, hire an arranger, rehearse the artist, and mix the product.

Remix To mix a multichannel product again.

Scale Union minimum pay.

Secondary market A market of some size, but not a giant population center—for example, Milwaukee as opposed to Chicago.

Sound track library Service that sells music to radio stations, television stations, or low-budget movie productions from preexisting tapes.

Standard A popular song that remains popular over an extended period of time, such as "Stardust."

Studio musician A free-lance musician who makes a living by playing in the recording studios.

Synchronization rights The rights for synchronizing of music to a picture, paid to the composer.

Subsidiary rights Rights for media other than the one specifically being contracted.

Taking care of business Payola.

Tour support Record company subsidies to an artist to support promotional tours.

Track record A person's history in the business.

Voice-over The voice of an unseen announcer for a commercial.

Annotated Bibliography

Recording

Carlin, Robert. *The Small Specialty Record Company in the United States*. John Edwards Memorial Foundation Quarterly. Summer 1976.

Chapple, Steve, and Garafalo, Reebee. *Rock 'n' Roll Is Here to Pay*. Chicago, Nelson Hall, 1977. A radical critique and analysis of the record business—stimulating and argumentative.

Davis, Clive. *Clive Inside the Record Business*. New York.: Morrow, 1975. Alive and intelligent, if egomaniacal.

Denisoff, R. Serge. *Solid Gold: The Popular Record Industry*. New Brunswick, N.J.: Transaction Books, 1975.

Dexter, Dave, Jr. *Playback*. New York: Billboard Publications, 1976.

Gillett, Charlie. *Making Tracks: The Growth of a Multi-Billion-Dollar Industry*. New York: E. P. Dutton, 1974. The fascinating story of Atlantic Records.

Hammond, John, and Townsend, Irving. *John Hammond on Record*. New York: Ridge Press/Summit Books, 1977.

Hurst, Walter E., and Hale, William Storm. *Record Industry Book: Stories, Text, Forms, Contracts*. Entertainment Industry Series, vol. 1. Hollywood: Seven Arts Press, 1974.

Jahn, Mike. *How to Make a Hit Record.* Scarsdale, N.Y.: Bradbury Press, 1976.

Karshner, Roger. *The Music Machine.* Los Angeles, Nash Publishing, 1971. More about payola than you'd ever want to know.

Morse, David. *Motown.* New York: Collier Books, 1971.

Shankman, Ned, and Thompson, Larry A. *How to Make a Record Deal and Have Your Song Recorded.* Los Angeles: Hastings House Limited, 1975.

Shemel, Sidney, and Krasilovsky, M. William. *This Business of Music.* New York: Billboard Publications, 1977. Be sure to get the 1977 edition. Invaluable.

————. *More About This Business of Music.* New York, Billboard Publications, 1977.

Spitz, Robert Stephen. *The Making of a Superstar: Artists and Executives of the Rock Music World.* New York: Anchor Press, 1978.

Stokes, Geoffrey. *Star-Making Machinery: The Odyssey of an Album.* Indianapolis: Bobbs-Merrill, 1976. A useful book. Contains an excellent description of recording and mixing.

History of Recording

Gelatt, Roland. *The Fabulous Phonograph.* New York: Collier Books, 1977. An absorbing history.

Read, Oliver, and Welch, Walter L. *From Tin Foil to Stereo.* 2nd ed. Indianapolis: Howard W. Sams, 1976.
  Two publications are available that provide listings of records. *Phonolog Reporter,* Trade Service Publications, 1710 Beverly Boulevard, Los Angeles, Calif. 90057, is a loose-leaf index of records, with supplements regularly added to reflect new record releases. It can be found in most large record stores. The *Schwann Record & Tape Guide,* 137 Newbury Street, Boston, Mass. 02116, is a monthly catalog of records and tapes, available by subscription.

Agents and Managers

Csida, Joseph. *The Music Record Career Handbook.* Studio City, Calif.: First Place Music Publications, 1973.

Frascogna, Xavier M., Jr. and Hetherington, H. Lee. *Successful Artist Management.* New York: Billboard Books, 1978.

Harris, Herby, and Farrar, Lucien. *How to Make Money in Music.* New York: Arco, 1978.

---

* I have commented on the books I feel are most important.

Shemel and Krasilovsky.   See Recording.

Spitz, Robert Stephen.   See Recording.

Young, Jean and Jim.   *Succeeding in the Big World of Music.* Boston: Little Brown, 1977.

Publishing, Performing Rights, Copyright

Berk, Lee Eliot.   *Legal Protection for the Creative Musician.* Boston: Berklee Press, 1977.

Hurst, Walter E., and Hale, William Storm.   *Your Introduction to Music, Record, Copyright, Contracts & Other Business & Law.* Hollywood: Seven Arts Press, 1974.

New York Law School Review.   *The Complete Guide to the New Copyright Law.* New York: Lorenz Press, 1977.

Pincus, Lee.   *The Songwriter's Success Manual.* New York: Music Press, 1978.

Racklin, Harvey.   *The Songwriter's Handbook.* New York: Funk & Wagnalls, 1977. An excellent guide.

Roth, Ernest.   *The Business of Music: Reflections of a Music Publisher.* New York: Oxford Univ. Press, 1969.

Taubman, Joseph.   *Performing Arts Management.* Book VI: *Forms—Music Publishing.* New York: Law Arts Press, 1977.

For addresses of the performing rights societies see the section on organizations in the Appendix.

Commercials

Cone, Fairfax.   *With All Its Faults.* Boston: Little Brown, 1963.

Diamant, Lincoln.   *Television's Classic Commercials: The Golden Years, 1948-1958.* New York: Hastings House, 1970.

————,ed.   *The Anatomy of a Television Commercial: The Story of Eastman Kodak's "Yesterday."* New York: Hastings House, 1970.

Galanoy, Terry.   *Down the Tube.* New York: Pinnacle Books, 1972. Simultaneously amusing and frightening.

Key, Wilson Bryan.   *Subliminal Seduction.* New York: Signet Books, 1974. Key finds sex is being used to sell us everything from alcohol to dark glasses.

Norbach, Peter and Craig.   *Great Songs of Madison Avenue.* New York: Quadrangle Books, 1976. Words and music for many famous commercials.

Robinson, Sol. *Radio Advertising: How to Sell It and Write It.* Summit, Pa.: Tab Books, 1974.

Schwartz, Tony. *The Responsive Chord.* New York: Anchor Books, 1973. Techniques of persuasion and communication.

Teixeira, Antonio, Jr. *Music to Sell By.* Boston: Berklee Press, 1974.

Wainwright, Charles A. *Television Commercials.* New York: Hastings House, 1970.

Welling, Si. *How to Sell Radio Advertising.* Summit, Pa.: Tab Books, 1970.

Radio

Barnouw, Erik. *A History of Broadcasting in the United States.* 3 vols. New York: Oxford University Press, 1966–1970.

Dolan, Robert Emmett. *Music in Modern Media.* New York: G. Schirmer, 1967.

Exploring Theatre and Media Careers: A Student Guidebook. Washington, D.C.: U.S. Government Printing Office, 1976.

Hall, Claude and Barbara. *This Business of Radio Programming.* New York: Billboard Publications, 1977. An extended analysis of programming followed by interviews with significant figures. Recommended.

Hoffer, Jay. *Radio Production Techniques.* Summit, Pa.: Tab Books, 1974.

Lujack, Larry. *Super Jock.* Chicago: Henry Regnery, 1975.

Passman, Arnold. *The Deejays.* New York: Macmillan, 1971.

Quaal, Ward L., and Brown, James A. *Broadcast Management.* New York: Hastings House, 1976.

St. John, Robert. *Encyclopedia of Radio and Television Broadcasting.* Milwaukee: Cathedral Square, 1970.

The public relations department of the National Association of Broadcasters (NAB), 1771 N St. N.W., Washington, D.C. 20036, offers the following free publications: *Careers in Radio, Careers in Television, If You Want Air Time, Radio and Television Bibliography,* and *Radio U.S.A.*

The Chronicle Guidance Publications, Inc., and the U.S. Government Printing Office publish a number of career guides to media and music careers. Their addresses are: Chronicle Guidance Publications, Inc., Moravia, N.Y. 13118; U.S. Government Printing Office, Washington, D.C. 20402.

Below are two useful books about television, among the many available.

Brown, Les. *Television: The Business Behind the Box*. New York: Harcourt Brace Jovanovich, 1971.

Shanks, Bob. *The Cool Fire: How to Make It in Television*. New York: Random House, 1976.

Studio Work

Faulkner, Robert R. *Hollywood Studio Musicians: Their Work and Careers in the Recording Industry*. Chicago: Aldine Atherton, 1971. A superb sociological study of studio musicians.

Audio Engineering

Aldred, John. *Manual of Sound Recording*. London: Fountain Press, 1971.

Burroughs, Lou. *Microphones: Design and Application*. Plainview, N.Y.: Sagamore, 1974.

Clifford, Martin. *Microphones: How They Work and How to Use Them*. Summit, Pa.: Tab Books, 1975.

Eargle, John M. *Sound Recording*. New York: Van Nostrand Reinhold, 1976.

Everett, F. Alton. *Handbook of Multichannel Recording*. Summit, Pa.: Tab Books, 1975.

Nisbett, Alec. *The Technique of the Sound Studio*. New York: Hastings House, 1971.

Runstein, Robert. *Modern Recording Techniques*. Indianapolis: Howard W. Sams, 1969.

Woram, John. *The Recording Studio Handbook*. Plainview, N.Y.: Sagamore, 1976.

Film Music

Baker, Fred, and Firestone, Ross. *Movie People: At Work in the Business of Film*. New York: Douglas, 1972.

Bazelon, Irwin. *Knowing the Score: Notes on Film*. New York: Van Nostrand Reinhold, 1975.

Eisler, Hans. *Composing for the Films*. New York: Oxford Univ. Press. 1947. Controversial and stimulating thoughts on the aesthetics of film music.

Evans, Marc. *The Music of the Movies*. New York: Hopkinson & Blake, 1975.

Fredericks, Marc. *A Summary of Film Mathematics*. New York: Comprehensive Publications, 1974.

Hagen, Earle. *Scoring for Films*. New York: Criterion Music, 1971.

Limbacher, James L., ed. *Film Music from Violin to Video*. Metuchen, N.J.: Scarecrow Press, 1974. A series of articles describing the history and craft of film score composition, and a long list of film scores with their composers.

Prendergast, Roy M. *Film Music: A Neglected Art*. New York, Norton, 1977.

Skiles, Marlin. *Music Scoring for TV and Motion Pictures*. Summit, Pa.: Tab Books, 1976.

Thomas, Tony. *Music for the Movies*. New York: A. S. Barnes, 1973.

Promotion and Publicity

Chapple and Garafalo.   See Recording.

Greene, Bob. *The Billion Dollar Baby*. New York: Signet, 1974. An enjoyable book describing the merchandising of Alice Cooper.

Meyer, Andrew H. *Dancing on the Seats: A Step By Step Guide To College Concert Production*. New York: Billboard Publications, 1972.

Plummer, Gail. *The Business of Show Business*. New York: Harper, 1961. How to promote concerts.

Rosenman, Joel; Roberts, John; and Pilpel, Robert. *Young Men with Unlimited Capital*. New York: Harcourt Brace Jovanovich, 1974. The peculiar story of the Woodstock festival, told by its backers.

Spitz, Robert Stephen.   See Recording.

Music Performance

This is a list of books on various facets of music. Not all of these books deal specifically with the performance of music, but all should be of some use to performers in the various styles listed.

Classical Music

Arian, Edward. *Bach, Beethoven and Bureaucracy: The Case of the Philadelphia Orchestra*. University, Ala.: University of Alabama Press, 1971. A hard look at symphony playing and the organization of the orchestra by a player who quit to pursue a career in political science.

Bing, Rudolf. *Five Thousand Nights with the Opera.* Garden City, N.Y.: Doubleday, 1972.

Carr, Janet Baker. *Evening at Symphony: A Portrait of the Boston Symphony Orchestra.* Boston: Houghton Mifflin, 1977.

Chase, Gilbert. *The American Composer Speaks.* Baton Rouge, La.: Louisiana State Univ. Press, 1966.

Elley, Derek, ed. *International Music Guide, '78.* New York: A. S. Barnes, 1978. Guide to festivals and music events, with some record reviews and some coverage of pop music.

Finell, Judith, ed. *The Contemporary Music Performance Directory.* New York: American Music Center, 1975.

Furlong, William Barry. *Season with Solti.* New York: Macmillan, 1974. A realistic picture of life in the Chicago Symphony.

Hart, Philip. *Orpheus in the New World.* New York: Norton, 1973. A study of American symphony orchestras, their organization, history, and finances. An important book.

Hurok, Sol. *Impresario.* New York: Random House, 1966.

Jacobson, Robert. *Reverberations: Interviews with the World's Leading Musicians.* New York: Morrow, 1974.

Kupferberg, Herbert. *Those Fabulous Philadelphians.* New York: Scribner's, 1962.

Mitchell, Ronald. *Opera—Dead or Alive: Production, Performance, and Enjoyment of Musical Theatre.* Madison, Wis.: Univ. of Wisconsin Press, 1970.

Roussel, Herbert. *The Houston Symphony Orchestra, 1913-1971.* Austin, Tex.: Univ. of Texas Press, 1972.

Rich, Alan. *Careers and Opportunities in Music.* New York: Dutton, 1964. Careers in the concert world.

Swoboda, Henry, ed. *The American Symphony Orchestra.* New York: Basic Books, 1967.

Temianka, Henri. *Facing the Music.* New York: David McKay, 1973.

Blues and Soul Music

Albertson, Chris. *Bessie Smith.* New York: Stein & Day, 1972.

Blesh, Rudi, and Janis, Harriet. *They All Played Ragtime.* New York: Oak, 1971.

Charters, Samuel. *The Bluesmen.* New York: Oak, 1967.

Dixon, R. M., and Godrich, John. *Recording the Blues.* New York: Stein & Day, 1970.

Garland, Phyl. *The Sound of Soul.* Chicago: Henry Regnery, 1969.

Heilbut, Tony. *The Gospel Sound.* New York: Simon & Schuster, 1971. The only thorough history of gospel music to date.

Jones, LeRoi. *Black Music.* New York: Morrow, 1967.

Leadbitter, Mike. *Nothing But the Blues.* New York: Oak, 1971.

Oliver, Paul. *Aspects of the Blues Tradition.* New York: Oak, 1970.

―――――. *Conversations with the Blues.* New York: Horizon Press, 1965.

Shaw, Arnold. *Honkers and Shouters: The Golden Years of Rhythm and Blues.* New York: Collier Books, 1978.

―――――. *The World of Soul.* New York: Warner Paperback Library, 1971.

Southern, Eileen. *Music of Black Americans.* New York: Norton, 1971. A marvelous book, intelligent and readable.

Walton, Ortiz M. *Music: Black, White and Blue.* New York: Morrow, 1972.

Country & Western Music

Artis, Bob. *Bluegrass.* New York: Hawthorn Books, 1975. An intelligent and well-balanced book.

Bart, Teddy. *Inside Music City.* Nashville: Aurora, 1970.

Cornfeld, Robert, with Farwell, Marshall, Jr. *Just Country.* New York: McGraw-Hill, 1976.

Dellar, Fred, et al. *Illustrated Encyclopedia of Country Music.* New York: Harmony, 1977.

Grissom, John. *Country Music: White Man's Blues.* New York: Paperback Library, 1970.

Hemphill, Paul. *The Nashville Sound: Bright Lights and Country Music.* New York: Pocket Books, 1971. An excellent guide to the music business in Nashville.

Malone, Bill C. *Country Music, U.S.A.: A Fifty-Year History.* Austin, Tex.: Univ. of Texas Press, 1968.

Shelton, Robert, and Goldblatt, Burt. *The Country Music Story.* Portland, Me.: Castle Books, 1966.

Stambler, Irwin, and Landon, Grelun. *Encyclopedia of Folk, Country and Western Music.* New York: St. Martin's Press, 1969.

Electronic Music

Deutsch, Herbert. *Synthesizer: An Introduction to the History, Theory, and Performance of Electronic Music.* Port Washington, N.Y.: Alfred, 1976.

Douglas, Alan. *The Electronic Musical Instrument Manual.* Summit, Pa.: Tab Books, 1977.

Friend, David; Pearlman, Alan R.; and Piggott, Thomas D. *Learning Music with Synthesizer.* Winona, Minn.: Hal Leonard, 1974.

Howe, Hubert S. *Electronic Music Synthesis.* New York: Norton, 1975.

Schwartz, Elliott. *Electronic Music: A Listener's Guide.* New York: Praeger, 1973.

Strange, Alan. *Electronic Music.* Dubuque, Iowa: Wm. C. Brown, 1972.

Wells, Thomas, and Vogel, Eric. *The Technique of Electronic Music.* Manchaca, Tex., Sterling Swift, 1974.

Folk Music

Ames, Russell. *The Story of American Folk Song.* New York: Grosset & Dunlap, 1960. A good brief history.

Brand, Oscar. *The Ballad Mongers.* New York: Funk & Wagnalls, 1961.

Nettl, Bruno. *An Introduction to Folk Music in the United States.* Detroit, Mich.: Wayne State Univ. Press, 1972.

Sandberg, Larry, and Weissman, Dick. *The Folk Music Sourcebook.* New York: Alfred A. Knopf, 1976.

Seeger, Peter. *The Incompleat Folksinger.* New York: Simon & Schuster, 1972. A fascinating memoir by America's leading folksinger.

Traum, Happy. *Folk Guitar as a Profession.* Saratoga, Calif.: Guitar Player Books, 1977. Include sample performer's contracts which will be useful to anyone booking himself.

Jazz

Case, Brian, and Britt, Stan. *The Illustrated Encyclopedia of Jazz.* New York: Harmony Books, 1978.

Collier, James Lincoln. *The Making of Jazz.* New York: Macmillan, 1978.

Feather, Leonard. *Inside Jazz.* New York: Da Capo, 1977.

Finklestein, Sidney. *Jazz, A People's Music.* New York: International Publishers, 1949. Concentrates on the social history of the music.

Hodeir, Andre. *The Worlds of Jazz.* New York: Grove Press, 1972. Translated by Noel Burch.

Leonard, Neil. *Jazz and the White Americans.* Chicago: Univ. of Chicago Press, 1962.

Ramsey, Fredric, Jr., and Smith, Charles E., eds. *Jazzmen.* New York: Harcourt Brace Jovanovich, 1977.

Schuller, Gunther. *Early Jazz: Its Roots and Musical Development.* New York: Oxford Univ. Press, 1968.

Sargeant, Winthrop. *Jazz, Hot and Hybrid. 3rd edition.* Roots of Jazz Series. New York: Da Capo Press, 1975.

Shapiro, Nat, and Hentoff, Nat, eds. *Hear Me Talkin' to Ya: The Story of Jazz by the Men Who Made It.* New York: Dover, 1966.

Spellman, A. B. *Black Music: Four Lives.* New York: Schocken Books, 1970. A beautiful if terrifying book about the lives of four jazz innovators.

Stearns, Marshall. *The Story of Jazz.* New York: Oxford Univ. Press, 1956.

Ulanov, Barry. *A History of Jazz in America.* 1955. Reprint. New York: Da Capo, 1972.

Williams, Martin. *The Jazz Tradition.* New York: Oxford Univ. Press, 1970.

There are also many autobiographical and biographical books of such figures as Armstrong, Bechet, Coltrane, Ellington, and so forth.

Rock

Belz, Carl. *The Story of Rock.* 2d edition. New York: Oxford Univ. Press, 1972.

Christgau, Robert. *Any Old Way You Choose It.* Baltimore, Md.: Penguin Books, 1973.

Clark, Sue C., and Kent, Douglas. *Rock, A World Bold As Love.* New York: Cowles Books, 1970.

Eisen, Jonathan, ed. *The Age of Rock: Sounds of the American Cultural Revolution.* New York: Vintage Books, 1969.

Fong-Torres, Ben, ed. *The Rolling Stone Rock 'N' Roll Reader.* New York: Bantam Books, 1967.

————. *The Rolling Stone Interviews.* Vol. 2. New York: Warner Paperback Library, 1973.

Gillett, Charlie. *The Sound of the City: The Rise of Rock and Roll.* New York: Dutton, 1970. The best history of rock I have seen.

Gelby, David. *The Facts About a Rock Group, Featuring Wings.* New York: Harmony, 1976.

Gleason, Ralph J. *The Jefferson Airplane and the San Francisco Sound.* New York: Ballantine Books, 1969.

Hopkins, Jerry. *Elvis, A Biography.* New York: Simon & Schuster, 1971.

Jahn, Mike. *Rock.* New York: Quadrangle Books, 1973.

Kooper, Al. *Backstage Passes.* New York: Stein & Day, 1977. Amusing reminiscences of the rock scene by the pianist-organist-producer.

Landau, Jon. *It's Too Late To Stop Now! A Rock and Roll Journal.* San Francisco: Straight Arrow Books, 1972.

Lawrence, Sharon. *So You Want to Be a Rock and Roll Star.* New York: Dell Publishing, 1976.

Logan, Nick, and Woffinden, Bob. *The Illustrated Encyclopedia of Rock.* New York: Harmony, 1976.

McCabe, Peter, and Schonfeld, Robert D. *Apple to the Core: The Unmaking of the Beatles.* New York: Pocket Books, 1972.

Meltzer, Richard. *The Aesthetics of Rock.* New York: Something Else Press, 1970.

Palmer, Tony. *All You Need Is Love.* New York: Grossman Publishers, 1976. A good history of the origins and evolution of rock.

Roxon, Lillian. *Rock Music Encyclopedia.* New York: Grosset & Dunlap, 1971.

Stambler, Irwin. *Encyclopedia of Pop, Rock and Soul.* New York: St. Martin's Press, 1976.

Vassal, Jacques. *Electric Children: Roots and Branches of Modern Folkrock.* Translated by Paul Barnett. New York: Taplinger, 1976.

Williams, Richard. *Out of His Head: The Sound of Phil Spector.* New York: Dutton, 1972.

Popular Music in General

Ewen, David. *All the Years of American Popular Music.* Englewood Cliffs, N.J.: Prentice-Hall, 1977.

Meyer, Hazel. *The Gold in Tin Pan Alley.* 1958. Reprint. Westport, Conn.: Greenwood Press, 1977.

Nancy, Charles, ed.   *American Music from Storyville to Woodstock.* New Brunswick, N.J.: Transaction Books, 1975.

Shapiro, Nat, ed.   *Popular Music, An Annotated Index of American Popular Song.* 6 vols. New York: Adrian, 1964–1973.

Whitfield, Ian.   *After the Ball: Pop Music from Rag to Rock.* New York: Simon & Schuster, 1974. Entertaining and informative.

Wilder, Alec.   *Popular Song: The Great Innovators, 1900–1950.* New York: Oxford Univ. Press, 1975. A book about popular songs before the rock era.

Songwriting

Boyce, Tommy, and Powers, Melvin.   *How to Write a Hit Song . . . and Sell It.* Los Angeles: Wilshire, 1974.

Brohaugh, William, ed.   *1979 Songwriter's Market.* Cincinnati, Ohio, Writer's Digest Books, 1978. A valuable list of places to submit songs with the names and addresses of company officials.

Cahn, Sammy.   *I Should Care.* New York: Arbor House, 1974.

Glaser, Hy.   *How to Write Lyrics That Make Sense and Dollars.* New York: Exposition Press, 1977.

Green, Bud.   *Writing Songs for Fame and Fortune.* Miami Beach, Fla.: Charles Hansen, 1976.

Hall, Tom T.   *How I Write Songs: Why You Can.* New York: Chappell Music, 1976.

Pincus, Lee.   See Publishing, Performing Rights, Copyright.

Pollock, Bruce.   *In Their Own Words.* New York: Collier Books, 1975. Useful interviews with a number of lyricists.

Racklin, Harvey.   See Publishing, Performing Rights, Copyright.

Sarlin, Bob.   *Turn It Up (I Can't Hear the Words).* New York: Simon & Schuster, 1973.

Whitfield, Jane.   *Songwriters Rhyming Dictionary.* Los Angeles: Wilshire Book Co., 1974.

Wilder, Alec.   See Popular Music in General.

Careers in Music

A useful introduction to this field is the book *Careers in Music,* available from the American Music Conference, 150 East Huron, Chicago, Ill. 60611. It gives brief sketches of the various careers available today in music. See also *Exploring Music Careers: A Student Guidebook,* Washington, D.C.: U.S. Government Printing Office, 1976.

Note: Alfred Music Co. of Sherman Oaks, Calif., puts out a series of cassettes on the following music industry careers:

Baker, Robert	*Careers in Church Music*
Gabriel, Col. Arnold	*Music in the Military Service*
Goldberg, Norman	*Careers in Music Retailing*
Herendeen, James	*Careers in Instrument Manufacturing*
Hume, Paul	*Music in Journalism*
Jones, Samuel	*Careers in Orchestral Playing*
Manus, Morton	*Careers in Music Publishing*
Wangerin, Richard	*Organization Management in Music and Arts*

Music Education

There are dozens of books available in the field of music education, and most colleges offer the music education major. I have therefore spent little time discussing music education careers in this book. Check with your local library or with a college offering a music education degree for more information.

Music Criticism

Music criticism is not offered as a major in any college in the United States. A student wishing a career in this area should take writing, journalism, and music courses. Very few books have been written that examine the field, and most books about music criticism are critical works about specific forms of music. The following books are some of the available works on music criticism.

Graf, Max. *Composer and Critic: Two Hundred Years of Music Criticism.* New York: Norton, 1971.

Rosenfeld, Paul. *Discoveries of a Music Critic.* 1936. Reprint. New York: Vienna House, 1972.

Thomson, Virgil. *The Art of Judging Music.* New York: Alfred A. Knopf, 1958.

See the Music Critics Association in the List of Organizations in the Appendix.

Music Library Careers

Bradley, Carol J. *Readings in Music Librarianship.* Englewood, Colo.: Service in Library and Information Services, 1973.

Redfern, Brian. *Organizing Music in Libraries.* 2d edition. Hamden, Conn.: Shoestring Press, 1978.

Music Therapy

A few of the important available works in the field.

Alvin, Juliette. *Music for the Handicapped Child.* New York: Oxford Univ. Press, 1976.

Bright, Ruth. *Music in Geriatric Care.* New York: St. Martin's Press, 1976.

Guston, E. Thayer. *Music in Therapy.* New York: Macmillan, 1968.

Gutheil, Emil. *Music and Your Emotions.* New York: Liveright, 1970.

Herbert, Wilhelmina K. *Opening Doors Through Music: A Practical Guide for Teachers, Therapists, Students, Parents.* Springfield, Ill.: C. C. Thomas, 1974.

Michel, Donald E. *Music Therapy: An Introduction to Therapy and Special Education Through Music.* Springfield, Ill.: C. C. Thomas, 1976.

Nordoff, Paul, and Robbins, Clive E. *Individualized Treatment for the Handicapped Child in Music.* New York: John Day, 1976.

————. *Music Therapy in Specialized Education.* New York: John Day, 1971.

Priestly, Mary. *Music Therapy in Action.* New York: St. Martin's Press, 1975.

Purvis, Jennie, and Samet, Shelly. *Music in Developmental Therapy.* Baltimore, Md.: University Park Books, 1976.

Schullian, Dorothy, and Schoen, Max, eds. *Music and Medicine.* 1948. Reprint. Plainview, N.Y.: Books for Libraries Press, 1971.

Tomet, Jean H., and Krutzky, Carmel D. *Learning Through Music for Special Children and Their Teachers.* South Waterford, Me.: Merriam Eddy, 1975.

Ward, David. *Hearts and Hands and Voices: Music in the Education of Slow Learners.* New York: Oxford Univ. Press, 1971.

Piano Tuning

Fischer, Cree J. *Piano Tuning: Registry and Repairing.* New York: Dover Books, 1976.

Reblitz, Arthur *Piano Servicing, Tuning & Rebuilding,* new ed. Vestal, 1976.

Church Music

Consult your local church or minister for more information about the music of each specific religion.

A Guide to Music for the Church Year. 4th edition. Minneapolis, Minn.: Augsberg, 1974.

Bauman, William A. *The Ministry of Music: A Guide for the Practicing Church Musician.* Washington, D.C.: Liturgical, 1975.

Davidson, James R. *A Dictionary of Protestant Church Music.* Hamden, Conn.: Scarecrow, 1975.

Davies, Henry W., and Grace, Harvey. *Music and Worship.* 1935. Reprint. New York: AMS Press, 1977.

Hunter, Stanley A., ed. *Music and Religion.* 1930. Reprint. New York: AMS Press.

Northcott, Cecil. *Hymns in Christian Worship.* Atlanta: John Knox, 1975.

Osbeck, Kenneth W. *Ministry of Music.* Grand Rapids, Mich.: Kriegel, 1975.

Phillips, Henry A. *Singing Church: An Outline History of the Music Sung by Choirs and People.* Hamden, Conn.: Archon, 1969.

Pratt, Waldo S. *Musical Ministries in the Church.* New York: AMS Press, 1976.

Rhys, Stephen, and Palmer, King. *ABC of Church Music.* Boston, Mass.: Crescendo, 1969.

Routley, Erik. *Twentieth-Century Church Music.* New York: Oxford Univ. Press, 1962.

Schmitt, Francis P. *Church Music Transgressed: Reflections on Reform.* Somer, Conn.: Seabury, 1977.

Stevenson, Robert. *Protestant Church Music in America: A Short Summary of Men and Movements from 1564 to the Present.* New York: Norton, 1970.

Square, Russel. *Church Music.* New York: Bethany Press, 1967.

Topp, Dale. *Music in the Christian Church.* Grand Rapids, Mich.: Eerdmans, 1976.

Law

Berk, Eliot Lee. See Publishing, Performing Rights, Copyright.

Hurst and Hale. See Publishing, Performing Rights, Copyright, and Recording.

New York Law School Review. See Publishing, Performing Rights, Copyright.

Shemel and Krasilovsky. See Recording.

Taubman, Joseph. *Performing Arts Management.* Book V: *Forms— Sound Copyright.* New York: Law Arts Press, 1977.

All of these books except the New York Law School book contain sample contracts. That book and the Shemel and Krasilovsky book, *This Business of Music,* contain the 1976 copyright law.

Arts Management

Chapin, Schuyler. *Musical Chairs: A Life in the Arts.* New York: Putnam's, 1977.

The Finances of the Performing Arts. Vols. 1 and 2. New York: The Ford Foundation, 1974.

Millions for the Arts: Federal and State Cultural Programs. Washington, D.C.: Washington International Arts Newsletter Editors, 1972.

Netzer, Dick. *The Subsidized Muse: Public Support for the Arts in the United States.* New York: Cambridge Univ. Press, 1978. A well-reasoned and clear viewpoint on a complex subject.

Reiss, Alvin. *The Arts Management Handbook.* New York: Law Arts Press, 1974.

Rockefeller, David, ed. *Coming to Our Senses: The Significance of the Arts for American Education.* New York: McGraw-Hill, 1978. A useful study for teachers, administrators, and artists.

Salem, Mahmoud. *Organizational Survival in the Performing Arts: The Marketing of the Seattle Opera.* New York: Praeger, 1976.

Taubman, Joseph. *Performing Arts Management and Law.* 6 vols. New York: Law Arts Press, 1973.

Toobin, Jerome. *Agitato: A Trek Through the Musical Jungle.* New York: The Viking Press, 1975. Arts management through the informed eyes of the manager of the defunct "Symphony of the Air."

The following books are all published by the American Council of the Arts, 570 Seventh Avenue, New York, N.Y. 10018.

ACA Yellow Pages 1977. 1200 U.S. and Canadian entries, a telephone directory for the arts.

Brownring, W. Grant. *Corporate Fund Raising: A Practical Plan of Action.*

Cities, Counties and the Arts. Information on what local governments are doing for the arts. Interbook, 1976.

Coe, Linda, ed. *The Cultural Directory: Guide to Federal Funds and Services for Cultural Activities.* Lists 250 federal programs.

Community Arts Agencies: A Handbook and a Guide. How to start and run an arts council.

Kreisberg, Linda. *Local Government and the Arts.* How to deal with local elected officials.

A Survey of Arts Administration Training in the United States and Canada. 1977. A description of college programs.

Wagner, Susan, ed. *A Guide to Corporate Giving in the Arts.* A detailed casebook.

Grants and Scholarships

A Directory of International Scholarships in the Arts. New York: Institute of International Education.

Federal Funds and Services for the Arts. Washington, D.C.: U.S. Government Printing Office.

Foundation Grants to Individuals. New York: The Foundation Center, 888 Seventh Ave., New York, N.Y. 10019.

Grants and Aids to Individuals in the Arts. Washington International Arts Letter, 1321 4th St. S.W., Washington, D.C. 20204.

Grantsy, R. O. *Register of Scholarships and Loans and Register of Fellowships and Grants.* New York: World Trade Academy Press, Simon & Schuster. Published annually.

Pavlakis, Christopher. *The Music Handbook.* New York: Free Press, 1974. Contains an extensive list of music grants and scholarships, lists of concert talent managers, musical instrument manufacturers, and a great deal of other useful information.

Ruth, Diane. *Post Baccalaureate: Grants and Awards in Music.* Washington D.C.: Music Educators National Conference, 1969. This forty-page booklet contains information about scholarship grants, trusts, and other awards.

The Foundation Center, which has national collections at 888 Seventh Avenue, New York, N.Y. 10019 and at 1001 Connecticut Avenue N.W., Suite 938, Washington D.C. 20036, offers much data on foundations, grants, IRS returns, foundation annual reports, and various reference materials regarding grants. It also has regional offices at 312 Sutter Street, San Francisco, Calif. 94108, and 739 National City Bank Building, 629 Euclid Avenue, Cleveland, Ohio 44114.

The following publications are all available from the New York office listed above.

Comsearch Printouts. An annual computer printout of grants by more than 340 major foundations.

Foundation Center Source Book Profiles. An annual loose-leaf subscription service.

Foundation Grants to Individuals 1977.

Margolin, Judith B. *About Foundations: How to Find the Facts You Need to Get a Grant.* 1977 revised edition, with 1978 addendum.

Martinson, Jean Alan. *International Philanthropy: A Compilation of Grants by United States Foundations.* 1978.

The Foundation Center National Data Book. 2 vols. 1977.

The following book is published by the Columbia University Press, N.Y., Lewis, Marianna O., ed. *The Foundation Directory.* 6th ed. 1977.

Women in Music

Chapple and Garafalo. See Recording. This book contains a good chapter on women in rock, but their percentage analysis of charts misses the point of the changes in women's music and its impact on the writing of men as well.

Cheney, Joyce; Diehl, Marcia; and Silverstein, Deborah. *All Our Lives: A Women's Songbook.* Baltimore: Diana Press, 1976. A fine study of women's music, yesterday and today. The focus is on American folk music.

Drinker, Sophie. *Music and Women.* New York: Coward McCann, 1948. A brilliant historical study of the oppression of women in Western music.

Felixson, Nancy, et al. *Women in American Music.* Aptos, Calif.: Written Word Collective, 1975. The result of a seminar in women's music at Kresge College of the University of California at Santa Cruz. A compelling study.

Hixon, Don L., and Hennessee, Don. *Women in Music: A Bibliography.* Metuchen, N.J.: Scarecrow, 1975.

Jepson, Barbara. *You've Come a Long Way: Women in Symphony Orchestras.* Vienna, Va.: American Symphony League, 1975.

Klever, Anita. *Women in Television.* Philadelphia, Pa.: Westminster Press, 1975.

Lynn, Loretta. *Coal Miner's Daughter.* New York: Warner Brothers, 1976. An autobiography.

Laurence, Anna. *Women in Notes.* New York: Richard Rosen.

Orloff, Katherine. *Rock 'n' Roll Women.* Los Angeles: Nash, 1974. A superficial book.

Smith, Julia, ed.   *Directory of American Woman Composers.* Chicago: National Federation of Music Clubs, 1970.

Sorrels, Rosalie, ed.   *Wine, Woman, and Who Myself I Am.* Sonoma, Calif.: Wooden Shoe, 1974. Poetry and song. A beautiful book.

Other Minority Groups

See also the book list on blues and jazz.

Abdul, Raoul.   *Blacks in Classical Music.* New York: Dodd, Mead, 1977.

Power in the Arts

Burns, Joan Simpson.   *The Awkward Embrace.* New York, Alfred A. Knopf, 1975. Studies of some key figures who wield great power in the arts. Intelligent and well researched, not much material on music.

Levine, Faye.   *The Culture Barons.* New York: Crowell, 1976. Some interesting material on the building of the Lincoln Center arts complex in New York, and some colorful material about promoter Bill Graham, but written in a peculiar and irritating style.

Metz, Robert. *Reflections in a Bloodshot Eye.* New York: Signet, 1977. A book about CBS.

Monaco, James. *Media Culture.* New York: Delta Books, 1978. The most interesting part of this book is the series of tables and analyses in the back relating to conglomerates and their various holdings.

Miscellaneous Music Books

Altman, Richard, and Kaufman, Mervyn.   *Making of a Musical: Fiddler on the Roof.* New York: Crown, 1971.

Amram, David.   *Vibrations.* New York: Macmillan, 1968. Amram is an unusual musician in that he is active in jazz, classical music, and pop-rock.

Baskerville, David.   *The New Music Business and the New Careers.* Los Angeles: Media Services Group, 1978.

Burt, Jesse, and Ferguson, Bob.   *So You Want to Be in Music.* Nashville: Abingdon Press, 1970.

Engel, Lehman.   *The American Musical Theatre.* Revised ed. New York: Collier, 1975.

————.   *The Making of a Musical.* New York: Macmillan, 1977.

Frankel, Aaron.   *Writing the Broadway Musical.* New York: Drama Books, 1977.

Goldmark, Peter C. *Maverick Inventor.* New York: Saturday Review Press/Dutton, 1973. Memoirs by the man who perfected the LP record. Contains amusing anecdotes about his struggle with the CBS bureaucracy.

Progris, Jim. *Language of Commercial Music.* Miami Beach: Hansen, n.d.

Rappaport, Victor D. *Making It in Music.* New York: Prentice Hall, Spectrum Books, 1979.

Rogers, Kenny, and Epand, Len. *Making It with Music.* New York: Harper & Row, 1978. Some interesting material about starting and keeping a group together.

Spaeth, Sigmund. *Opportunities in Music Careers.* New York: Universal, 1966.

Toffler, Alvin. *The Culture Consumers.* New York: Random House, 1973.

Periodicals

Music Trade Papers

Billboard, 1515 Broadway, New York, N.Y. 10036

Cash Box, 1780 Broadway, New York, N.Y. 10019

Daily Variety, 6404 Sunset Blvd., Hollywood, Calif. 90028

Melody Maker, PC Specialist & Professional Press Ltd., 161 Fleet Street, London EC4, England.

Music City News, Box 975, 1314 Pien St., Nashville, Tenn. 37203. Weekly.

Radio and Records, 1930 Century Park W., Los Angeles, Calif. 90067

Record World, 200 W. 57th St., New York, N.Y. 10010

RPM, 6 Brentcliffe Road, Toronto, Ontario, Canada M4G 3Y2. Weekly. Deals with records, promotion, and music in Canada.

Variety, 154 W. 45th St., New York, N.Y. 10036

Other Periodicals

AAMOA News, Afro-American Music Opportunities Assoc., Box 662, Minneapolis, Minn. 55440

American Choral Review, 130 W. 56 St., New York, N.Y. 10019

American Music Center Newsletter, American Music Center, 2109 Broadway, Suite 15–79, New York, N.Y. 10023

American Music Teacher, 408 Carew Tower, Cincinnati, Ohio 45202

American Record Guide, Box 319, Radio City Station, New York, N.Y. 10019

American Recorder, American Recorder Society, 141 W. 20th St., New York, N.Y. 10011

Association of College, University, and Community Arts Administrators Bulletin, Box 2137, Madison, Wis. 53701

Audio, 134 N. 13th St., Philadelphia, Pa. 19107

Black Perspectives in Music, P.O. Drawer 1, Cambria Heights, N.Y. 11411

Bluegrass Unlimited, Box 111, Broad Run, Va. 22014

Broadcasting, 1735 De Salle St., Washington, D.C. 20018

Cadence Magazine, Rt. 1 Box 345, Redwood, N.Y. 13679. A review of jazz and blues.

Canadian Music Educator, Canadian Music Education Association, 34 Cameron Rd., St. Catherines, Ont., CP2 3E2, Canada

The Choral Journal, P.O. Box 17736, Tampa, Fla. 33602

Church Music, Concordia Publishing House, 3558 S. Jefferson Ave., St. Louis, Mo. 63118

Church Musician, Southern Baptist Convention, 127 9th Ave. N., Nashville, Tenn. 37234

Clavier, 1418 Lake St., Evanston, Ill. 60204

Coda, Box 87 Station J, Toronto, Ontario, Canada. Lists many obscure new jazz records. My favorite jazz magazine.

Contemporary Keyboard, P.O. Box 615, Saratoga, Calif. 95070

Country Music Magazine, P.O. Box 2560, Boulder, Colo. 80322

Country Rambler, P.O. Box 1080, Skokie, Ill. 60076

Country Song Roundup, Charlton Publications, Charlton Bldg., Derby, Conn. 06418

Country Style, 11058 W. Addison St., Franklin Park, Ill. 60131

Crawdaddy, 72 Fifth Ave., New York, N.Y. 10011. Critical journal of contemporary popular music.

Creem, 187 S. Woodward Ave., Birmingham, Mich. 48011

Cultural Post, National Endowment for the Arts, Mail Stop 550, Washington, D.C. 20504

Current Musicology, Music Dept., Columbia University, New York, N.Y. 10027

DB, 1120 Old County Rd., Plainview, N.Y. 11803. A sound engineering magazine.

Disc & That Magazine, P.O. Box 228, Kingsbridge Station, Bronx, N.Y. 10463

Downbeat, 222 W. Adams St., Chicago, Ill. 60606

Drum Corps News, P.O. Box 146, Revere, Mass. 02151

Ethnomusicology, 201 South Main St., Ann Arbor, Mich. 48108

Foundation News, 888 Seventh Ave., New York, N.Y. 10019. A magazine about grants.

Gig, 415 Lexington Ave., New York, N.Y. 10017

Good News, Gospel News Association, Box 1201, 816 19th Ave. South, Nashville, Tenn. 37202

Guitar Player, Box 615, Saratoga, Calif. 95070

Guitar Review, Society of the Classic Guitar, 409 E. 50th St., New York, N.Y. 10022

Harmonizer, Society for the Preservation and Encouragement of Barber Shop Singing in America, 6315 Third Ave., Kenosha, Wis., 53141

Harrison Tape Guide, 143 W. 20th St., New York, N.Y. 10011

High Fidelity/Musical America, 130 E. 59th St., New York, N.Y. 10022

Hit Parader, Charlton Pub. Inc., Charlton Bldg., Derby, Conn. 06418

The Instrumentalist, 1418 Lake St., Evanston, Ill. 60204

International Guitar & Violin Makers Journal, 403 W. Maple, Jeffersonville, Ind. 47103

International Musician, 1500 Broadway, New York, N.Y. 10036. AFM journal, but contains many interesting articles on nonunion matters.

Journal of American Folklore, University of Texas, Austin, Tex. 78212

Journal of American Musicological Society, Wm. Byrd Press, 2901 Byrdhill Rd., Richmond, Va. 23228

Journal of Church Music, 2900 Queen Lane, Philadelphia, Pa. 19129

Journal of Country Music, Country Music Foundation, 700 16 Ave. S., Nashville, Tenn. 37203

Journal of Jazz Studies, Dane Library, Rutgers University, Newark, N.J. 07102

Journal of Music Therapy, National Association of Music Therapy, P.O. Box 610, Lawrence, Kans. 66044

Journal of Popular Music & Society, Bowling Green State University, Bowling Green, Ohio 43403

Living Blues, Box 11303, Chicago, Ill. 60611

Modern Recording, 14 Vanderventer Ave., Port Washington, N.Y. 11050

Music Clubs Magazine, Nation Federation of Music Clubs, 600 S. Michigan Ave., Chicago, Ill. 60605

Music Connection, 6381 Hollywood Blvd., Hollywood, Calif. 90028

Music Educators Journal, Music Educators National Conference, 1902 Association Drive, Reston, Va. 33091

Music Journal, 370 Lexington Ave., New York, N.Y. 10017

Music Ministry, United Methodist Publishing House, Graded Press, 201 8th Ave. S., Nashville, Tenn. 37202

Music Retailer, 210 Boylston St., Chestnut Hill, Mass. 02167

Music Trades, Box 432, 80 West St., Englewood, N.J. 07631

Music Works, 83 McAllester St., Room 403, San Francisco, Calif. 94102. A good magazine with articles on recording, managers, agents, and other music business topics.

Musical Merchandise Review, Peacock Business Press, 200 S. Prospect Ave., Park Ridge, Ill. 60068

Musical Newsletter, 654 Madison Ave., New York, N.Y. 10021

Musical Notes Magazine, Ace & Wonk, 408 S.W. Second Ave., Portland, Ore., 97204

Musical Quarterly, 866 Third Ave., New York, N.Y. 10022

Musicanada, Canadian Music Council, 287 MacLaren, Ottawa K2 PUL9, Ontario, Canada

Musician, P.O. Box 701, Gloucester, Mass. 01930. Published eight times a year. Articles on musicians and on specific instruments in the popular music field.

NARAS Journal, NARAS Institute, 505 N. Lake Shore Dr., Chicago, Ill. 60611

National Music Council Bulletin, 250 West 57 St., New York, N.Y. 10019. Semiannual magazine concerning music clubs, contests, and activities, of national music organizations.

New on the Charts, 1500 Broadway, New York, N.Y. 10036

New Records, H. Royer Smith, 2019 Walnut St., Philadelphia, Pa. 19103. Record reviews, mostly of classical music.

Notes, Music Library Association, 343 S. Main St., Ann Arbor, Mich. 48108

Opera Journal, Hotel Wellington, N. 823, 55th St. & Seventh Ave., New York, N.Y. 10019

Opera News, Metropolitan Opera Guild, 1865 Broadway, New York, N.Y. 10023

Paid My Dues, Women's Soul Publishing Co., P.O. Box 11646, Milwaukee, Wis. 53211. Journal of women's music.

Percussionist, Percussion Arts Society, 130 Carol Dr., Terre Haute, Ind. 47805

Perspectives of New Music, Annandale-on-Hudson, N.Y. 12504

Piano Quarterly, P.O. Box 815, Wilmington, Vt. 05363

Piano Technicians Journal, Box 1813, Seattle, Wash. 98111

Pickin', Universal Graphics Corp., 1 Saddle Rd., Cedar Knolls, N.J. 07927. Magazine about bluegrass.

PTR Journal, National Association of Educational Broadcasters, 1346 Connecticut Ave., Washington, D.C. 20036. Journal about public radio and television.

Recording Engineer-Producer, P.O. Box 2440, Hollywood, Calif. 90028

Record Week, 216 Carlton St., Toronto, Ontario, Canada. The Canadian record trade paper.

Rock, 166 Lexington Ave., New York, N.Y. 10016

Rock Scene, Four Seasons Publications, Fairwood Rd., Bethany, Conn. 06525

Rock and Soul Songs, Charlton Pub., Charlton Bldg., Derby, Conn. 06418

Rolling Stone, Straight Arrow Publications, 625 Third St., San Francisco, Calif. 94107

Sacred Music, Church Music Association of America, 548 Lafond Ave., St. Paul, Minn. 55103

School Music Notes, Box 2620, Schnectady, N.Y. 12309

The School Musician, 4 E. Clinton St., Joliet, Ill. 60437

Sing Out, 106 W. 28th St., New York, N.Y. 10001. Specializes in American folk music.

Singing News, 2611 W. Cervantes, P.O. Box 5188, Pensacola, Fla. 32505

Songplugger, P.O. Box 3839, Hollywood, Calif. 90038. Lists artists and producers looking for songs. Intended for songwriters and publishers.

Songwriter, P.O. Box 3510, Hollywood, Calif. 90028. Useful articles on songwriting and allied subjects.

Stereo Review, Ziff Davis Pub. Co., 1 Park Ave., New York, N.Y. 10016

Symphony News, American Symphony Orchestra League, Symphony Hall, Box 66, Vienna, Va. 22180

Synapse, 2829 Hyans St., Los Angeles, Calif. 90026. Journal of electronic music.

Talent & Booking Agency Rosters, Specialty Publications Inc., 7033 Sunset Blvd., Suite 222, Los Angeles, Calif. 90028. A bimonthly alphabetical listing of booking agents. Also includes articles on agents, managers, and promoters.

Trouser Press, 147 W. 42 St., New York, N.Y. 10036. A rock magazine.

Tunesmith, P.O. Box 3839, Hollywood, Calif. 90028

Upbeat, 222 West Adams St., Chicago, Ill. 60606

Violincello Society Newsletter, 140 W. 57th St., New York, N.Y. 10019

Washington International Arts Letter, 1321 4th St. S.W., Washington, D.C. 20024

Woodwind World, 17 Somerset Terrace, Oneonta, N.Y. 13820

The World of Music, 434 S. Wabash Ave., Chicago, Ill. 60905

Index

A & R men, 39, 42–44. *See also* Record producers
Advances against royalties, 50, 53–54, 58
Advertising, 64, 65, 96, 97. *See also* Commercials; Publicity
concert promotion and, 127–28
Advertising agencies, 89–92
Agents (agency), 8–9, 15–17, 63, 68–74, 219–20
Air check, 121
Air play, 83, 86–87, 141
Alternative media, 197–200
American Federation of Musicians (AFM), 7–8, 15–17, 91, 98–103
dues and initiation fees of, 100
phonograph labor agreement, 99, 101
standard contracts, 72–73
union scales, 211
American Federation of Television and Radio Artists (AFTRA), 56, 73, 86
commercials and, 91
dues and initiation fees for, 103–4
union scales, 211
American Guild of Authors and Composers (AGAC), 78
American Guild of Musical Artists (AGMA), 73, 98, 104, 211–12
American Guild of Variety Artists (AGVA), 98, 104

American Society of Composers, Authors, and Publishers (ASCAP), 92–96, 143
American Songs Festival, 144
American Symphony Orchestra League, 181
Armed forces, music in, 177–78
Arrangers, 122-24, 194
Arts management, 180–82, 206–7, 233–34
Associated Council of the Arts, 181
Attorney. *See* Lawyers
Auditing of royalty statements, 57–58, 78
Automated format, radio, 107–8

Band teacher, 151
Billboard, 65, 95, 96, 237
Black musicians, 192–94, 236
Booking agents (booking agency), 15–17, 63, 68–74, 126, 219–20
Broadcast Music Inc. (BMI), 82–86, 143

Cash Box, 65, 95, 96, 237
Cassette tapes, 21, 143. *See also* Demo tapes
CETA (Comprehensive Employment and Training Act), 195
Chamber music ensembles, 138
Charts, trade papers', 95–97
Chorus melodies, 140

Churches, 133
Church music, 178, 206, 232
Classical music. *See also* Symphony
    orchestra
    agent-managers in, 73
    black musicians and, 194
    books about, 224
    careers in, 135–38
    performing rights societies and, 86
    promotion of, 128–29
    recordings, 34
    record producers and, 48
    women and, 190
Classical record companies, 39–40
Click track, 90–91
Clinicians, 159–60, 169
Club dates, 132–34, 139
Collaboration, 142, 143
College programs, 145–49
    in arts management, 149, 206–7
    in church music, 206
    in music industry, 145–47, 149
    in music therapy, 149, 204–6
Commercials (jingles), 88–94
    advertising agencies and, 89–92
    books about, 220–21
    click track for, 90–91
    demo tape for, 90, 91, 93
    drop-ins, 89, 93
    radio, 109
    singers of, 92–93
    test-marketing, 91–92
    writing of, 91
Commissions, agents' and managers',
    72–73
Composers, 122
    black, 194
    careers for, 124
    of commercials (*see* Commercials)
    of film music, 123–24
    women, 190
Compulsory license, copyright law
    and, 80
Concert promotion, 126–29
Conference of Personal Managers, 74
Contractors, 113–16
Contracts
    with agents, 16, 17
    cross-collateralization in, 78–79
    with managers, 17
    with music publishers, 77–79
    between promoter and a group, 129
    with record companies, 52–59
Copyright, 14, 79
Copyright law, 159
    books about, 220
    new, 79–80, 86
    old, 80
Copyright notice, 79, 80

Cover records, 44, 76
Crawdaddy, 97, 239
Creative services department, 66
Critics, music, 161–64, 230
Cross-collateralization in contracts,
    78–79
Cutouts, 66

Dalcroze system (eurythmics), 151
Dashon (ozalid), 143
Demo records, 42, 143
Demo tape, 14–16, 17, 20–29
    for commercials, 90, 91, 93
    number of tunes on, 20
    opening cut of, 21
    original songs on, 21–22
    quality of, 22–23
    recording, 24–26
    selling the, 27–29
Direct-to-disc records, 34
Direct-mail record sales, 62
Disc jockeys, 106–9, 120–21
Discounting of records, 172
Distribution of records, 35, 60–63, 95,
    96
Doubling, 90, 99, 113
Drop-ins, 89, 93
Dylan, Bob, 141–42

Education. *See* Music education
Engineers (audio), 47–48, 117–18, 222
Equalization, 32
Ethnomusicologists, 152
Eurythmics (Dalcroze system), 151

Fakebooks, 156
Federal Communications Commission
    (FCC), 105, 108–10, 188
Film music, 123–24, 222–23
First-call list, 113
Ford Foundation, 196
Free-form format, radio, 107
Full-service music stores, 170

Gavin Report, 65, 110
General manager of radio station, 105,
    121
Grants and scholarships, 183–86, 234–
    35

Instruments, 167–69, 177
International Musician, 136
International   Talent   Associates
    (ITA), 7–8
Internships, 145, 146

Jazz performance, 138–39, 227
Jingles. *See* Commercials
Jobber

music, 154–55
rack (records), 61–62, 66, 95, 96

Kodály system, 150

Lawyers, 17, 52–53, 59, 178–79, 233
Lead sheet, 14–15, 77, 79, 143, 214
Leasing songs, 159
Leiber, Jerry, and Spoller, Mike, 40–41
Liaison people, 64–65, 96
Logging, 83, 105

Manager, general (radio station), 105, 121
Manager, personal, 16–18, 28, 53, 54, 56, 59, 68–74. *See also* Arts management
 agents distinguished from, 17, 68–71
 books about, 219–20
 commissions for, 72–73
 contract with, 17
 power of attorney of, 71
Manuscript for music books, 156–59
Mastering, 33, 49, 50
Mechanical use fees, 75, 76, 79
Media, the
 alternative, 197–200
 books about, 236
 concentration of power of, 195–98
Method books, 156, 157
Miller, Mitch, 43–45
Minorities in music business, 187–94
 black musicians, 192–94
 women, 187–92
Mixing down the tape, 49, 50
Motown, 193
Moviola, 123
Musical hook, 21, 43, 140, 141
Music book, creation of, 157–58
Music critics, 161–64, 230
Music director (radio), 105, 106
Music education (teaching), 150–52, 230
Music engraver, 158–59
Music house, 89–91
Music industry programs in college, 145–47, 149, 201–4
Music jobber, 154–55
Music law, 178–79, 233
Music library work, 165–66, 177, 231
Music performance. *See also specific types of music*
 books about, 223–29
 careers in, 131–39
 women in, 189
Music Performance Trust Fund (MPTF), 101, 186
Music publishers, 154–60
 list of, 210–11
Music publishing, 75–76. *See also* Me-
chanical use fees; Performing rights; Printed music; Sheet music
 books about, 220
 careers in, 159–60
Music publishing contracts, 77–79
Music therapy, 173–75, 204–6, 231

National Endowment for the Arts (NEA), 182–86
National Organization for Women (NOW), 188, 191
News and public service announcements, 105–6
Newspaper Guild, 161
Noise-reduction systems, 32, 33

One-stop, 61, 172
Open stages, 134
Operatic singers, 136
Operations manager (radio), 105, 121
Orchestra. *See* Symphony orchestra
Orff system, 150–51
Overdubbing, 31
Ozalid (dashon), 143

Payola, 65, 108, 163
Performance royalty, 86–87
Performing experience, 12–13, 131, 135
Performing rights, 75, 82, 220
Performing rights societies, 82–87, 208
Periodicals, 237–42
Personal manager. *See* Manager, personal
Piano Technicians Guild, 176
Piano tuning, 176, 232
Practice teaching, 150, 151
Printed music, 75, 154–57, 210–11. *See also* Sheet music
Private teaching, 152–53
Producers. *See* Record producers
Production manager, 66, 158
Program director (radio), 105, 106, 108, 120
Promotion (promoters)
 books about, 223
 concert, 126–29
 of records, 60, 63–67
Promotion records, 60–61, 63
Public service announcements, 105–6
Publicity (public relations), 130, 223
Publishing. *See* Music publishing
Publishing rights, 56, 58, 124

Race records, 192
Rack jobbers, 61–62, 66, 95, 96, 154–55
Radio and Records, 65, 110, 238
Radio (stations), 105–10
 AM, 106, 107, 110
 automated format, 107–8

books about, 221–22
careers in, 119–21
commercials on, 109
departments of, 105–6
disc jockeys on, 106–9, 120–21
FM, 106, 107, 110
free-form format, 107
Top 40 format, 106–8, 110
trade papers for, 110
Recitalist, 135–36
Record companies, 35–41
Record distributors, 35, 60–63, 95, 96
Record industry, history of, 30–34
Recording, books on, 218–19
Recording contracts, 20, 52–59
  auditing provisions, 57–58
  for groups, 56
  number of albums, 55
  release of recordings, 55–56
  royalties, 50, 53–54, 58
  verbal agreements, 54, 56
Record producers, 20, 42–51
  creative life-span of, 50–51
  functions and responsibilities of, 46–51
  independent, 45–46, 57
  traditional, 45
Records, 31
  air play, 83, 86–87, 141
  as career vehicle, 19
  distribution process, 60–63, 95, 96
  promoting, 60, 63–67
  promotion copies, 60–61, 63
Record World, 65, 95, 96, 238
Reel-to-reel tape, 77
Residuals, 90, 93
Retail music stores, 170–72
Retail record stores, 60–62
Reuse fees, 93, 99
Reviewing music, 161–64, 230
Riders, 129
Rock 'n' roll, 44, 45, 192
Rolling Stone, 97, 126, 134, 242
Royalties, 52–55, 80
  advances against, 50, 53–54, 58
  auditing of, 57–58, 78
  mechanicals, 75, 76, 79
  performance, 86–87
  for print rights, 75, 76
  of record producers, 50
  for sheet music sales, 77–78
  for written music, 155–57

Scholarships and grants, 183–86, 234–35
Screen Actors Guild (SAG), 91, 98, 104, 212
SESAC, 82–86
Session fees, 90, 91

Sheet music, 77–78, 154, 155. *See also* Printed music
Showcases, 134, 143
Songbooks, royalties paid on, 155
Song sharks, 78
Songwriting, 140–44, 229
Sound equipment, 15–16
Specialty music stores, 170, 171
Specialty record companies, 36, 40–41
Sponsorship, 112
Studio, renting a, 26
Studio work, 112–16, 194, 222
Suzuki system, 151
Symphony orchestra
  arts management specialist with, 180–81
  auditions with, 136–37
  jobs with, 136–38
  recording a, 99
  women in, 190
Synchronization rights, 76

Tag, 91
Tape
  cassette, 21, 143
  demo (*see* Demo tape)
  mixing down, 49, 50
  reel-to-reel, 77
Tape recorders, 31–34
Teaching music, 150–53, 230
Television, 110
Therapy, music, 173–75, 204–6, 231
Top 40 format, 106–8, 110
Trade papers, 95–97, 126–27, 237–38
Turntable hit, 95

Union payments, 56
Union rules, 102–3
Unions, 48, 98–104, 132–34, 138, 199. *See also specific unions*
  agents and, 72–73
  benefits, 101–2
  list of, 208
  local, 99–101
  national, 98–99
  pensions from, 101
  regulations of, 102
  wage scales and working conditions set by, 98–99, 211–12
Union scales, 211–12

Vanity records and books, 199
Variety, 95–97, 238
Verbal agreements, 54, 56
Verse melodies, 140

Wholesaling, 172. *See also* Music jobber; Rack jobbers
Women, 187–91, 235–36
Work dues, 100